HOMESCHOOLING
AND WORKING

While Shaping Amazing Learners

by

LM
PRESTON

Contents

SECTION 2: DAY TO DAY WORKING AND HOMESCHOOLING

HOMESCHOOLING AND WORKING

While Shaping Amazing Learners

Editor: Cindy Davis
Content Editor: LeNyia Preston
Proof Reader: Dawn Yacovetta
Cover Design by We've Got You Covered. All Rights Reserved.
Interior Design and Formatting by Stephany Wallace.
All Rights Reserved.

A Phenomenal One Press publication, July 2019
www.phenomenalonepress.com

SYPNOSIS

Jumpstart Your Working and Homeschooling Journey with LM Preston

Free Mini-Course: www.empoweredsteps.com
Join our Facebook Group: https://www.facebook.com/
groups/homeschoolwhileworking/
Read the blog: http://homeschoolandwork.blogspot.com/
Visit the website: www.EmpoweredSteps.com

Homeschooling and Working While Shaping Amazing Learners is a nuts and bolts guide for working parents who want to groom exceptional learners through the flexibility of homeschooling. Learn to juggle working and homeschooling your kids while maintaining your sanity. Also, use aspects of homeschooling for after-schooling when traditional school isn't working. Single parents are given options for executing homeschooling or after-schooling methods that work in practical bits for the busy parent. Learn how to take your child from an average student to an exceptional student by exploring the possibilities shown in the section on acceleration of learning. From pre-K to Homeschooling College, open your eyes to the many options in flexibility this approach to learning can give. You can homeschool and work to shape amazing learners by exploring the possibilities.

Presented by: www.empoweredsteps.com

LM Preston is an author, engineer, former college professor, and working mother who's is married for over twenty-five years. She homeschooled 3 of her 4 children from elementary school and beyond while she and her husband worked outside their home. Three of her kids graduated with degrees by the age of 17. Her blog: http://homeschoolandwork.blogspot.com/ details her homeschooling while working journey.

HOMESCHOOLING AND WORKING

While Shaping Amazing Learners

ALSO BY L.M. PRESTON

NON FICTION

Building Your Empowered Steps

Team Wave Surfing

FICTION

PURGATORY REIGN SERIES

Purgatory Reign, Book 1

Deviant Storm, Book 2

Fierce Tides, Book 3

THE PACK SERIES

The Pack, Book 1

Retribution, Book 2

THE BANDITS SERIES

Bandits, Book 1

Wastelands, Book 2

DEDICATION

This is dedicated to my husband, parents, and my Nana, for molding me and shaping me into not just a survivor, but a conquerer of all of my fears and roadblocks.

I couldn't have made it without witnessing what true tenacity of spirit would bring.

ACKNOWLEDGMENTS

To all of my friends and family who constantly told me I should write this book and others. Your belief in me was the best motivation anyone could ask for, and it fed me.

To my readers who keep cheering me on by reading and reviewing my books.

To my many friends and family who encouraged me to write this book and create the courses that support my radical way of doing things, I thank you.

And to God, who guided and shaped me through many of life's adventures.

SECTION ONE

PREPARING TO HOMESCHOOL WHILE WORKING

WELCOME FROM THE AUTHOR

I am happy to be in the position the help others on the path to homeschooling, after-schooling, and acceleration of learning while working a full-time job or business.

All of my life, I have been around and observed inspiring women and men that lived their lives in triumph and determination without complaint about their struggle. They just buckled down and did what needed to be done to support their family in any way necessary. My parents were teen parents and never married each other, but that didn't stop my mom from funding my private school education with the help of her sisters, the church, and sometimes social services. She didn't give up on my brother or myself and pushed us to do much with the gifts we'd been given.

I had never considered homeschooling my children until my youngest child suggested it to me when he was in the 2nd grade. At that point in his young life, he'd had a bad opinion of school, had been bruised by a teacher, was mentally beat down by many others, and wanted something different. I don't know where he got the idea. It was divine intervention. It hurt my heart that my youngest child hated school so much. He wasn't thriving there. The traditional method of education he attended was beating him down. Numerous visits to the principal and the school frustrated my husband and me. They constantly tried to convince us to pursue testing then medicating of our son for his overactivity.

My husband and I enrolled him in a private school. There his behavior improved, but his self-esteem and fear of not being good enough didn't. At that point, I told my husband I would research ways to work and homeschool him. Then, my oldest and youngest daughters voiced their desire to homeschool. I couldn't find any information on homeschooling while working, which is why I decided to create this book.

We are almost at the end of this journey as a family. My home-schooled children have excelled beyond our wildest expectations. All who were homeschooled finished their college degrees as early as 17 years old. Our daughters even pursued their Master's degrees while working full-time. One daughter finished hers at 21 years of age while working as a Data Scientist, and the 17-year-old is on her way to earning her Masters at 19 years old while working as a software developer. Believe it or not, both my husband and I worked outside of the home the entire time we homeschooled them. I am an engineer by trade, an author and business owner while homeschooling my children with my husband. My husband is an Engineer and had a real estate business for ten years while we raised our kids. We did what some people considered impossible. It wasn't impossible. Challenging, yes, but definitely possible.

Juggling Working and Homeschooling

BECOME EMPOWERED

The theme of this book and my personal motto is to, "Own your flexibility in homeschooling!" This journey of working while home-schooling and creating this book to help others has been rewarding. I was asked to write this so many times and desired a book like this when I started this crazy ride with my husband and three of my four children. I originally started writing this as a diary of sorts on my blog (http://homeschoolandwork.blogspot.com/) for my children, hoping that they would learn from all we tried to accomplish with them.

This is a guidebook to those parents who want to try another method of education for their children. The chapters are short, well outlined, and specific with overviews to spark the reader to customize the principles for their personal homeschool and work exploration. It's best used by reading in its entirety first, then going to the chapters or appendixes that serve you and your family through your educating journey. Use this book to spawn further research into the areas needed for your homeschooling or after-schooling journey while working it into your life.

These lessons come from my experience in many types of education scenarios with my four children. I selected this method as a last resort. My youngest son planted the seed that fed himself and two of his sisters through an exciting adventure in learning. My oldest son went the traditional route to school, but many of these lessons can be used even if your child decides to return to a traditional school setting. Use the time home with them wisely.

This book is a tool in creating your own recipe for home-schooling.

2

Definition of Homeschooling

Homeschooling means many things to different people. The reason is that when a child isn't schooled in the traditional method, people create an opinion of the validity of that method based on their own specific circumstances.

Homeschooling is a big movement in the United States where parents take their children out of traditional schools—public, private, charter brick and mortar schools—to teach them at home or through other methods that are independent of a typical school setting.

During the 1970s, this phenomenon became popular again. It wasn't an easy choice to sustain for many families. Now homeschooling is a legal form of education in the United States and other countries.

Legal requirements differ from state to state and country to country. These laws must be researched and adhered to according to where the parents live.

In homeschooling, the child learns outside of a typical school setting, and their learning is supervised by their parents, not a school board or government entity. The child's family decides on the curriculum, the expectations, and the style of teaching that adhere to the government regulations of the state where they live. The parents certify the transcripts and the high school diploma which can be used for college admissions, the military, and job entry.

The public school online scenario is not considered homeschooling. When the state school system controls the curriculum, the child's grades, and the child's path to graduation, it is not considered homeschooling. Homeschooling is when the parent makes all the decisions on curriculum, course selection, methods of teaching, grading and progression through the grades, and graduation. The school board of that state still sets the standards that parents should follow, but they don't determine the graduation status of the child.

Due to legal issues that arose for homeschoolers, the Home School Legal Defense Association (HSLDA, https://hslda.org/content/laws/) was formed in 1983. It was started by two homeschooling fathers who sought to provide affordable legal advocacy for homeschooling families. This organization is invaluable in providing legal awareness, support, advocacy, and guidance to homeschooling families.

```
┌─────────────────────────────────────────┐
│                                         │
│                    3                    │
│                                         │
│        Preparing To Homeschool          │
│                                         │
└─────────────────────────────────────────┘
```

Taking the plunge and deciding to homeschool doesn't come easy to most parents. Making sure you properly prepare yourself for this adventure will ensure that you have gained what your child and you plan to get out of it.

Research Your State's Requirements for Homeschooling

The foremost step in preparing to homeschool is to get to know your state requirements. Homeschooling is allowed and legal in all fifty states. A great source for this information is the HSLDA (HSLDA, https://hslda.org/content/laws/) as mentioned earlier. Visit the HSLDA website then your school board website for rules for homeschooling in your state. Then, align yourself with the laws.

Find Local or Online Homeschool Groups

Research to find online and in-person homeschool groups that offer a wealth of information and support. As a working and homeschooling parent, it may seem there is no place for you, but times are changing. The homeschooling communities are becoming more diverse than ever before. Finding a local group affords your family many resources and others that can give you some great in-person tips. These resources can be found in a Google search, Yahoo group search, Facebook search, homeschool.com, and hslda.org, and are a good place to start.

Search for Homeschooling Options

Different states offer services for Homeschoolers. Research online whether your state has any government-funded programs for homeschoolers. The local library is a great source for homeschool curriculum, information, and help. Magazines like *Homeschool Today* and *Practical Homeschooling* can help jumpstart your journey into homeschooling.

Preparing Your Child for Withdrawal from School

You should prepare your child for their withdrawal from school by walking them through some of their fears, concerns, and challenges. Play games to get them to express their feelings towards the change. Address their fears by working through solutions and their concerns about homeschooling. Some games to consider are Totem, StrongSuit, and Mindfulness (from Amazon) that can be used to gain positive affirmations. This includes talking through the change with them. Have them get contact information for their friends. Let them connect with friends or favorite educators prior to their last day.

Requesting Child's Transcript

This should be done at the school prior to homeschooling or notification that you plan to homeschool. Request this in writing via an email, form they provide, or a signed letter per the school's protocol for transcript request. Ask them for an unofficial copy first. Then when you've decided to homeschool, ask for an official transcript to be sent to your home or handed to you in a sealed envelope.

Withdraw Child from School

Before withdrawing your child, verify that you have in-hand your requested official and unofficial transcript of the courses your child took at the school. It gives you an idea of what your child had accomplished up to the point of the withdrawal. Also, it serves as a record in case you send your child back to school at some point that school year.

Many people who consider homeschooling after enjoying the benefits of traditional schooling models may ignore the risk of making a quick, knee-jerk response to problems their kids are having in school by jumping into homeschooling without proper consideration and planning. Doing so is a recipe for disaster that can frustrate parents and be a detriment to the child if not well planned. Making the decision to homeschool, especially when both parents need to work to sustain a household, is nothing to take on lightly. This should be researched, tested, and considered from social impacts on the family, financial effects, and the emotional changes to come from this decision. Mainly, parents who are working parents use the structure of a traditional school model to provide resources, childcare, education, and more for their kids. Childcare is a major issue that has to be solidified before taking children out of the school system to homeschool them. Even though risks are apparent, planning and preparation can ease all of them.

**Returning To Traditional School
May Set Child Backwards
Or Cause them to Slip Back if Ahead of their Peers**

In the case of high school, taking a child out to homeschool could be a detriment to the child if they plan on returning to traditional high school. Most high schools will not accept homeschooling credit, or even dual enrolled college courses for courses. Some schools will not accept testing or any parental proof of courses, classes, or educational knowledge.

As far as elementary and middle school, it depends on the school. However, middle school is when most schools separate the honors students, advanced students, and the general education students. Those categories follow the child through high school, and if the school doesn't allow for testing into those areas upon registration, those opportunities for placement in the 'Gifted and Talented' courses may not be offered. The parent can check with their school board to see if testing is available out of cycle to properly place their child on the correct grade level based on their test scores.

Also, note that various types of homeschooling methods (such as unschooling, see Chapter 18) cause a deficit of learning in core subjects such as math, reading, writing, and comprehension. Those learning styles may force the parent and child to work hard to bring the child's abilities back to grade level skills prior to going back to traditional school.

Socialization Challenges

Although many homeschoolers fight this stigma on homeschooling, it isn't a stigma – it's a reality. It is a fact that kids who are homeschooled spend less time in settings with kids their own age. The setting and circumstances are very different than if they went to traditional school. Ways to mitigate this (see Chapter 48) take creativity on the part of the parent. Every one of my kids, at some time or another, desired what they perceived as exposure to their peer age group. They wanted what they'd experienced in traditional school without the drama that came with it. Socialization exposure affects *both* the parents and the child. Especially, working parents. As a working and homeschooling parent, one gives up many friendships, time to cultivate work relationships, and more to homeschool their child. This can cause depression in both children and adults, so be mindful to acknowledge this risk.

Lack of State Funded Benefits and Educational Support

When a family depends on state benefits and public school structure to assist children with disabilities or challenges, it is likely that when homeschooling, the family forfeits these benefits and services. Take the time to research with your medical doctor, social worker, school board, and other educational services if some of the services provided in public school can still be used if homeschooling. If one resumes traditional school, gaining benefits lost may be difficult.

Public Opinion and Defending the Right to Homeschool

The public opinion on homeschooling isn't positive. A homeschool is different as every other type of school. Therefore, it is hard for a consensus to be made regarding the success of homeschooled children when re-entering public school, entering college, or even the workforce. Some homeschooled kids have excelled, others made the grade, and some fell grossly behind. Most public opinion is that the child is missing a key factor in their education that most parents are not qualified to give. Navigating against the bias is difficult. Therefore, be prepared for it coming from many avenues. Use instances of homeschool successes to respond to naysayers. Be confident in your decision when those who oppose it feel the need to disagree with your method of schooling your child.

Discomfort in Educating Child in Unfamiliar Subjects

Many parents are not well versed in all subjects from kindergarten to 12th grade. Intimidation on teaching topics in which one isn't well versed, or topics undesirable to the parent, is intimidating to homeschool parents. To alleviate that discomfort, consider hiring a tutor, having another teacher for the topic, obtaining a curriculum that teaches the topic, or even take the time to learn with the child while they are being taught. The risk that children will falter in subjects' parents are uncomfortable teaching is a challenge that can be overcome.

Childcare Challenges

It's a major challenge for a working parent to consider home-schooling. Childcare options (see Chapter 11) are limited, and parents must have some flexibility. Being creative with work schedules, finding jobs to work from home, budgeting for childcare, and having backup childcare are very important. Without childcare, the decision to work and homeschool may be difficult.

If the Parental Structure & Support Changes

One may believe that homeschooling can only be possible with two parents in the home. That isn't the case. A growing number of single-parent households (see Chapter 38) are homeschooling children. However, if a marriage fails or a support system changes, this affects the outcome of one's homeschool support and decision.

Burnout

Burnout is a trap where most working parents find themselves, and if you add on the responsibility of homeschooling a child, it can feel like quicksand. Management of burnout (see Chapter 58) is an ongoing battle for most parents, but the truth of it is, it is a matter of perception, organization, delegating, and realizing you can't, and shouldn't, try to do it all. It's important to anticipate the chance of burnout of the teaching parent, the spouse, and the child ahead of time by slowly adding goals, subjects, and expectations to gauge what is enough and what is too much for everyone involved. If it gets stressful, cut back, re-direct, or take breaks.

5

Benefits to Working and Homeschooling

Freedom and flexibility rule a working and homeschooling parent's journey. The benefits in controlling your own schedule, your child's learning, and your family's ability to be flexible can't be beat. Homeschooling while working permits you to be able to work and build a learning environment that will allow your child to thrive in a non-traditional way. The key to it all is thinking in a fluid manner and making sure finances, childcare, and stress remain manageable.

Flexibility

Flexibility is a key part of homeschooling that many parents don't use to the fullest. When you homeschool your child, you get to decide when schooling takes place, how it happens, and the contents of the curriculum. Instruction takes place for a working parent when they are home from work, when the child can learn independently, and on the weekend and evenings. Curriculums that teach the student and allow for the parent to do the follow up and supplementary instruction work best for working and homeschooling parents. The ownership of flexibility depends on the career or business that the parent works in and the type of childcare options the parent is able to afford. The child's education and schooling can take place at any time, place, or circumstance that fit within environment set by the parent.

Building a Closer Relationship with Your Children

The best part of homeschooling for most working and homeschooling families is the ability to build deeper relationships with their children. Ways to do so can be found in Chapter 59. When a child is in school all day while the parent is at work, both are usually tired in the evenings. Even though I'd considered myself an involved parent, participated in many events, and volunteered at the school, there were many aspects about my kid's personalities I didn't see until I was their teacher. After overcoming those challenges, our relationship and theirs with their siblings have a deeper connection.

Turns Your Child into an Independent Learner

Children that are homeschooled, especially with working parents, have to be taught the skill of self-learning and time management (see Chapter 19). Taking the baby steps to encourage your child to seek their own answers, work through problems, and communicate their questions helps the parent better understand their child's challenges. Many homeschool students that venture into high school are great self-starters and learners that make the transition to college, career, or military with ease.

Customization of Education

Homeschooling while working allows both parents and children to customize education to fit their interests, explore interests, deep dive into areas of curiosity, stop or start when needed, and more. Parents can build a curriculum that feeds their child's learning style, personality, limitations, and areas of excellence when needed. It can allow parents to build an education based on experiencing life in new ways but taking a deeper inspection of it day to day. If a parent travels for their work, they can take their children with them to explore and customize education based on child's maturity, level of interest, work and travel schedules. Also, if a child needs to focus on filling in educational gaps before moving forward in certain subjects, they can while proceeding in topics that they show advanced skills. In instances where your child is gifted or curious about any topic, you can build an entire curriculum around their passion while integrating math, science, writing, and reading into that topic for as long as the child is interested.

More Hours in the Day ~ Let's Compare

As working parents who have kids in traditional school, the day is longer than one may realize (see Chapter 8). It includes preparing everyone in the morning, the drop off to daycare or school, the school and work day, then the after-school program travel, stuffing in dinner, finding time to finish homework, and finally falling into bed. When you homeschool and work, you make your time count. Also, school for homeschoolers is condensed into two to four hours, depending on the age of the student. That five day a week schedule can be broken up into a yearlong school year of just three to four days of schooling a week, or a block schedule where the focus is on only a few subjects at a time. When comparing homeschooling to a traditional school schedule, you will see there is much more freedom with homeschooling. The children do not have to do homework or have long school days and are better rested (sometimes more than the parents).

Having Money, Networking & Resources to Accomplish More

Being a working parent who also homeschools offers great advantages. It is less draining if the job is something that is enjoyed and where you can network with other working parents. Having a second income does help with the possibilities and can afford private tutors, other opportunities for your kids, and a place to have adult friends. Homeschooling while working allows the parents the ability to afford assets their family needs in order to live comfortably. Both parents become positive role models for their children in regards to setting career possibilities examples. Kids witness how parents are maintaining a job or business while having a family. Working and homeschooling encourages kids to become more independent and see a reason to help. It is a proven fact that children of working moms tend to do better at their studies and have less separation anxiety while learning independently. Lastly, it can benefit the union of those married and raising kids to have outlets to use as conversation starters that don't revolve around their household.

6

Documentation Requirements

Many states, and sometimes cities, require reporting from home-schoolers. You can find the updated laws and requirements for each state on the HSLDA.org website.

Notebook or Portfolio to Document Child's learning

Documentation involves keeping the evidence of teaching, learning, and meeting the state requirements in one location so it can be presented to the state, county, or official at the time of a review. These artifacts from your homeschooling efforts are proof of the execution of learning. In addition, this can be an adequate review if the family finds themselves separating and one spouse challenges the validity of continuing to homeschool. Also, it's a great way to review with your student how far they have come. The easiest way to keep all the information together is to use a large notebook. Each child should also have their own notebook.

Break up the notebook sections into areas noted below:

1. *State Required Documentation*: Have a section for state-required documentation and anything you've had to sign, letters sent, and contacts.
2. *Curriculum*: A curriculum list sheet that outlines what sources of curriculum were used to educate your child, and for what courses.
3. Include even activities done that could reinforce the topic. For example: videos, projects, field trips, hands-on exposure, exercising, sightseeing, songs, and even activities like paying for groceries at the store.
4. *Reading*: Reading list for the student can include audio books, video books, or reading to the student.
5. *Math*: Provide a sample of math activities with pictures of child doing them, or the actual sheets, quizzes, and or test.
6. *Language Arts/English*: This can include grammar, writing practices, essays, quizzes, and tests.
7. *Science*: A list of projects completed, pictures of projects, quizzes, and tests.
8. *All other subjects*: Each subject covered for the year should have its own notebook tab.
9. *Synopsis* of growth noted during the school year regarding knowledge, critical thinking, and an overview of accomplishments.
10. *Additional items*: quizzes, test results, papers written, pictures of the child working on projects, and small projects that fit in the binder.

Testing Options Required By Some States

Most states don't require standardized testing for students until 3rd grade. As a homeschooler, you usually have the option to select the type and method of testing for your child. Getting the test is easy, and some providers are Abeka Homeschool, BJU Press Testing and Evaluation Service, or Seton Testing (see Chapter 16 for more information). Some tests to consider are Stanford Achievement Test,

California Achievement Test, or the Iowa Standardized Test. Taking practice tests during the year to get your child comfortable is a good exercise and takes the anxiety out of the process. These tests can be administered by a parent and sometimes require that the administrator has a degree. See the HSLDA Homeschool Laws in Your State (https://hslda.org/content/laws/) website for states that require testing.

Report Cards

Homeschooling does not require report cards for grades until high school when a transcript needs to be created for the child to enter college, military, or the workplace. If a parent wants to create a report card for elementary or middle school, they can although it will only be for the child's personal homeschool records. In cases where the parents decide to enroll their child into an online school, which is similar to a private school, those grades and report cards may be considered accredited. The accreditation of the report card and school should be researched and confirmed by the parent if they are seeking an accredited form of reporting from their curriculum source.

Options in which the parent may want to have a report card:

1. *Plan to Return to School the next year*: If the child is in elementary or middle school, no report card is typically needed since schools will either test the student or put them in class to evaluate them. However, it does make a difference if the parent desires to have their child placed in a *gifted and talented* program, which usually starts at 3rd to 5th grade, depending on the state.
2. *Student is in High school*: If the student is going into 9th grade and doesn't desire honors courses or gifted and talented courses, no former middle school report card is needed. The student will be placed in the average grade

level and will be moved around as needed after that. However, after 9th grade, many high schools do not accept a homeschool transcript. Therefore, the student will have to possibly repeat classes such as English 9th through 12th grade, Algebra 1, Algebra 2, and Geometry if they have taken it in homeschool. A work around to this is for the parent to enroll their child in an accredited online school that acts as a private charter school so the high school will accept the transcript.

3. *Parent Desires Yearly Accountability*: This personal choice may be helpful by unmarried parents to show child's progress.
4. Use of transcript services
5. Private schools with online options
6. Parent can provide report card that is backed by list of curriculum, standardized testing scores, and student's completed work and notebook.

Transcript

The transcript is a list of all coursework and can be tracked to the state's requirements for each level of schooling. When considering transcripts, coursework should include traditional forms of coursework as well as non-traditional forms of courses. In most cases, transcripts are mainly for High school, more so than Elementary and Middle school. The best way to confirm you don't miss anything the student has accomplished is by keeping a weekly, monthly, or yearly track of all tasks and exposure to knowledge.

Transcript should have:

- Student's name, date of birth, graduation date
- Homeschool name
- Homeschool address
- Parents' phone number
- Number of credits earned

- GPA and GPA scale
- Course information (check your state required course list by which to build transcript)
- Name
- Grade earned
- Course weight on the scale
- Number of credits earned (typically 1 per class or 0.5 for half of year course)
- GPA for course

Examples can be found on the HSLDA.org website as well as templates. Also, see **Appendix J** for more examples.

7

How to Manage Homeschooling and Working

This isn't a journey for the weak at heart. However, it can be extremely rewarding and bring a parent closer to their child than they thought possible. The major challenges with homeschooling while working is (1) Childcare (2) Scheduling (3) Being realistic (4) Learning to focus on what's important (5) Daring to be different from other homeschoolers and traditional schoolers or even your co-workers.

Childcare Considerations

The initial issue for many working parents considering home-schooling is childcare. Here is how to access your childcare needs.

1. How old are the children?
2. Can they stay home alone?
3. How many people can assist with childcare and during what hours?
4. Can I afford to pay for childcare? If so, for how many hours?

5. Can my spouse and I alternate work schedules? Work at home? Work part-time? Take child to work with us?
6. Do you have a relative or stay-at-home parent, who is a friend, who can help with childcare? At what cost?
7. Is the current job stable?
8. What is the backup plan if work schedule or circumstances change?
9. Can I change jobs or careers that would make homeschooling easier to administer?
10. Can I work multiple part-time jobs to cover childcare?
11. Do we want to pay for someone to educate our child, have the child attend an online school that manages their work, or teach them ourselves? What is the budget?

Budget

Take time to do a budget to see where you can find money to get childcare and emergency childcare if you need it. Or if you need to hire a tutor for a specific topic. Curriculum cost can be budgeted in to know in advance how much you have to spend on curriculum.

Tentative Schedule

Creating a tentative schedule of when you can spend one-on-one time with your child in regards to teaching or helping with work will give you an idea of the actual time for homeschooling. How much time do each of you have to focus on schooling needs?

Once you have answered the questions above, then write up a schedule from the child's perspective. What time will they be spending doing schooling? Realistically, homeschoolers usually spend 2 hours a day for elementary school, 2.5 to 3 hours for middle and four hours a day for high school. See the schedule in Appendix A: Weekly Schedule Work & Homeschooling.

- MS Excel or any workbook software you can purchase or use for free on Google docs. Also, for computer savvy students, using Google Classroom, which is free, can make it completely online and available for the entire family. You can also use Excel spreadsheets, Power Point, or just create a schedule in a notebook.

- Write down your and your partner's work schedules.
- Write down any activities that happen after work.
- Include commute time
- Dinner prep time
- Bath time
- Extracurricular time

8

Traditional School vs Homeschool Working Schedule

Realize the pros and cons to every scenario by looking closely at the time it costs to implement. We did private schools, traditional public schools, and homeschooling. Once we realized the freedom we had in homeschooling, the consideration to go backwards never worked for us. However, assessing all scenarios may help in the decision-making process.

Please do this for your household while considering what works best. Also, realize that time can be freed up by hiring out certain activities. Please see Appendix A for an example from the parent's point of view.

Questions To Ask Yourself about Public or Private School

- Do you and your child spend over 90 minutes a day on homework, makeup work, or supplemental work?
- Are you seeing your child negatively affected by their time at school?
- Is the child's school meeting their educational needs?
- Do you want your child to have more time to cultivate

other talents such as dance, gymnastics, music, art, a skill, or area of interest?

- Does your family want to travel outside of the restrictions of a public or private school schedule?
- Do you feel out of the loop when it comes to what your child is learning at school?
- Do you want a private and customized education for your child but can't afford it?
- Do you want to streamline your child's college career with dual enrollment opportunities not offered in school, or that they won't have the time to pursue while taking public school classes?
- Are you all right with being the person to create your child's transcript and diploma?
- Have you exhausted other options?

When you have considered all of these questions, take a look at the schedules below and create one like it for your family. See where the benefits of homeschooling can fit in.

Our Schedule
Private School

Both Hubby and I switched. My husband would drop of the children and I picked them up. I had all of my kids at one time in private school.

*Required MORE homework
*Parental support (financial and physical)
*Ad hoc costs came up frequently
*Quality of education wasn't always worth money paid
*Lack of extracurricular and college transition programs

My schedule when kids were in Private School and we worked

- **5:30 a.m.**-Wake up kids
- **6:30 a.m.**-Drop off two younger kids at morning care (with their own breakfast – tell provider what homework they weren't able to finish the night before so they can do it there). Older kids finish any homework not finished the night before.
- **3:00 p.m.**-Kids get out of school and go to aftercare in same building
- **6:00 p.m.**-Pick kids up from aftercare
- **6:30 p.m.**-Grab dinner
- **7:00 p.m.**-Go to sport activity, Kumon (after school tutoring) three days a week
- **9:00 p.m.**-Do homework. (They usually didn't do a good job of it in extended care-only time to play.) In private school there is A LOT of homework for all grades.
- **10:45 p.m.**-Put them to bed (if they didn't finish their homework)

Our Schedule
Public School

*Never knew what my kids were learning in class
*Kids were spread out over different schools (I had one in Daycare, Elementary, Middle, and High school for several years)
*Unplanned costs came up for support, supplies, or activities
*Quality of education depended upon the location where we lived

My schedule when kids were in Public School and I worked:

- **6:00 a.m.**-Wake up kids
- **6:30 a.m.**-Drop off two younger kids at morning care
- **6:30 a.m.**-High school student walks to school bus pickup

- **7:00 a.m.**-Middle school student gets dropped off at school bus pickup
- **3:00 p.m.**-Elementary School kids go to aftercare
- **4:00 p.m.**-Pick up Middle school student from bus stop
- **5:00 p.m.**-Pick up High school student from High school Sports (football, track or lacrosse)
- **6:00 p.m.**-Pick younger kids up from aftercare
- **6:30 p.m.**-Grab dinner
- **7:00 p.m.**-Go to sport activity, Kumon (after school tutoring in math and English) three days a week – Kumon while in public school for educational gaps, so we paid extra for supplemental education
- **9:00 p.m.**-Do homework (if they had any). In public school they didn't have much if any homework—we had no real idea what they did during the day.
- **9:30 p.m.**-Do AFTER-SCHOOLING to teach them what they didn't learn in school
- **10:45 p.m.**-Put them to bed (even if they didn't finish their homework)

Our Schedule
Homeschool

*Finding the curriculum that can be pulled off by two parents
*Childcare/tutors that will come to my home
*Schedule has to be flexible

My homeschooling schedule, and yes, I still work outside of the home:

- **5:00 a.m.**-Mom gets herself up and goes to work
- **9:30 a.m.**-Dad gets up and dresses
- **10:00 a.m.**-Dad wakes kids to start their independent work then leaves for his job
- **11:00 a.m.**-At-home helper comes over
- **2:30 p.m.**-Mom home, relieves at-home helper

- **3:00 p.m.**-Kids do online or DVD curriculum /streaming courses start and Mom present to help or instruct
- **6:00 p.m.**-Eat snack and leave for sports
- **7:00 p.m.**-Go to sport activity
- **9:00 p.m.**-Late and light dinner
- **9:30 p.m.**-Dad helps kids with work they didn't understand or watch a movie, play video games with kids
- **10:45 p.m.**-Kids finished, either go to bed or hang out with Dad

Working In or Outside the Home

Many people believe that working inside the home is a better option for homeschooling than working outside the home. Where a person works is a matter of perspective, but the benefits to both working at home and being outside of the home depends on the circumstances. My husband and I have done both scenarios, and we were less stressed when we worked outside the home. The pay was also better when we found jobs outside of the home. The best scenarios were a blended mix where we could work from home a few days a week or we had a flip-flopped schedule that covered childcare needs. In other words, we transitioned our careers so we could work some days from home and some days in the office.

Benefits for working inside the home for a homeschooling parent:

1. Save money on childcare costs and can easily find an in-home babysitter while the parent is home working.
2. Less time spent on commuting to work, which gives the parent more one-on-one time to homeschool.
3. The cost of working outside the home makes a

difference in the cost of time and money for transportation, business clothes to wear, which makes the transition from work to home easier and faster.

4. In some cases, it gives an overall flexibility to your schedule for work and home life.
5. Work possibly while your children are working by providing a setting where you can watch them, but they can't disturb your work. Sometimes kids just like having a parent around, and they know that you are present.
6. You can travel while working, and it opens up opportunities for homeschooling on the road, being able to work from any location in or outside the home that has Wi-Fi.

Benefits for working outside the home:

1. Work time is focused on work without distractions. Also, gives parent time away to be less obsessed with homeschooling and maybe even go out to lunch with co-workers for fun. It forces the parent to separate and organize scheduling time.
2. It reduces isolation and depression that comes with never leaving the house. Less chance of feeling trapped or stagnant by always being at home.
3. It's easy to make the transition from work to homeschooling and home life.
4. The pay is usually higher for certain jobs when you work outside the home. There is no stress to constantly prove that you are being productive like many employees who work at home have to combat.
5. The opportunity to network with other working parents can open opportunities for your children and yourself outside of work.
6. More likely to work less hours than employees that work from home do. It's easier to get help for technical issues and work closely with teams.

7. It gives parent the mindset to raise independent learners.

The options above give you some aspects to judge what may work best for your family. Sometimes, all it takes is asking your employer for the flexibility of changing your job requirements to allow some days working from home. Remember that a work-from-home job has requirements that may not allow you to be home with your children. They require that childcare is outside of the home. In those cases, hiring home childcare is what many parents do to meet their employer's expectations.

10

Employment Considerations

The type of job you have makes a difference in the ease with which you will be able to maintain homeschooling and working. Consider changing careers, changing jobs, or augmenting your schedule to accommodate your work/life balance. Both my husband and I changed careers after finishing college in order to accommodate our growing family needs. Being flexible in your career choices gives a huge boost to the accommodation of the lifestyle you want to maintain with your family. In those cases, money doesn't always matter as much as the flexibility in schedule.

Evaluate Career and Job Type for Homeschooling and Working

Having flexibility in your job will help lessen the cost of child-care and is an important step toward making homeschooling a reality. Just know that you will have time to do it all and do it well. It will take some creativity. Think about your current career and whether it allows you the ability to come home from work and devote 1 to 2 hours with hands on time with your child, at least three to four times a week (include nights and weekends). That's the least amount of time realistically that you will need to home-school your child in core subjects. If you can't devote at least that amount of time during the weekday, ask yourself: does the income you gain from your job afford you the ability to hire out a course or tutor?

Openness to Changing Career to Take Job with Flexibility

Being open to changing your career to find a work-from-home opportunity, or a work at night job, or several part-time jobs that supplement income and support the family dynamics to homeschool can help. Discuss and evaluate each parent's careers, goals, benefits, needs, and see if a career pause, change, or another type of job would pay close to what they are making to accommodate the change of direction and career focus. This doesn't have to be a permanent diversion from your or your spouse's goals; it is a small change to make while homeschooling your children and bringing in two incomes.

Places to Find Reputable Work-at-home Job and Flexible Job Opportunities

Finding work-from-home opportunities where you get job bene-fits and work for a reputable company is a challenge for most people. Apply for many jobs, at least five to ten a day, until you get opportunities. Be flexible with pay to gauge the market.

My favorite websites to find WAH opportunities are:

- Flexjobs.com (a yearly membership has a small fee, but it's worth it)
- VirtualVocations.com
- Indeed.com (search locations as: Remote or Work From Home)
- Wahadventures.com (Work from Home Adventures)
- Remote.co

Businesses That Pay Good Commissions with Little Start-Up

Many have the multi-level marketing businesses out there as a go-to, but the situation is they usually are over-saturated. Be creative and find different ways to make continuous money as a micro-business if you have skills to support it. Here are some businesses that pay good commissions and have flexible schedules.

Please understand that all businesses take some start-up cash for investment. You may have to work a part-time job to fund the kickoff of a new business.

- Realtor
- Hairstylist, pedicurist
- Esthetician
- Hair removal threading
- Dog walker
- Babysitter
- Tutor
- Web developer
- Housekeeper
- Virtual assistant
- Marketing professional
- Graphic artist
- Editor/writer
- Computer programmer
- Online instructor
- Transcriptionist
- Customer service representative
- Tax accountant
- Nurse (independent, own nursing home)

These were just a few; continue to search for more opportunities that offer flexibility if you seek them.

Working Multiple Jobs for Flexibility with Full-Time Job Pay

To cover childcare, my husband worked several jobs to allow him to be home during the day with the kids while I worked early mornings and maintained the home during the evening hours. You have to disassociate yourself from the career or job you think defines you as a person, and seek out opportunities that meet your family's needs in income and flexibility. Sometimes multiple part-time jobs meet the family's needs. One person to carry the household benefits and the other to flex their jobs around the family childcare schedule. Many spouses complain that with this schedule, they don't get much time together, but it can be done if they have one day a week that neither party works, and they use the extra savings to get childcare to spend time together.

Moving Career to Overnight and or Weekend Work

Working a night and a weekend job may pay a little less but free up the cost of childcare. Working early mornings and late afternoons may allow for less childcare. The purpose is to put together a job combination that meets the pay and the schedule you are seeking. Many people can find similar careers that pay even better when done overnight and weekends.

11

Childcare: Think Outside the Box

Childcare is a major issue for many working parents. For working homeschooling parents, it gets even more complicated. Until a certain age and level of maturity, proper childcare is important but also costly. Childcare when a kid is in school is covered for at least six to seven hours and is free if you want to consider public, private, or charter schools as a form of childcare. This covers most parents' babysitting concerns for children ages four until eighteen years of age. So how does a working and homeschooling parent find care for their child so they can work?

In-Home Daycare

Consider searching for home daycare providers that have the flexibility to watch older children during the day. It's a benefit to your child who can get help throughout the day. All the work will be done by the time you get home from work to pick them up. There are 24-hour daycare providers and centers that can accommodate any schedule.

Flip Flop work schedule with Spouse

In this case, a parent works a regular 9 a.m. to 5 p.m. schedule, and the other parent works a job around that schedule so that there is always a parent home. In this scenario, the family saves money in childcare costs.

- One parent works full-time standard hours; the other parent works full-time night hours.
- One parent works full-time standard hours, the other parent works part-time weekend and/or some nights.
- Both parents work part-time hours around the other, maintaining the ability for someone to always be home with the children.

Flip-Flop work schedule with another Parent

Consider working with other homeschooling parents or family members who also need childcare. Barter with a friend who will watch your kids for another form of payment. This works well for single-parents and can be a viable option for family members and friends who have kids, work in a commutable distance, and will share childcare.

Create a Babysitting Co-op

Network with other working parents who may own a business, work hours opposite yours, work part-time, and you build a team who provides childcare for the kids throughout the week. Make a schedule, contract, and agreement on who does what days and how the Co-op works.

Babysitter Swap and Nanny Share

If you have a friend with a standing babysitter, you can share the expense and days of the full-time spot with the other parent. Sharing a nanny with another family is a great way to save on costs and to get the childcare you need for only the hours needed. You can interview both the person you are sharing the nanny with and the nanny. Also, you can go through nanny services that you find online to inquire about nanny sharing in your area.

Co-Work Spaces with Childcare

For work-at-home parents, getting out of the house and finding a co-work space to rent can be worth it, especially if the place includes or has onsite childcare. It can also offer nanny-share spaces.

Place Child in Daycare, Aftercare, or Before-care Programs

Just because your child doesn't attend traditional school, realize that you can still utilize the same daycare situations as when your child was in traditional school.

- Private home daycare providers will be flexible in this type of scenario.
- Before and after school care centers will accommodate kids that aren't in traditional school settings.

Find a Nanny or In-home Tutor

This may take a small hit on a homeschooling parent's budget, but having an in-home nanny or tutor can be a lifesaver. This allows the family to get childcare, some light cleaning, and someone to cook dinner.

- Using an au pair that is between the ages of eighteen and thirty from another country. Research nanny services that offer au pair which can also open your child up to learning another language by having an onsite teacher living within the home. An au pair can also expose your child to different languages and cultures.
- Using a high school or homeschool teenager to watch

your children is good when it's not a full day, but you need a fill-in babysitter for when your schedule leaves no childcare coverage.

- Using a college student that you find in community colleges or universities. A parent can place ads at these establishments for nannies and home-helpers.

Utilize Spring Break, Summer Camps, and Winter Camps

Some daycare centers offer camps to cover long breaks in the school system. These Spring Break or Winter Fun camps are great for homeschooling parents and kids to get some childcare help. It offers an opportunity for kids to socialize with other children their ages.

You can find these by dropping into the local school and picking up some of the publications the kids get to share after school and on break enrichment activities. Summer camp offers great support during the summer months for childcare and learning opportunities, and can focus on the child's specified areas of interest.

Your Gym's Daycare

Some gyms offer licensed daycare for parents while they work out in the gym. However, in some cases, they do allow for kids to be there for up to a certain amount of time. If you are able to work from anywhere, utilize the gym and all the optional daycare hours by working while at the gym.

State Provided Childcare Development Funds

Many states have babysitting monetary assistance programs that are funded by the government. It is for low-income parents or the primary caregiver of kids below thirteen years old. Read more about this benefit at benefits.gov.

Move-in Grandparents or Aunts or Cousins for Childcare Help

Multi-family living arrangements used to be a main source of childcare. Moving in grandparents, or sharing childcare with a cousin, sibling, and their family, or bringing in a relative's college student can be a way to get childcare and have a home backup. Offering payment can even sweeten the deal. Be specific about expectations of the living arrangement, and avoid abusing the convenience.

Enroll child in a Tutorial or Homeschool Hybrid

This option is available for families in some states where it's popular. You have to search your location to see if a Tutorial or Homeschool Hybrid is available. It offers in-classroom teaching only two to three days a week and school online days the other days of the week. The two such schools in my current state are state-funded charter schools with educational flexibility.

Other Unique Ways to Gain Childcare

Parents that need childcare at odd times, or in unique situations like homeschooling, get creative by thinking outside of the norm. Don't be afraid to ask other trusted homeschooler their ideas on childcare.

- Ask a stay-at-home parent; they may like the opportunity to make extra money.
- Consider jobs where you can take your child to work with you.
- If your children fit the legal age to stay home alone, consider allowing them to.
- Ask your spouse or the children's father or mother to keep them.
- Inquire if your employer has onsite childcare.

- Ask your employer to allow you to work from home some days.

Start your own childcare business

Creating your own childcare related business can be the answer to making money and staying at home. You can set your own hours, have tax benefits for doing so, and create flexible income. You can also offer your own nanny service where you go to a client's house that is lenient with you bringing your child along. Starting a childcare business can be a transitional business for people in teaching careers.

Whatever form of childcare out of the box you use, always have a backup plan in case your situation changes. Life happens, and childcare needs change with it.

12

If Child is Home Alone While You Work

Leaving your child at home alone to do their homeschool work while you are at your job is possible. It is not uncommon for kids to stay home alone. Many working parents, even those that do not homeschool, have a latch-key child. Many children leave their house to walk to school or take the school or public bus to and from school. In some cases, kids hire an Uber or Lyft taxi service to take them to and from school. They are usually home alone either before or after school.

Not many states have laws regarding this, and of the three known at the time this book is written, the youngest age for allowing a child at home alone is 7 years old.

General Age and Guidance for Length of Time Alone

Verify the Laws in Your State

The law applies regarding age and length of time a parent should be able to leave their child home alone. The consensus is: seven years of age and younger, the child should not be left home alone for any time period. As of the ages eight years to ten, the child shouldn't be home alone more than 1.5 hours during that day, but not at all during the night. From age eleven to twelve, up to three hours during the day only. Teenagers from thirteen years to fifteen can be left alone all day, but not overnight. When a child reaches sixteen to seventeen years old, they can be left alone for a few days at a time. It is in the best interest of the parent to verify this fact with local law enforcement to avoid confusion if it is found that the child is home unsupervised.

Safety Measures

When you leave your child home alone, you must prepare them for any possible situation that may occur while you aren't there. Such as: someone knocking at the door, calling on the home phone, trying to get into the house, a fire in the home, and behavior for online and interaction with someone that may or may not know that they are home by themselves.

Here are some tips for you to use if your child will be home unsupervised. These actions can give you a level of comfort.

- Do not tell anyone that your child is home alone, and ensure that your child does not share this information either.
- Install a home security system.
- Teach child to work the locks and security and to make the home secure.
- Get a dog that the child can train or will be available for protection and companionship.
- Create a list of home-alone rules to place in their bedroom.
- Do fire drills.
- Have child memorize your address, cellphone number, work number.
- Have a list of people your child can contact in an emergency.

- Don't allow them to open the door or have company over without approval.
- Teach them emergency safety care and CPR.
- Use security cameras to communicate/check on them.
- Communicate with them during the day, hourly if possible.
- Don't have guns, car keys, medications, and matches in easy-access locations.

Know Your Neighbors

Get to know your neighbors. Know who is home during the day and the times your child is home. Check the Child and Sex Offenders Registries to ensure there aren't any nearby your home. Also, show your child the person's picture in case they notice someone lurking around.

Child Maturity

Every child is different, and maturity is very important when considering leaving the child home alone. Work through scenarios with your child to gauge their maturity. Teach them to understand their responsibilities while home alone. Take your time making this transition, and have measures in place to give the child the ability to tell you what they are uncomfortable with doing while alone.

Home Rules for Child
Hang on Your Child's Bedroom Wall

The major rules for children home alone are the following, no matter what the age:

- Lock all windows and doors
- No answering phone or door (have cellphone for communication with parent)
- Look at the video cameras occasionally to see if anyone

is lurking around the house and to view who may be at the door

- No friends over
- Tell no one you are home alone
- Do not cook on the stove
- Know emergency evacuation rules (where to go)
- Know emergency call for help phone numbers
- Know all parents' phone numbers and phone number of several people nearby that can pick up or drop over to check things if parent not home

13

Alternatives to teaching at home

Many homeschooling parents try to provide an environment for their kids to learn outside of their home. That's where Cooperatives (Co-ops), Tutorials, and Umbrella schools come in. None of them are created equal and are as different and diverse as can be.

These don't always fit the needs of parents with jobs outside the home since they may require parental involvement during school hours. Parents in these groups tend to mostly be stay-at-home mothers who may not understand the challenges of a working parent. It can be awkward if trying to build a community of friends to network with but can be an opportunity to find possible paid childcare. In some cases, these groups can also be cliquish. No matter what the challenges may be, it would be best to visit some and make your own decision whether it is a good fit for you and your child. However, it can be a way to extend a child's learning and give a parent somewhere for their child to be while they are at work.

Commonalities

The few things that Co-ops, Tutorials and Umbrella schools have in common: costs, rules, and curriculum are selected by the organizing party. None of the transcripts or courses offered will give the student a state school grade. However, they may give a home-school grade if requested by the parent.

Co-ops

The Homeschool Cooperative (Co-ops) involves several families, even organizations like churches or groups that like a particular curriculum. They come together to co-teach and get together with their kids. Co-ops aren't a typical class or teaching environment. Most times, the age groups are mixed and the teachers are usually not licensed teachers but are homeschooling parents who are passionate about a particular topic or subject. Parents take turns or schedule in a cohesive environment where they do curriculum, play dates, arts, crafts, and more. These meetings may happen a few days a month or a week and change from year to year. You cannot get formal school credit from a Co-op in most states.

Tutorials

Tutorials are classes for service. They run a few days a week, are not deemed as a private school, but have certified teachers or teachers with advanced degrees. The tutorial provides curriculum, teaching, grading, and transcripts only for the classes taught there. They aren't the same as a transcript from a private school but can save the parent effort in creating one. There is no accreditation usually, so the parent still controls the final transcript. No parental volunteering is usually necessary although it is appreciated in most cases.

Homeschool Umbrella

For families who enjoy some type of oversight, want an organi-zation to be their middle person, or want mentorship in educating their child, Umbrella Groups are a great option. The prices are usually very reasonable and can include curriculum or not. They can offer transcript creation, mediation assistance, and ensure that the children meet government education requirements. All are as different as one private school is to another. There isn't a board-associated accreditation for most of them; consider researching what is offered or expected.

14

Setting Realistic Expectations

The first and foremost expectation and goal of homeschooling and working should be to build a close and loving relationship with your child. Don't ever let educating your child get in the way of that. Remember, as long as they are growing to perform well in their core courses or anchor courses, all the rest will fall in place.

Before diving into homeschooling, being realistic is the first step to managing your expectations. Sometimes, just letting learning happen without expectations can allow your children to exceed them.

In order to start from a good place, create a list of your bottom-line goals for the school year, and build your mindset to be happy that, at the very least, you've met them.

1. List what must be accomplished this year of homeschooling.
   ~Examples:

   - Improve my relationship with my child
   - Help my child overcome their anxiety
   - My child must memorize their addition, multiplication, division, and subtraction rules

- My child must know how to phonetically sound out and read short vowel words
- My child must have the ability to write his name, our address, and phone number
- My child must work independently for thirty-minute intervals
- My child must know how to write a research paper without help.

2. Ask your child what they want from the school year.
   ~Examples:

- Child wants two field trips a month
- Child wants to participate in a camp or sport
- Child wants to study animals

Make the First Goal Unrelated to School but on Self-Esteem

Most working parents only consider homeschooling when their child has some negative experiences at their traditional schools. Likely, the child was exposed to, expressed, or was hurt by events that have taken place. Many of their challenges aren't understood or witnessed by parents while the child is home. It takes the child some time to get to the level of comfort, when homeschooling with their parent, to display some behaviors that may have gone unnoticed. Realistic expectations for your first-year homeschooling and working should be to focus on the basics—first and foremost, to get your child to a good emotional and mental place.

Games can be a way to encourage kids to speak up about their feelings. Some board games to consider are:

- Mindfulness Therapy games
- Totem the Feel-Good game
- LetzTalk Conversation Starter
- Mad Dragon game

- You Know game
- Playing CBT game

Also, other self-esteem building curriculums:

- The Big Life Journal curriculum

Teach your child how to relax, calm anger, reinforce their positive affirmations, and talk through stress

- Create a Calm Down List of phrases for a child to control their emotions: Please visit Chapter 30 for more details.
- Build a list of actions that specifically reduces your child's stress, and act them out with them.
- Have the child recite their positive affirmations to re-establish their positive self-esteem.
- When the child makes mistakes or gets in trouble, ask them: "How could you have turned your day around? What could you have done differently? Are you willing to consider a positive action?
- Teach your child to make their own choices but to discern a better choice for next time.
- Let them feel comfortable sharing their thoughts in a respectful manner without worrying about punishment.

Filling in the Gaps and Building Foundation Should Be #2 on your list

Coming from a traditional school setting, most kids have skated by without retaining what they have learned. This can be problematic in subjects that build on each lesson, such as math, reading, english and writing. In order to have a successful learning journey, use the time while homeschooling to rebuild the bridges of gaps in your child's education. This should be done after rebuilding their self-esteem. They have to be reprogrammed to think about working for grades and know that it's all about them learning at their pace, in their space, their way.

Focus on Behavioral Growth

Behavior is a major obstacle for most parents. Homeschooling gives a parent the chance to redirect behavior problems. The importance of seeking tools, trying scenarios, and adjusting these behaviors in an age appropriate manner will alleviate roadblocks later in their learning.

Remember, as far as teens go, you should transition them to an adult mindset. That happens with challenges. Considering that a sixteen-year-old is virtually going to be a grown man in just two years, he should be comfortable expressing his opinion in a respectful manner. He should also be held responsible for his mistakes, then to consider them in a logical way that assesses the areas for improvement. Whereas a child from age sixteen and below should respect and expect direction from their parents.

Behavioral growth should be about getting the child to understand the importance of following rules and communicating their questions or concerns. They should not become robots that can't express the way they feel about circumstances.

Knowing Their Personal Information

Kids should know their personal identifiable information. Their home address, their parents' full names, directions to their home from a main highway, the home and cellphone numbers of parents, the work numbers of parents. Knowing their address, emergency phone numbers, where they were born, and even their social security number is important. Writing their name in cursive and all of their personally identifiable information is an asset to children in all situations.

15

Child's Learning Style and Personality Type

The best part about homeschooling and being a working parent is that since you are their main educator, you get to learn more about your child than ever before.

It is important to get to know your child's learning styles and personality type. This can change over time, so evaluate and discuss with your child what worked for them and what didn't, or why.

There are seven known learning styles that your child may fit into. Some kids learn by way of a combination of them.

Child's Concentration and Need for Sleep

Building an approach that is customized to your child's learning ability starts with understanding what they are able to focus on, how long, and at what age. Sleep is a major part in the child's ability to concentrate. According to WebMD, a school-aged child needs 9 to 11 hours of sleep. Keep these factors in mind when selecting a method to educate them.

The amount of sleep a person needs*

Age		Hours of sleep a day
Infants	0-3 Months	14-17 Hours
Infants	4-11 Months	12-15 Hours
Toddlers	1-2 Years	11-14 Hours
Pre-school Children	Ages 3-5	10-13 Hours
School-age Children	Ages 6-13	9-11 Hours
Teenagers	Ages 14-17	8-10 Hours

* According to WebMD

Types of Learning Styles

Use your knowledge of your child's learning style to better determine the methods of instruction and the curriculum to use for their success.

Type	Learning Style
Visual	A visual learner absorbs information best by use of pictures, different images, and three-dimensional understanding (spatial)
Aural	This learner does best with using music or sound to absorb information (auditory-musical)
Verbal	A verbal learner needs to be spoken to or learns from speech, lectures, and written works (linguistic)
Physical	The physical learner does well using their body, hands, and touch in learning (kinesthetic)
Logical	A logical learner needs to think through things and uses logic, reasoning, and methods to learn (mathematical)
Social	A social learner needs to work with groups or other people to learn, even with the parent, to be able to express what they learned and be excited about learning (interpersonal)
Solitary	The solitary learner prefers to be left alone to work undisturbed and uses self-study to understand subjects as they go (intrapersonal)

Ways to Evaluate Learning Styles

Observation of your child is an easy way to evaluate their learning style. Take time to note, and watch your child's interactions for these:

- How do they express themselves? If they are visual learners, they show their emotional responses in their faces or by watching others' facial cues. For a kinesthetic learner, they like to move hands, expressions through movement.
- Talk to them about their interests, what they find exciting, watching a show, doing a hands-on project, reading a book and other activities associated with each.
- Observe their methods of problem solving.
- Note what sparks their interest, motivation, excitement.
- Talk to others who have taught or interacted with your child.
- Ask your child what they prefer and how they prefer to learn.

Another way of evaluating their learning style is to do a test. There are several tests and services that can be utilized in defining your child's learning styles. Here are some below:

- *School Family*: This website has twelve questions that the child checks to show their interests to define the child's learning style. (Teacher Lists: Learning Styles Quiz: https://tinyurl.com/y9xqxnsl)
- *EducationalPlanner.org*: This website gives a choice of three different learning styles it tests for: visual, auditory, and tactile Education Planner Org: What's Your Learning Style: https://tinyurl.com/7oh89lq
- *Love To Know*: It is a fast quiz for you to answer for your child. (Learning Style Quiz for Kids: https://tinyurl.com/ybytugco)
- *VARK Questionnaire*: It tests four of the learning styles (http://vark-learn.com/the-vark-questionnaire/)

- *Kid Telligent:* A deep diving test that will help identify child's learning style and personality type: (http://www. kidtelligent.com/)

Knowing Your Child's Personality Type
For Understanding and Communication

Personality tests can give a parent an edge when understanding the best communication methods to use with their kids and to dissect some challenges when doing so. Here is a great website for taking a personality test, 16Personalities (https://www. 16personalities.com) will give the test and show the different personality types. Take the test with your child; ask them the questions, and you can put in the answers if they aren't old enough to do it. Try doing it every year. It's fun and gives them a bit of insight on themselves and how they interact with their world.

Understanding what makes your child want to learn, communicate, and the best methods to teach them will make a selection of a curriculum much easier.

16

Child's Learning Gaps and Levels

The evaluation of learning gaps is an important step in building realistic expectations for your child and solidifying a firm base in their learning going forward. Whenever you take a student from one learning system to another, you will find that there may be some unknown learning gaps.

Use this evaluation when it comes to selection of your curriculum, planning of expectations, and while building the list of growth to accomplish.

Testing is a great way to assess your child's gaps. You can conduct a self-made test, purchase a test, or do a free test found on various education-based sites.

Test at the beginning and end of a school year. Sometimes every quarter if you want to evaluate whether your child is progressing with the new curriculum the way you'd hoped. The educational gaps should be addressed early on in homeschooling in order to solidify a firm base.

Deciding to Conduct an Assessment Test

The best time to do the assessment test is when you first start homeschooling your child. Do it at the beginning of the school year and then again at the end of the school year to chart your child's growth. It will help you evaluate what worked and what didn't. Also, it gives you an idea of what growth may have been lost during the school break periods. After your child has mastered math, reading, writing, and comprehension, testing isn't needed as much to measure growth. You would test through 8th grade Math and English. Then, only if your child starts homeschooling in high school, you would do an initial school year assessment.

When Child Suffers from Testing Anxiety

As a homeschooling parent, you can approach testing in many different ways. If your child is afraid of the expectations of the test, here are some tips.

- Let your child know that the testing isn't something he could fail. It's a test for you to see what you need to help them with in order for you to be a good teacher for them.
- Read the directions of the test, and walk through how to solve the questions with them. Be calm during this and supportive.
- Ask them if they feel comfortable finishing the rest of the test themselves. If they aren't, continue to walk through it with them. Reiterate to them that the test isn't about them; it's about helping you to help them.
- Do not answer the questions with them or get frustrated. If they are stuck, ask them the question in a different way.
- Give them positive speak and affirmations during the testing process.
- Continue this method, and slowly do less and less questions with them by letting them know the exact number you will help them with to get them started.

- Show them how to use calming techniques like breathing exercises, stretching, holding their hands wide for a few minutes, smiling, petting their animal, writing down positive words and phrases.

Where to get Assessment Test

There are several test and services that can be utilized in defining your child's learning styles. Here are some that I've personally used below:

Abeka Testing Service (1-888-772-0044) Call to ask about the service. The parent administers the written test to the child. Online testing is available for kids when parents don't qualify as testing administrator. Offers test grading and interpretation.

Academic Excellence (1-866-960-9331) California Achievement Test (CAT) is made for homeschoolers, and no training or certification is required. It's online, and an untimed version is available with a practice test. Offers test grading and interpretation.

Bayside Testing Service (1-900-723-3057) A TerraNova in a complete battery of tests or short format for cognitive assessment. Offers test grading and interpretation.

BJU Press (1-800-845-5731) Offers three test choices, including the Stanford 10. Offers test grading and interpretation.

For additional and a more extensive list, please refer to **https://hslda.org**

Other Options

Before we homeschooled, I took my kids for free assessments at several tutoring and learning centers. My favorite was:

Kumon (https://www.kumon.com/) which teaches kids core math and reading skills by rapid memorization and drills. I personally used this for all of my kids through elementary school, and it was the help they needed to solidify facts up to 8th grade and Algebra. Also, it is a great way to reinforce and clear up learning gaps in these subjects if this works for your child's learning style.

Sylvan (https://www.sylvanlearning.com/) A tutoring franchise that I used for my kids when they were in traditional school and also somewhat during homeschooling for subjects I didn't feel comfortable teaching or administering.

17

The Least My Child Needs to Learn for Educational Success

Keep your eyes on the basics. Sometimes as homeschooling parents, we want to keep up with the traditional school way of teaching and thinking. In homeschooling and being a working parent, you want to focus on building the foundation for success and allowing your child's interests, strengths, and new discoveries to fuel their path, which will be easy when they can read, write, comprehend, be comfortable with math, and effectively communicate.

First order of business is to focus your initial start in homeschooling on filling in gaps and building the core anchor courses that feed success in all other areas (math, reading, comprehension and writing).

The Subjects That Influence Proficiency in All Others

The subjects in school, any school, that are the building blocks to education and can help them to succeed in any topic if they are mastered by your child are reading, writing, comprehension and math. If you learn to read and comprehend, you can teach yourself anything just by reading about it. Learning logic and test-taking skills with the ability to memorize allows your child to absorb anything and show understanding. Lastly, if you learn logic and reasoning, you have developed a thought process to take what was learned, process it, and create your own approach.

Here are the courses I found that, once my kids mastered them, allowed them to soar.

Reading and Comprehension

The most powerful tool in learning is to have the ability of reading with comprehension. It's the ability to teach oneself by reading directions and understanding them. Also, reading a story and retaining the main points.

Elementary school: Teaching your child to read is the first most helpful step in building their ability to self-learn later. We started by teaching the kids the vowel sounds then the consonant sounds. After that, we taught the name of the letter, but by then, the child was already learning to read phonetically. We used *Hooked on Phonics* and taught them to read in three months by working on it daily (even weekends) for about twenty minutes a day.

Some methods to consider when teaching children to read:

- Phonics: Learning the sound and name of each letter and blends to sound out words.
- The Whole-word Method: The child learns to memorize or recognize the word—not the sound of the letters—to read. They don't decode by sounding the words as with learning phonics. This method is a good companion method to use after phonics is taught. It can also be used for children with good capacity for memorizing.
- Orton-Gillingham Method: This form of teaching reading is usually used for children with dyslexia. It teaches by showing the word connection to an action, place, or thing.
- The Read Naturally Method: Teaches kids to learn by using audio books, software, and books to do read along.

The child basically learns by memory and the rhythm of the writing.

- The Read, Write and Type Method: Use this for teaching older kids to read by using software that teaches the child to read while teaching them to type words.
- Reading Recovery Method: A focused short tutoring curriculum for struggling readers. It is to work on areas where the child has gaps.

Middle school: Start to introduce speed reading drills at this stage. This was practiced with timed read out loud and silent reading and comprehension drills. In addition, we used vocabulary builder tools like *membean.com* to increase the child's understanding of words.

High school: At this point, we enrolled our kids in formal speed-reading courses. Some were in person, and others were online. The online program we used was Ace Reader and 7speedreading.com, which helped our kids improve their reading and comprehension.

Math: Instant Recall of Addition, Subtraction, Multiplication and Division

Math is a struggle for most students. Realize that traditional school spends the majority of middle school reinforcing elementary school taught math skills. If your child needs extra time to build instant recall, give it to them. Those skills will allow them to soar in advanced math.

Three of my four children took a long time to have the core topics solidified. The truth was memorization worked, and it included drills. My oldest three kids used a tutoring service named *Kumon,* and it was a big help, but after a point, they hated the monotony of it. My oldest girl stuck with the program until they got her to Algebra 1(She was in 7th grade when she stopped.), and I have to say she is my best math student and was a math teacher's assistant in high school and college. My other students used Saxon

Math with video lessons, CTCMath and Xtramath.org for drills as well as math sheets.

IMPORTANT NOTE: Kids must learn to do quick recall of the facts, to recall verbally, visually, and written.

1. To see the problem and respond verbally via flash cards held by parent
2. To answer problem quickly on a computer
3. To write the answer quickly on paper
4. To verbalize or write the steps involved with solving the problem

The reason I note the above is that math recall happens in different forms: by memory with visual and verbal answers, by written response which processes in the child's mind differently than verbal recall. However, if you test your child these few ways, you will see that the recall may be slower in some instances or completely wrong in others.

Elementary school: By the end of elementary school, your child should be able to recite their addition, subtraction, multiplication, and division facts. They should be comfortable doing timed drills up to the double digits.

Middle school: In middle school, the child should be able to complete stacked addition problems, complex subtraction, long division, and multiplication **without a calculator**. If your child can do this and do this without a struggle, you can move them easily to Pre-Algebra and on. **Note: Work towards knowledge that builds mastery. Don't move on until they are really comfortable and accurate with these skills without a calculator.**

High school: When the student reaches high school, having a grasp on at least Algebra 1, Algebra 2, and Geometry is to their benefit even if they aren't planning on attending college. Also, **keep up with daily basic math drills** for prep of standardized tests required for colleges and some career fields. These skills may be tested if they are going to trade school, the military, or even to work a career.

Grammar and Writing

Did you know that 80% of college work includes writing papers? It's unbelievable that this seems to be the one subject most people don't realize has a major effect on their child's success in all other classes. In addition, writing folds into many career fields and is a tool used in everyday life.

Elementary school: We usually started with sentence writing, then paragraph writing when the kid was a good reader and could comprehend what they were reading. This was usually at grade 3 or 4 (age ten years). The curriculum we used was heavy in grammar; however, we did supplement with some great tools. Our base curriculum was strong in language arts and grammar. We selected Junior Analytical Grammar and Mechanics as it had a video companion teaching tool with it. The child should know how to write, edit, and understand grammar facts.

Middle school: At this point, the child should be able to write essays, research papers, edit their work and others' effectively. We then moved to Analytical Grammar curriculum with Time4Writing.com and Sandiego Scribbler online courses to teach and test them in this area. We expected timed essay writing by age fourteen years, for the child to be able to write (by hand) a legible and well written 300-word essay within thirty minutes.

High school: It is expected that the child can write a detailed research paper or study within two days with valid sources.

Logic

The development of reasoning and logic will be a great tool in tests-taking, attacking problems and finding solutions. Logical thinking is a lifelong skill that truly benefited my children.

Elementary school: To build logic at this stage, we used puzzles, games, and played what-if scenarios. We used the tool called math grids for kids.

Middle school: We introduced logical thinking processes, the historical figures of the school of logic, and a curriculum like Fallacy Detective, The Thinking Toolbox, Introductory Logic, and the Art of Reasoning.

High school: At this point, we had our children exposed to debate clubs and groups. They also took Intermediate Logic courses online and with Compass Classroom logic curriculum. The student should learn how to make an argument, dissect the argument, write papers, and verbally defend an argument or study.

Verbal Communication and Logical Debate

At this point your child can bring together all of their skills and share comfortably with others. Public speaking and debate are good ways to give them this comfort. Giving speeches comfortably communicated with others is a life-skill that will help your child succeed in all areas of learning.

Elementary school: Your child should be comfortable sharing their explanation of work to others within the family and outside the family. Doing projects and science experiments that they have to present is a good way to develop this skill.

Middle school: When middle school ends, the student should be able to give a three-minute speech on any topic, answer questions, complete a mini-interview with someone, interview another person for a topic, and be able to prepare for the presentation.

High school: The student should feel comfortable giving a ten-minute speech and presentation, participating in debates where they defend their point and counter another's view. A ten-minute speech that they write, develop a presentation for and can deliver easily should be something that they practice during their high school years.

18

Styles of Homeschooling

Homeschooling styles are a classification of more than eight top methods to conduct school at home. We will review them, but the truth is, many don't mix well for working parents who will be out of the home or unavailable for their students. However, everyone's working and homeschooling experience is unique, so review these styles to see what may fit.

What to Consider as Working Parent

To save yourself from disaster, consider these points when evaluating what style will work for you.

- How much time would parent teacher have to spend doing the below?
- teaching lessons
- administering lessons
- checking or reviewing lessons
- Does this fit with my child's learning style?
- Will I be able to meet our minimum goals with this approach in the timeframe desired?

- Can this style be combined with another to meet our family's needs?

Top Styles for Homeschooling

Additional styles of homeschooling than listed can be explored, but these are the main types you will find when you talk to other homeschoolers. Don't be afraid to combine styles.

School at home or traditional: This approach is that homeschooling is the same structure as a traditional school with the child being at a desk or table doing a full curriculum from a curriculum provider in some cases, or doing an online school program that follows strict adherence to subjects and topics. This approach takes about two to three hours for elementary and four to six hours a day from middle school and up. This approach may have long days and lots of additional work or homework. School at home usually doesn't work because this is the structure that doesn't fit well with the child's development and attention span.

Points to note from a homeschool and working standpoint

- Time consuming
- Rigorous
- Some flexibility
- Longer day (two to five hours)
- Works well for students that desire this type of experience and structure when transitioning from traditional schools

Online or Virtual Traditional/Public School: Legally these students aren't homeschoolers as they are enrolled in a public-school system or private school system that is accredited. This approach may have long days and lots of additional work or homework.

Points to note from a homeschool and working standpoint

- Time consuming

- Rigorous
- No flexibility
- Longer day (two to five hours)
- Homework (or work in addition to the day of school)

Classical: An age-old teaching style that focuses on tools such as reason, record, research, relate and rhetoric. Grammar based with logic and rhetoric. The classical based curriculum is a language-based curriculum and rarely includes videos or hands-on approaches. The subjects are woven together by the works to read for the school year. Includes memory work, lots of reading by the child, and parent to child, practice, copy work and narration.

Points to note from a homeschool and working standpoint

- Lots of reading for the student
- Rigorous and systematic
- Some flexibility
- Longer day (two to five hours)
- Combines many subjects during reading sessions

Charlotte Mason: In this style, use 'living books' instead of textbooks. The point is to make the literature interesting yet challenging to the student, and it wraps learning into the reading and journaling. The point is to have short periods of instruction and mix it with active learning through field trips, reading, and acting out lessons in plays.

Points to note from a homeschool and working standpoint

- No lectures
- Lots of reading for the student
- Flexibility as you can use audio books to assist in reading
- Shorter day (fifteen to twenty-minute classes for Elementary and Middle and no more than forty-five minutes for High school)
- Combines many subjects during reading sessions

Eclectic: Relaxed homeschool. The most popular form of homeschooling is eclectic and combines many styles to fit well within household dynamics. This method adheres to the state required subject standard and mixes in whatever curriculum or style works best for the child.

Points to note from a Homeschool and Working Standpoint

- Different methods combined
- Flexibility
- Length of day is dependent upon the parents' choice of curriculum mix
- Can be challenging for a parent to organize

Unschooling: An extremely relaxed homeschool method that is completely led by the child, their interests, and their motivations. The parent acts as a facilitator and places opportunities to spark interest in their child. In some extreme cases, children aren't made to read, write, or do math unless they are interested in it.

Points to note from a homeschool and working standpoint

- No method really but determined by a child's interest and learning style
- Flexibility
- Parent has to put forth facilitation as requested by the child
- May cause serious gaps in learning that will be difficult to recover from if faced with the need to return to traditional school setting without preparation
- Child may show anxiety when placed in a formal learning setting with rules and expectations
- Parent may get frustrated if a child doesn't want to pursue interests considered relevant such as reading, writing, or math
- Some children whose parents partake in extreme unschooling will not learn to read until they want to, which can be upwards to middle school age.

Montessori: Montessori is all about free movement and interest-based learning that is structured more so than unschooling as parents lead the approach. The child is encouraged to learn at their own pace with use of wooden figures, hands-on activities, discovery, and reading. Discourages television and computers for younger students.

Points to note from a homeschool and working standpoint – this does take a lot of prep time to set up.

- Action and reading based
- Parental interaction and prep needed
- Flexible
- Shorter day
- Student led

19

Create an Independent Learner

In a working and homeschooling environment, creating an independent learner is a must. Several methods can be used, and it takes a lot of time, patience, and effort to groom some kids to that point, but it can be done. All aspects and learning styles can be shaped to cater to the independent learner.

Understanding What Independent Learning is

Know that an independent learner is not expected to do everything on their own, without a parent, any questions, or accountability. Know that your student should ask questions and learn at their own pace. **Don't expect a child to basically teach themselves everything** without any help or guidance when needed. To do so is not fair to the child, nor is it realistic. Adults don't even operate that way when learning, so we must not expect our children to be able to do so without support.

- Not the child teaching themselves everything.
- Not the child performing at 100% without accountability or guidance.

- The child will have questions and will need to be comfortable asking them.
- The child should already know how to read, comprehend, and write. These skills initially have to be taught by a parent, teacher, and tutor. They can't teach those skills to themselves with perfection.
- The child should not be responsible for teaching younger children in place of parental support in learning.
- They should have some one-on-one attention per subject each day.
- It's best that they are nurtured to the point of being on grade level with peers in reading, comprehension, writing, and math.
- Parent should impose accountability that involves parental interaction.

Organization is Key in Encouraging Self-Learning

Taking the time to prepare and organize your child's environment to support independence in learning is the key to keeping everyone on the same page, moving the child forward, and giving the child ownership in their scheduled activities and goals.

- Use a Scheduling System for the day and the week that the child can refer to and check off accomplished lessons, actions, or tasks completed.
- Organize by subject items the child should use to get through their goals or lessons for the day and week.
- Involve them in the goal setting, lesson planning for the week and day.
- Set up bookshelves, moving drawers, accordion folders, or anything that holds their materials, allows them to see their schedule posted, and is their master center for learning materials.

Help Less and Less

It's difficult to watch your child struggle. However, to teach them to learn independently, you have to encourage them to work through the steps, or learning, failing, and re-learning. Each time you help them, show them how you are getting your answers.

- Have them re-read any directions.
- Have them explain what they understood from the directions to you the parent educator.
- Write down a lecture.
- Review their work.
- Compare work with a textbook.
- Have them explain what the lesson was, what they didn't understand before, and what they understand after your help.

Teach Them How to Research Answers to Their Questions

The best tool a parent can give a child in learning independently is the lesson in researching their own answers. Have the child read the issue, dissect the parts and questions in the issue, seek methods to solve the questions, then write the steps to forming their conclusions. After they've accomplished those steps, let them check their work with teacher's books or manuals, and create notecards or notes on what they didn't grasp. Allow them to explain the lesson, the questions they got wrong, why they think they got them wrong, and whether they agree with the answer. It will teach them to process corrective ways to learn material, find the right answers, and to take notes to review problem areas later. Asking them open-ended questions that lead them to the right answers is the key.

Have them check their own work

Once they are taught to research their answers, allow them the freedom to check their own work (through open book or internet search – not the teacher's manual). However, make them write down or tell you how they got their answers. When the work and their wide check of it is done against the book or internet, then give them the teacher's manual to check their work, and correct their notes.

Find Curriculums that have a Teacher via Online, DVD, or Teaches through Discovery

As a working parent, time is of the essence, and finding curriculum that comes with a teacher, tutor, or learning assistant works best. However, try to match your child's learning style in the selection of the curriculum.

Take time to teach your child to take notes and keep a notebook handy if they are learning this way. It makes recall easier and allows the parent to review notes without having to watch the lecture if the child has questions or lack understanding in an area.

Separate Work in Groups to Do Independently and With Parent

Always have topics the child can do themselves but that they can share what they've learned with others. Put a separator in the schedule so they know what work is theirs to work on independently and what work they will do with a parent. This can start as young as kindergarten.

As they Mature, Give Them Freedom in These Areas

Kids are constantly growing and changing. Giving them the freedom to do their work when and where they want in the day garners independent learning and responsibility for their task. Just add an accountability measure that lets them know work will be reviewed by the parent the next morning or at the end of the week.

Even though the below are offered areas of independence, having time and someone to talk about what they learned is very important. Make it a point to have that as part of the accountability. Allow them to grow into having a voice and to plan the areas below.

- When they'd like to chat about what they learned
- School day times
- When to complete their work
- How they will finish their work
- What topics to work on which days
- What to study and focus on
- The type of curriculum they want to use
- Selection of books to read
- Where to go on field trips

The Workbox System

This system saved my homeschooling and working adventure. It does take time to set up weekly, but it is a great way to teach kids independence. It saves you time during the week, helps your kids prioritize tasks, and is flexible and versatile while being scheduled. It will assist more than one educator with staying on task and keeping the kid focused while giving them a sense of control of their progress. (Based on the 2008 book by Sue Patrick *Sue Patrick's Workbox System A User's Guide*)

How it works:

1. Use a drawer set with a separate drawer for each subject.
   (Note: you can use an accordion folder, shoebox,
   magazine rack, file folders, crates, or baskets to hold
   daily work for each separate class subject.)

Place Velcro on each drawer for the #card that the child can remove and take with them while working on the specified box. Then, the child Velcro's it back on when they are finished with the drawer.

Two pieces of Velcro on the box. Left side for work not done, then the child moves it to right side when they are finished with the box.

1. Create a **weekly schedule** for the child with the #number on each line. Correspond that #number with the drawer (or whatever you are using to store the work for each subject). If the child can't read, the numbered schedule and corresponding numbered box can be pictures instead.
2. Place weekly schedule on top of drawer set or on wall above drawers.
3. Put work for each separate subject in its specified #numbered workbox drawer with instructions within on what to do. Each workbox drawer should have everything the child needs for the lesson.

Note: Direction cards (if laminated) can be used over and over so that the child knows what to do. If the child can't read, the direction cards can be pictures.

1. The child is to take Velcro #number sticker of the box with them and their work.
2. The child is to complete one box before moving on to the next.
3. When the child completes their work, they are to stick the Velcro #numbered sticker to the right side to show that they are finished.
4. After the child has completed all of the boxes, school for them is finished for the day.
5. The parent can check the work, and if the child has to work with the parent, then a parent can set aside time to do so.

(**Note:** The extra drawer is for the child to place the Velcro of a #numbered drawer with which they need help.)

Methods

Independent learning methods are plentiful. However, the

workbox method will easily assist in this. It keeps the child on task by redirecting them to their schedule when they are working through their boxes. Teach them the method of using workboxes. Also, have a place for them to tell you if they need help. If you have a dry erase board, you can have Velcro there for the kids to put on the box numbers where they need help.

- Use of a timer per box.
- Use of dry erase boards for kids to write down questions to be answered when a parent is available.
- Give rewards for when boxes are finished in a timely and orderly manner.
- Create a poster that the child can put a sticky tab or magnet on per subject to show they need help.

The Power of a Timer

A timer gives a child a frame of reference for starting and ending an assignment. You want the time set to be realistic and in line with the amount of work to be completed.

20

Curriculum Types for Your Schedule & Child's Needs

Curriculums are being created every day and offer different variations that are compatible to many types of learning styles. The best option is to decide what to use based on your child's learning styles, your level of time that you can spend facilitating, and whether it works for your child that school year.

Working Parent Challenges

When considering a curriculum as a working parent, you may have to find ways to make the curriculum that works for your kid fit in your schedule. If you are working outside the home, some of these methods may not be conducive to your needs.

We used video based learning and online curriculum with workbooks in order to make it work. In addition, we hired tutors for some of the curriculum, who gave our child positive confirmation of his work (until we taught him to self-affirm).

Working parents have to find curriculum their kids can do with as little oversight and handholding as possible. If the child requires a curriculum that doesn't have those qualities, then the parent may have to only use the curriculum for the child's more hands-on learning style in core subjects like math, reading, and writing where they are available to facilitate instruction.

Types of Curriculum

- **Traditional Schooling with Textbook and Lecture:** The child will watch a lecture, follow up with lessons in a textbook, and have quizzes and tests administered and checked by the teacher.
- **Interactive Online Schooling:** Interactive schooling is usually online and is a dynamic lesson and response method that assesses the student constantly to see if they remember the information, then introduces it over and over again in different ways.
- **ACE (American Christian Education) Pace Based Schooling:** The curriculum breaks up each part of the lesson into small booklets the student works through in order to learn the information. As they finish each section or unit, they move onto the next as each topic builds on the prior topic. The work is completed by hand with small text.
- **Video Based Schooling:** The curriculum is on CDs or sometimes online with the lecture being pre-recorded. It's completely video-based teaching by lecture, movies, short video skits, and usually with written books or text for quizzes or tests.
- **Textbook Based Schooling:** The student will read the textbook, answer questions in each section, and complete chapter tests, then move on until they have finished the textbook.
- **Online Based Schooling:** Students complete the courses online, and the information is shared either in videos, movies, or interactively that have quizzes and tests for each lesson.

- **Workbook Based Schooling:** A curriculum based on workbooks will have lessons for the child to read, then activities and practice of the lesson within the same book.
- **Topic Scavenger Hunts:** These aren't out-of-the-box curriculums. The parent will put together a scavenger hunt based on the child's interests and initiate a search for clues or information about the topic and present their adventure and discovery to the family.
- **Game Schooling:** The parent can use different games to build a curriculum. My child loved Minecraft, and I found an online Minecraft class for math and science. Games like Scrabble for spelling and Telestrations for writing.
- **Project Based Schooling:** A child can do a project independently and share the findings with the family.
- **Movie Based Schooling:** Movies can teach children most anything. You use interesting movies, documentaries, or even fiction to build a curriculum. The child can help by selecting the films for viewing with the family.
- **Unit Based Schooling:** The focus is in small chunks where you deep-dive through a subject. It can include any of the other methods.
- **Note booking or Lap booking:** Ways to express learning. The student will learn or focus on a particular subject and will build a notebook diary of their interpretation of the lesson. It can include artwork, craft work, pictures, journaling, copywork, postcards, maps, or photos from trips to the museum.
- **CopyWork:** The act of copying written works to learn by writing. The student will copy poetry, spelling words (Spelling You See is a copywork spelling program.), historical facts, or science facts as an alternative way to solidify what they read.

- **Experience-Based Schooling:** This works well with history and science where the student builds an experience by either cooking food from a country or time period, doing field trips about the subject, creating items from that period, or whatever they want to experience a topic.
- **Visual Learning and Exposure to Topic**: Watch a movie, documentary, quick video on a topic that covers the lesson.
- **Audio Exposure**: Listen to an audio book, historical rendering, podcast, or reading out loud that covers the same lesson.
- **Activity**: Create an item to depict the lesson, project, craft, food, Lap book.
- **Reenact**: Play a game that solidifies the lesson, act out a play of what the lesson discussed, play a game that reinforces the lesson.
- **Write About it**: Create a paper, journal entry, report on the lesson and reflection.
- **Read More on the Topic**: Read and discuss comprehension of the lesson.
- **Interest Led Curriculum:** Usually eclectic in nature where the parent pieces together several curriculums that are focused on the child's areas of interest and passionate enthusiasm.
- **Question Based Curriculum:** Not a formal curriculum but can be used as the basis of any subject to teach your child to answer a set of core questions on any topic or lesson. The Question Based approached is derived from the classical conversations by Leigh Bortins' curriculum. Having them answer from a scientific method point of view. They define and describe the object, subject, or interest. Then they compare the lesson to another philosophy and consider the relationship with the topic to other topics. They will research the topic,

prove their point. See: The Teach Thought of Learning Taxonomy (Heick, 2019)

- **Ask them to define the subject or topic**: Ask them questions that get them to define the topic or subject using all five senses or as many as applicable.
- **Compare**: Ask them to find or speak from experience on an item or topic they can compare with the subject matter.
- **Cause and Effect**: Have them give a probable cause and effect from the topic being studied.
- **The Factors Feeding the Topic**: Have them name the factors that feed the topic, the environment at the time, the stressors.
- **Question the basis of the Topic**: Validation of the topics source. Is the author qualified to give the information? Is the circumstance valid given the source?
- **Integrated or Cross-Curricular Curriculums:** This curriculum works well for working and homeschooling households as it combines several subjects into one topic area. It focuses on combining several skills into one academic topic. For example: reading and comprehension are a part of almost all curriculums as students are usually required to read then understand to apply the directions given. The four ways that cross-curriculum subjects can be designed:
- **Parallel integration:** Your focus is on the same theme through different subject areas. For example: Greek history that includes reading mythology, studying logic, word vocabulary, science of the time in history, then combining those lessons to see how their literature and beliefs impacted their scientific thinking.
- **Infusion integration:** Focuses on a main subject but makes references to other subjects to solidify the lesson. For instance: a math teacher using several historical events to discuss the progression of math and scientific discoveries in a mathematical format.

- **Multi-disciplinary integration:** A theme-based focus on a topic that spans several subjects. For example, using different perspectives from other disciplines or subjects to debate and argue facts in a specific topic area.
- **Trans-disciplinary:** This completely integrates two or more subject areas into one course and offers a combined and condensed course of two or more subject areas.

Use Curriculum Review Sites for Feedback

Before selecting a curriculum, take the time to go to various websites, and research the curriculum from another homeschooler's point of view. Find reviews on homeschool blogs, message boards, and forums that have a wealth of information. Here are a few that were favorites.

- **Cathy Duffy Reviews**: https://cathyduffyreviews.com/
- **Homeschool Review Crew**: http://schoolhousereviewcrew.com/

Curriculum Should Fit Child's Learning Style

For best success, consider how the curriculum fits with your child's unique needs. Their learning style (Chapter 15) and educational gaps (Chapter 16) are other factors in deciding on the curriculum that will work for your child. When the curriculum doesn't complement your child's learning style, it will be a recipe for disaster. If there is difficulty in finding curriculum that works for multiple children that will gain the best results for all, customize each child's curriculum at least for Math, Writing, and Reading.

Easiest Methods for Working and Homeschooling

Every household is different, however. As a working and homeschooling parent, there are some forms of educating that just work easier and take the actual teaching of the topics off the hands of the parent who has limited time to administer topic explanations.

- **Video Based Curriculums:** Shows the lesson taught by a teacher for the specific subject, and it can be rewound to review facts and can be separate from the computer if the parent wants the child to focus only on the instruction.
- **Online Instruction (live or video)**: Instruction is computer-based and allows the student to review, enter answers, get responses, and sometimes gives a parent the student's status.

Types of Online Courses Formats

- *Synchronous*: Student has to log on and interact in the class at a specific day and time. It's similar to a traditional course except it is online.
- *Asynchronous*: Student can log on and do the course work at any time they want. It has a specific day of the week that work, projects, papers have to be turned in, but the student can review the course lectures, reading, and examples when they want.
- **Interactive Online Curriculum**: These types of learning tools and curriculum have a teach/do/grade/redo aspect that interacts with the student to integrate practice and learning customizations.
- **Adaptive Curriculums**: These curriculums start by testing the student's level of understanding in the subject. Then it builds the lessons based on the student's responses and weaknesses. It skips the topic area the student knows well and is usually computer- or online-based.
- **Integrated Curriculums**: Using or building a

curriculum that combines several subjects into one main course (trans-disciplinary) is the most efficient type of curriculum for a working parent who has limited time to focus one-on-one with their student.

21

Create Your Own Curriculum

Sometimes there is no box, online, or video-based curriculum that works. In a few cases, we had to create our own curriculum in order to inspire our children to rely less on our intervention.

If you are building a curriculum, make sure you take into consideration your child's learning style, your available time for the lesson, and whether you want to facilitate the lesson or have someone administer.

Verify Your Child's Learning Style and Get Kid Inputs

When building a new curriculum, your child's opinion matters. You don't want to work hard at organizing a curriculum only for your kid to hate it. Assess their learning style and your time restraints. Focus on creating an independent learning course, or if you are using several sources, create a method for the child to access all pieces from one location. You can create a blog page, Google classroom, a link list within a schedule, and many other quick access pieces directly from the curriculum list you build.

Decide on the Number of Lessons
and Course Type

The number of lessons per a full year course is 140 – you can cut the number into four quarters if you desire to make the course a half credit or quarter credit course. If you want to complete a full year course but complete it in half a year, the student would need to complete two lessons a day. When creating a customized curriculum, it can be condensed to a one-hour and two-lesson day for the student.

Outline the Syllabus

If you need to share the course specifics with another educator, a syllabus is helpful. Here is an outline of one of ours.

Having a syllabus is a great way to outline a course before you put it on Google Classrooms, a blog for your child to go to for their lessons, your daily and weekly schedule for your child or sharing it with your co-teacher.

Required Materials:

Required Course Materials and Resources

Tool	Title	Author/Publisher	ISBN
Book	Classical Africa	Dr. Mulefi Kete Asante	1-56256-900-7
Book	African American History: A Journey of Liberation	Dr. Mulefi Kete Asante	978-1562569037
DVD	A History Of Black Achievement In America, narrated by James Avery		ASIN: B000B69TEG
DVD	Slavery and the Making of America, narrated by Morgan Freeman		ASIN: B0007IOTJ8

Stating the objectives helps to keep
everyone on track

Course Goals/Objectives
After completing this course, you should be able to:
* Recall major historical impacts to the African American race

Cross-curricular initiatives

Cross-curricular initiatives	Activity in this class that fulfills the initiative
Writing	Communicate in various forms of writing from Essays, to Blog Post, to Presentation
Historical Perspective	Understanding the evolving growth of the African American race and their unique struggles to obtain that growth.

Then, fill in what task to complete and the weeks of class.

III. Schedule Information *Classes are from July-May*

Week	Date	(3 Day Weeks) Day and Topic	Reading Assignments or Video Assignments
		Lesson 1 – Classical Africa – Chapter 1, African Beginnings Lesson 2 – Classical Africa – Chapter 2, Nile River Lesson 3 – Classical Africa – Chapter 3, The Rise of Egypt	Lesson 1 – Chapter 1 Homework: *Read* Chapter 1 *Create blog* on http://edublogs.org/ *Write Explanatory* 2 page blogpost on your thoughts *Answer Questions* in the Center Your Thinking Box put on blog Lesson 2 – Chapter 2

Lastly, break down weekly activities into individual lessons depending on how many you'd like to have.

Break Lessons into Small Weekly and Daily Segments

The syllabus is the initial outline for the course. Review each planned lesson, and try to keep them short (under twenty minutes) for instruction, reading, or digesting information. Then add some active component to the lesson that will take no more than ten minutes in order to solidify the lesson. A complete lesson should be about thirty minutes. Then, build this into your weekly plan for the school year to evaluate how successful your student will be in completing the material.

Focus on Building the Lesson and the Important Facts

Make the lessons concise and clear for the student. Try not to give information dumps or overloads. Keep it in their grade level and reading ability. Interpretation should be within their maturity level.

22

Schedules: School on Nights, Weekends, on the Go

As a working parent, you have to be flexible and realize that getting it all done during the week, at normal working hours, just isn't possible. Build your schedule to include nights, weekends, and times when you and your kids are on the go.

Use the freedom in homeschooling and working to your benefit. Break those rules, and get your kid used to working at odd hours; just remember never to make them feel like they are working too many hours for school. They will revolt.

You have the power of flexibility – use it or lose it

Never forget that you are the one in control of the schedule, the goals, the direction, and flexibility. Do not allow yourself to set rigid standards for how your week or day has to fit into the box that you were used to before you started homeschooling. Traditional school isn't homeschooling. Create your own path and flavor of schooling.

- Don't have a set time for school when writing the schedule.

- Pad time to finish coursework by fifteen minutes or days depending on the type of schedule you are creating.
- Assess the previous weeks to make sure the schedule isn't over-ambitious or under-performing for the students.
- Find and search creative ways to learn that don't involve books at all. Give kids a nudge to be creative.

Typical Hours in a Day Spent on Schooling

A homeschool day is much shorter than a traditional public school or private school day. Consider the difference in time of a full traditional school day against how long you want your day to be when planning the schedule.

Typical Vigorous Homeschool Times of Instruction

(Abeka and BJU vigorously rigid schedules and timeframes for instruction that are similar to a traditional private school curriculum.)

- **Kindergarten:** 1 hour a day homeschooling vs 4-hour day at traditional school
- **First Grade:** 1.5 hours a day homeschooling vs 8-hour day at traditional school
- **Second Grade:** 2 hours a day homeschooling vs 8-hour day at traditional school
- **Third Grade:** 2 hours a day homeschooling vs 8-hour day at traditional school
- **Fourth Grade:** 2 to 3 hours a day homeschooling vs 8-hour day at traditional school
- **Fifth Grade:** 3 to 4 hours a day homeschooling vs 8-hour day at traditional school
- **Sixth Grade:** 3 to 4 hours a day homeschooling vs 8-hour day at traditional school
- **Seventh Grade:** 3 to 4 hours a day homeschooling vs 8-hour day at traditional school

- **Eighth Grade:** 3 to 4 hours a day homeschooling vs 8-hour day at traditional school
- **High school:** 4 to 6 hours a day homeschooling vs 8-hour day at traditional school

Relaxed Homeschool Times of Instruction
(eclectic, relaxed homeschool, unschooling)

- **Kindergarten:** 30 minutes a day homeschooling vs 8-hour day at traditional school
- **First Grade:** 1 hour a day homeschooling vs 8-hour day at traditional school
- **Second Grade:** 1.25 hours a day homeschooling vs 8-hour day at traditional school
- **Third Grade:** 1.50 hours a day homeschooling vs 8-hour day at traditional school
- **Fourth Grade:** 2 hours a day homeschooling vs 8-hour day at traditional school
- **Fifth Grade:** 2.5 hours a day homeschooling vs 8-hour day at traditional school
- **Sixth Grade:** 2 to 3 hours a day homeschooling vs 8-hour day at traditional school
- **Seventh Grade:** 3 hours a day homeschooling vs 8-hour day at traditional school
- **Eighth Grade:** 3 hours a day homeschooling vs 8-hour day at traditional school
- **High school:** 4 hours a day homeschooling vs 8-hour day at traditional school

Types of Schedules you can have

There is so much freedom in homeschooling as far as scheduling is concerned. The problem is that it takes many homeschooling parents a while to use that freedom to their benefit. The approach to schedules is all about what works for your homeschool, and it can change monthly, quarterly, by semester or year.

Traditional Five Day a Week Schedule: A five-day schedule is typical of a school-at-home option. It follows the traditional public or private school model of instruction. During the day, four to six subjects are reviewed.

Three or Four Day a Week Schedule: This schedule allows for four days of four to six subjects and one day off for makeup work, field trips, or just relaxing. However, most people with this schedule plan on schooling year-round with limited long-term breaks.

One Subject A Day, Plus (core class): For families that like to deep-dive into subjects, they may have a four- or five-day week, but only work on one main subject that day and maybe a core subject like Math or Writing as a plus to the original topic for the day.

Block Schedule: This schedule is flexible where a block of time is set for a specific subject, and the student only does that topic for the set period of time. The parent can create a two-week or three-week block for two subjects and a nine-week block for another.

A Checklist Schedule: With this schedule, weekly planning may not be necessary. The student's lessons and assignments are placed in a notebook, and they check off the assignments as they go. The parent may do accountability checks weekly.

Need-to and Want-to Schedule: It is a variation of the checklist schedule. Subjects like Math and Writing are listed as daily Need-To, but every other subject is in the Want-To list, and depending on what or where the family is, it gets done or not. The Want-To list can be completely kid-interest and motivation-inspired. The Need-To listed items could be the topics where parents want to offer more oversight.

Loop Schedule: A loop schedule lists each subject and the tasks or assignments within them, and the student checks off what's done for a set amount of time, focuses on a different set of subjects, then loops back to the original set, checking off assignments as they are finished. It's great for subjects the family wants to try out or squeeze into a core schedule.

College and University Schedules: Colleges have at least four different types of schedules. It really depends on the college attended, but using these options for homeschool gets kids in a higher learning mindset. It is best to only focus on three to four classes for each semester when utilizing this condensed schedule.

- **Semester System:** 90% of colleges allow four to five classes every fifteen weeks with a Spring and Fall and Summer Semester.
- **Quarter System:** Four quarters are in fall, winter, spring, summer for ten weeks each – start in September and end in June.
- **Trimester:** Three terms lasting nine to ten weeks for fall, winter, and spring. Does not include summer.
- **8-Week Schedule:** colleges usually allow three classes every eight weeks.
- **4-Week Schedule:** colleges usually allow two classes every four weeks.
- **Continuous:** Has no large breaks. The schedule is continuous, and students will take two classes at a time then start another two when they are done.

Things You Give Up by Adding Nights and Weekends

This is where it can hurt some parents and kids who try to over-schedule themselves. When doing school in the evenings and weekends, both kids and parents give up a lot of sports and extra-curricular activities. This can be augmented by using a block schedule, and when a child's preferred sport of choice is in season, school can be cut down to a curriculum that is less time intensive. Change your scheduling types to accommodate what your family wants to accomplish – remember, you the parent are in control.

Combinations and Change-Ups Are Okay

We worked hard in the fall and winter so the kids could go to several weeks of Spring Break Camp. That meant turning our four-day school schedule into five days, compressing topics into one lesson, skipping topics that the kids were comfortable with or will learn the following year. Then, starting school instruction three days a week from 4 p.m. to 8 p.m. and weekends on Saturday and Sunday from 12 p.m.-2 p.m. We did that schedule for years, through my kid's elementary school and middle school, with the traditional school-at-home method. It worked for us, and the kids thrived. It allowed them to sleep in late, play all day, and we usually watched a show or movie after class ended at 8 p.m. during the week. Then when Spring Break camps and sports started, our school week shifted to just Saturday, Sunday, and Tuesday for several months.

Road Schooling

For families that travel—from sports, recreational events, with a parent who owns their own business, or vacationing—schooling on the road will keep skills current. The parent will make sure they have a portable curriculum. Workbooks, writing, audiobooks can be placed in the car and done while the family is driving from place to place. If there isn't any ability to plug in a computer with an adapter, use a tablet, or books on tape, or the parent's cellphone.

Considerations When Scheduling

Take inventory of what your subjects will be for the school year. Focus on your homeschooling goals and make sure the schedule and subjects fit the plan. Don't skimp on math, reading, and writing. Your family is different than everyone else's, so take comfort that you know how to schedule best for their unique needs. Know how much time your kids basically work well independently and how much time you have to spend doing hands-on work with them. Build a schedule of their independent tasks, your time helping them, and time you spend checking their work. Don't let scheduling become a stressful chore and involve both educators and children in the process. Try something new once in a while to keep everyone from getting bored. Remember to stay within the homeschooling guidelines of your state and county.

23

Build Making up Work into Your Schedule

In reality, every homeschool parent and educator starts with the glorious idea that they will get everything done in the school year that they've planned. Well, that's not true. Plan for the worst, and hope for the best.

Scheduling for Flexibility

When you review most boxed curriculum, they will have at least 120 to 140 lessons that complete the school year. Most schools don't even meet those days in instruction. However, in homeschooling, you have some flexibility to play with the lessons. Plan to efficiently finish four lessons a week. If your child is having a good week, then add the fifth lesson to the schedule, but be open to only finishing four. Therefore, making your schedule weekly helps you to slide in work that has to be made up at a later time.

Give the Kids Homework

I know, I know, the best part of homeschooling is that there usually isn't homework. However, if your child is off schedule, revert back to what you would have done in traditional school. Consequences teach valuable lessons. Also, for kids that decide to go to college or the military – they will have homework, and being exposed to the concept is a life lesson.

So, when my kids decided they didn't want to finish their work for the week, I allowed them to make the choice to give up their weekend or an activity in order to finish the work. I wanted them to see the sacrifice they were making when they didn't stay on task. Sometimes this worked well, and other times my kids got carried away with it until we had to push their school year into the summer, which meant no summer camp for May or June. The year they gave up summer camp, I posted pictures of it on the refrigerator to show them the results of their procrastinating. That was the last school year that they misused the homework clause.

Present the Curriculum in a Different Way

Presentation in various ways are great for history, science, literature, social studies, or even English lessons. Find a movie, book, game, play, or experience that will teach the points of the lesson and make the learning seem like it was just an activity, a fun thing to do, a field trip, or whatever. Then, chat about the discovery with your child. You can create many lessons this way. Make sure you document how you taught it or take a picture of the moment.

Notate What You Can Just Skip Altogether or Combine

With a limited timeframe for school; sometimes you may just have to skip a missed lesson. When reviewing the topic or curriculum, put a sticky tab on lessons that the student will catch up on later. Note if the lesson will be repeated another year. Highlight if the lesson can be added to another to do two lessons in one day. You can also remove a topic that isn't relevant to the overall purpose of the course.

Combining lessons is another way to shorten time spent on

school instruction. You want to condense where you can so you can add in time for extra practice on topics that your child isn't as comfortable working on.

```
┌─────────────────────────────────────┐
│                                     │
│                 24                  │
│                                     │
│                                     │
│      Create a Working Parent        │
│          Friendly Schedule          │
│                                     │
└─────────────────────────────────────┘
```

The moment of truth. The customization of your schedule. This should include the work schedule of the parents teaching, the child's expected independent learning, and the time the parent spends doing hands on teaching or interaction with the child. See Appendix A for examples.

Create a Basic Template

As a working and homeschooling parent, your schedule will change weekly. It's always good to make a master template of your schedule so that you know what your week will likely look like and how much time you actually have for hands-on instruction.

Template should have the following: (Use MS Excel on Google Docs or use a dry erase board for making changes.)

	Mon	Tue	Wed	Thu	Fri	Sat	Sun
5am	Mom Work	Mom Work	Mom Work	Mom Work	Mom Work		
6am							
7am	Dad Wakes up kids	Dad Wakes up kids	Dad Wakes up kids	Dad Wakes up kids	Dad Wakes up kids		
8am	Kids wk with dad	Kids wk with dad	Kids wk with dad	Kids wk with dad	Kids wk with dad		Morning Service
9am	Kids wk with dad	Kids wk with dad	Kids wk with dad	Kids wk with dad	Kids wk with dad		
10am	Dad Work	Dad Work	Dad Work	Dad Work	Dad Work	Sports Practice	Sports Practice
11am	Kids with nanny	Kids home alone	Kids with nanny	Kids home alone	Kids home alone		
12pm	Kids with nanny	Kids with nanny	Kids home alone	Kids with nanny	Kids with nanny		
1pm	Kids with nanny	Kids with nanny	Kids home alone	Kids with nanny	Kids home alone		
2pm	Kids with nanny	Kids home alone	Kids with nanny	Kids with nanny	Kids home alone		
3pm	Mom Home	Mom Home	Mom Home	Mom Home	Mom Home		
4pm	Kids wk with Mom				Make up work day		
5pm	Sports Practice	Sports Practice	Sports Practice	Sports Practice			
6pm	Sports Practice	Sports Practice	Sports Practice	Sports Practice			
7pm	Dad Home - Dinner	Dad Home - Dinner	Dad Home - Dinner	Dad Home - Dinner	Dad Home - Dinner		
8pm		Kids wk with Mom	Kids wk with Mom	Kids wk with Mom			
9pm		Kids wk with Mom		Kids wk with Mom			
10pm	Movie with Dad		Movie with Dad				

Break Down your Subjects into Daily Lessons

This will require taking a detailed assessment of each curriculum item. If using a boxed curriculum or online curriculum, you have to review the syllabus that comes with it and break down each day or lesson to see if it realistically fits in the time frame available for homeschooling. This also means you must understand your child's learning style to make valid assumptions on their ability to complete certain tasks. Note: if your child can't focus for a thirty-minute lesson, cut it into fifteen-minute segments. Make sure you aren't being too optimistic and overloading the scheduled daily lessons if your child isn't able to handle the load.

Outline Your Year per Curriculum

Outlining your year can be the tedious part, but don't stress; take your time and allow for flexibility. Don't make your plans for curriculum and the school year so rigorous that you set yourself up to fail.

1. Use a calendar that spans two years.
2. Add vacations, birthdays, any other time off.
3. Add sports or activities and what days or how many hours a week anticipated.
4. Use a notepad or sticky notes to show the total days in each month you will have school and how many days you won't be doing school.
5. Create a scratch sheet for each child that shows.
6. Number of each lesson. I put the first letter and number on the scratch paper
7. Curriculum. Note the total number of lessons to be attempted
8. Lessons planned/time for each lesson per day
9. Break down to lessons planned for each week, then each day
10. Estimate the number for each month against your free days

Schedule in Time to PLAY with your children

Parents forget how important it is to just hang out and play with your kids. Fun games like hide and seek, musical chairs, capture the flag, tug of war, or jumping jacks can get the family outside and create serious bonding time. Schedule this in each week to remind yourself and your kids that it's not all about school but building a relationship with each other. Plan a weekly family game night to encourage play and interaction.

Draft Your First Month Schedule

Completing each weekly schedule for the first month will help tremendously. Then, create the schedule weekly since there will be some days or goals not met or overachieved from the prior week. Use an Excel spreadsheet that will be easy to update and change as you go. We create a shared document in Google Docs that we send to all educators. (My husband and I share the schedule.) Also, having a Google Classroom is free and allows the child to just go through the curriculum planned easily. It is also easy to integrate with other online free schools such as Khan Academy. This schedule follows the work box system that is discussed in Chapter 19.

25

Prepare Your Space for Homeschooling

Your home setup is an important feature in organizing your home-schooling and working environment. Be realistic and to build a home of consistent learning that doesn't box yourself or your kid into a room or location in your home. The truth is, when we started this journey, many of the resources found had elaborate school-rooms. It was really intimidating. We attempted this school room concept; it worked for them when they were younger. After the first year, my kids wanted to move their work areas to different places on different days. We did start with a schooling area but made sure it was easily mobile so if the kids, or even we, didn't want to stay in that space, it was not a problem to move somewhere else.

Remove Distractions

Distractions are the largest time thief of productivity. It's a difficult topic, but having television, access to computers, cellphones, and video games is a major distraction. These items should be out of the way of the areas where the child focuses on work. If the child likes music or background noise while working, then a player that doesn't have the temptation of a quick social app would be best.

Placing items of distraction in a closet, safe, or another room can remove the temptation.

Make It Moveable

Purchase foldable desks, chairs, rolling workbox drawer sets or accordion folders that can be put away when school is done. Having a designated school space is okay. Going through the motions of closing down school or putting those items away gives students and parents a sense of accomplishment. Also, having the freedom to roam encourages learning. Having a way to move their items from room to room, even outdoors, allows a level of freedom. It teaches them to learn what and where in the house works best for them.

Inspire Learning

Pictures mean, and can speak, a thousand words. Put pictures of things they are learning about all over the house. Have the children select the pictures with you. Place their key principles and encouraging words around the house for easy memorization and reciting.

Don't Pick a Dark and Out-of-the-way Place

We made a major mistake of making our basement the schooling area. The kids hated working down there, both with us and alone, even though it was well lit and had a sliding glass door out to the backyard. It didn't inspire learning. We allowed them to move their portable desks and work boxes where they wanted—they selected the dining room.

Create Places with Great Lighting and Inviting Feel

Colors and shades matter in stimulating learning. Lighter and brighter colors make an impact on getting kids in the mood to tackle a problem. Don't just focus on one spot for schooling; change the entire house to make it comfortable, colorful, and a place that will inspire creativity. Some colors to use would be blue, red, yellow, and green.

Scents that keep the mind focused

Playing with essential oils, scents, and textures make the environment more kid friendly. Peppermint, lavender, eucalyptus, lemon, and rosemary can be a calming tool in homeschooling to set the mood for what is planned for the day. Creating blends: with one drop of lemon and lime, two drops each of tangerine and grapefruit can boost their mood and get them focused. To wake them up, try blending three drops of orange and peppermint. Make sure not to overdue the use of scents and oils as some can cause medical side-effects.

Pick it up and Take it with you

At times, we have to take one child to an event, and another child doesn't have anything to do. We take all the children with us with the mindset of bringing their school on the road. We had a backpack that allowed them to take their video player, workbook, tablet, or laptop with them. They would do their work outside on the playing field, in the car, at a restaurant, or even a friend's house.

26

Separate Roles as Parent & Teacher

It is important to separate your roles as parent and teacher. The problem most homeschooling and working parents have is to allow their homeschooling parent role to become their identity for every other aspect of their lives. Try to set clear boundaries in those roles and to make sure that the child understands those boundaries. Being a parent is different than being a teacher.

Your Main Role Should Always Be as Parent

At the end of the day and this journey with your kids, remember that you are always a parent. To love your child, building a relationship and bond with them should come before getting the schoolwork done, keeping a perfectly clean home, or even getting dinner on the table. Don't waste time and energy around completing a curriculum; spend it on building a relationship with your child.

Your role as teacher and facilitator

As a homeschool educator, you have to find the way to teach your child whatever subject, topic, or area that is in your curriculum. This means in some cases to facilitate finding the right people to teach. To make your life less stressful, working parents can find people to teach subjects to their child and use their time with their child to help them through understanding the topic further. Acting as in the role of a principal by hiring the teachers for their child's schooling can make the transition to homeschooling less daunting.

Your role as counselor

Your child's emotional wellbeing should outweigh the push to get the work done. Find time to reassess progress once a week to make sure they can express their feelings, both positive and negative, about their week. Listen to their opinions on their academic, social, and environmental contributions to their expression of learning. Reinforce that the journey of you homeschooling and working is one that you all are traveling and growing in together. Mitigate their angst, even if it means, cutting some subjects or making a play date instead of working. If your child is comfortable talking to you about what bothers them, it's easier to notice signs of distress.

Several games that initiate discussions:

- Letz Talk: Conversation Cards
- Our Moments: 100 Thought Provoking Conversation Starters for Great Parent – Child relationship building

Your role as educational coach

If you ever had a coach or a mentor to keep you positive and motivated, then realize that as a working and homeschooling parent, being an educational coach is your most powerful role in your child's success. Many times, my kids complained about not being able to accomplish something, and I turned it around to let them know that they can do anything, they may just have to do it a different way than others. Helping them to keep focused on the positive voices to keep moving forward is one valuable lesson for a young person who is going against the norm of traditional schooling.

Separating Roles with List Description

Create a list of three to five focus areas for each role you and your co-teacher will play in the school year. Share that list with your kids and post it on the wall. Your kid can point to the role that they need at that time. Having it there to see keeps everyone on the same agenda and even can be a little fun.

27

Daily Phrases for Mindful Success

Words have real power and can help put your family in the mood to do something great. Reciting phrases that define the way you want your student to approach work, how to keep a positive attitude, rules that work in your household during schooling time, and songs that put your kids in their happy place make a mindset for learning a real and tangible thing. Please consider reading my book, **Building Your Empowered Steps** (www.empoweredsteps.com) to get tools to use for yourself and your children in gaining a positive perspective and guiding your direction towards meeting your goals.

Start the Day off Reciting a Power List

Have a daily school reciting of the School Power List that will put your kid in the mood to get the work done. You can put this on the wall to recite with them when it's time to start the day. Create one that is specific to where you want to focus your day.

Have a board or poster that has positive sayings like:

- I am enough.

- I can do amazing things.
- All my problems have solutions.
- Today, I will be a leader.
- I forgive myself for my mistakes.
- I choose my own attitude.
- I am deciding to have a great day!

Positive Phrases to Frame the Day and the Walls

The use of positive phrases or pictures to show the meaning of a positive attitude are a subconscious way for setting the child's attitude about themselves, others, and peers. Place these positive phrases throughout your home, and read them with your kids when you walk past them. Then have them repeat or recite the phrases on their own.

Have a positive saying in a box that the child can pick from:

- You are loved.
- We are lucky to know you.
- Trying is a success.
- Never give up.
- You can do this.
- You are ready for this.
- Own your decisions.

Have a Starting Work Poem

Having a poem that you and your child read, listen to, or watch unfold in a video is a positive way to start learning. It can be a spiritual psalm, a book of poetry, a series of poetry set to music and phrases. Also, encourage them to create their own poems that speak to them personally.

28

Prepare Your Child for First Day of School

The first day of school arrives, and neither you nor your kid has any idea what is expected. It happens all the time, even with traditional school's first day. That's the reason you need to take several days before you intend to start your curriculum to show your child how the day should go when they start homeschooling.

The week before you plan to start focused schoolwork, go over your school power list (chapter 27), phrases of affirmations, the workbox method or organizational method you will use to administer their work, the roles that you play as the parent, and the different curriculum that you will be using.

The School Tour

Take a school tour two times to include the week before starting and the day before starting to homeschooling. On the week before, ask your child questions about their thoughts on the school area, their workboxes, the schedule, where to find everything. The day before starting to homeschool, play a game of treasure hunting with your child to get them excited about starting homeschooling. Hide all the school supplies, give them a clue list, and have a school supplies treasure hunt. Take a picture of them after they've found all of their supplies and finished the tour. Walking through the school helps everyone to start on the right foot when beginning this new journey together.

Review of the Rules and School Phrases

Prior to beginning school, put the school rules and phrases up in places the kid occupies daily, and walk them through reciting the rules with you in order to start with tools to focus their day.

Have a theme Song

It's fun to have a school theme song. We had one that we sang to start the day. Some fun songs to consider are, "Don't Worry, Be Happy." Or "We are a Family," "Stronger," and "I believe I can Fly."

Create a Homeschool Empowered Steps Picture and Journal

The week before school, have your child work on a homeschool dream board with you (see LM Preston's book, *Building Your Empowered Steps* as a guide, www.empoweredsteps.com). The child adds what they hope to accomplish with their homeschooling year, and you put what you hope to accomplish. Place this where you both can see it daily. Go over your vision board the first day of school and weekly thereafter.

29

Can My Kids Just Teach Themselves Everything?

Children that are exceptionally good learners and self-motivated can grasp instruction independently when they have a clear ease of reading and comprehension. Even with being bright, kids still need some direction and assistance. As for most other kids, this isn't the case. At least it wasn't for any of mine. To be honest, most adults aren't even self-motivated. There is nothing wrong with not being a self-starter and focused to the point of being able to teach yourself everything. We can teach our children – to a point.

Age to Expect Ability to Self-Teach

Most kids are able to cognitively understand and process complex concepts around twelve or thirteen although that is totally dependent on each child's independent learning style and maturity.

Every single student, no matter what age, will need an adult available to assist them when they get stuck, to give them account-ability, and to challenge them to reach higher into the unknown. Remember, they have only been on this earth a short time; parents are there to guide them into directions beyond their understanding.

Children will not be able to Self-Teach Some Subjects Effectively

Some subjects or topics that aren't easy to understand through self-teaching. These subjects require hands-on interaction and learning with an adult to guide and encourage.

- Reading
- Comprehension and Vocabulary
- Spelling
- Math
- Writing

Once the child can do the above proficiently, they are capable of interpreting learning materials, searching for and researching things they don't understand.

Tools Needed for Children to Teach Themselves Effectively

Start with a curriculum where it is self-teaching and the parent is the facilitator. If the curriculum comes with a tutor, it will assist in support.

The truth is, everyone, at one time or another will need a little help. However, for a kid to effectively self-teach, they need to do the following:

- Read well (to include some complex words and definitions).
- Use a dictionary (the ability to research words or phrases they don't understand).
- Follow directions.
- Research a topic or presented piece of information they don't understand but to find other sources that can help them decipher the problem.

- Communicate well when they don't understand something.
- Seek help when they don't interpret a topic.
- Test their knowledge and be comfortable reworking an issue.
- Study skills that include: taking notes, reviewing information, memorization of facts, then learning the how and why.

30

Creating a Calm Down List and Kits for Your Kid

Kids haven't learned specific methods or ways to control their impulsive and cascading emotions. When you have the opportunity to homeschool your children, this should be one of the first and foremost areas to focus their growth as it will affect all aspects of their ability to learn, communicate, and act.

My youngest son used to have a terrible temper. At nine years old, he was still having tantrums. He was the youngest of my four kids, and we hadn't had this problem with the others. Every child is different. We'd decided against getting him tested since, for our own personal reasons, we are both opposed to medicating our children. The pressure to test and medicate was so strong in the traditional school system that it was a major factor in us deciding to work and homeschool him specifically.

Impulsiveness and lack of control in children can be caused by anything, and it's sometimes specific to the child. Our son didn't appear to have any routine triggers. The odd thing was he was a great kid who listened and rarely had tantrums at home—with Mom and Dad. However, when he was in traditional school, it was a different story. Until we brought him home to homeschool. Those behaviors and mechanisms for responding to stress shifted when we transitioned to our homeschool.

We brainstormed for a few weeks and decided we had to change our son's way of thinking. He needed words and direction that would eventually change his behavior. It takes time and patience and sometimes even the parent following the rules of this method in order to be an example to their child in calm reactions. We accomplished this change by using the 'Calm Down List' and the 'Calm Down Kits' as combined therapy for our son over the course of our first few years of homeschooling. Once he memorized the list, the actions became second nature.

So, Your Kid's Got Issues

Understanding the cause and reaction to the behavior can pinpoint the root of it. Behavior that includes stomping to the time-out corner, mumbling under his breath, and, when I wasn't looking, throwing something to the floor were actions that we wanted to curb. Another challenge was his mean and disrespectful mouth, which was followed by some type of distress or impulse reaction to something he didn't like. We realized he was displaying anger when he felt threatened, like when he didn't understand something, was being blamed or confronted, or didn't know how to respond.

The List

We came up with the idea of the CALM DOWN list. Take your child's personality and style of learning into consideration to make their list specific to your kid's issues. For our son, we focused on: controlling a temper, not having a tantrum, not yelling, learning to calm down, and not internalizing things when they don't go the way they want. The list came with research then trial and error.

We built a list of ten things that he needed to do or say to calm down. The list also had actions for evaluating of the problem, opening communication, and ways to gain forgiveness.

The Daily Repetition

Read the list every single day before starting homeschool. Parents should read it with the child even if they just mumble it. Try singing it sometimes, or chat about it. When a child is having an issue, read it prior to stating the redirection. The child can either spend time in a time-out corner, on the couch, on the floor, with a stuffed animal, jumping up and down somewhere in the room, with his head on his desk—or on the parent's lap with arms around them.

An entire Village

This will work best when everyone in the house knows about and refers to the list when the issues arise. Take the list with you when you go out. The purpose is to turn those words into actions so the child knows instinctively how to calm down.

Talk About How They Can Turn the Day Around

Having a moment of retrospect helps the child to consider how they could have acted to garner a different response. Ask them, "How could you have acted differently for a positive outcome?" and "How are we going to turn the day around?"

The List

Make it specific to the needs of your child. Research solutions and actions that will mitigate the behavior. This was the list we used for my son.

1) It is not so bad.
2) Breathe slowly. Relax your shoulders. Count to ten.
3) Don't beat yourself up. Hit a pillow instead of YOURSELF
4) Pray or make quiet time chant for peace inside your head.
5) Tell your story - slowly and respectfully.

6) Take control. "I am in charge of my own choices and actions."

7) Find small physical distractions. Squeeze a stress ball. Pet our dog. Flex your fingers; jump up and down or stretch.

8) Talk. Be respectful though. Don't suffer in silence.

9) Tell how you want to turn the situation around.

10) You're not always going to get your way, so don't expect to. Don't plan on everything to come out perfectly.

After an episode, it was followed by a hug and a calming song sang by mom or dad.

Calm Down Kits

The calm down kit or box is a box of soft toys, tools, and items that help the child to regulate their frustrations without acting out. The kit or items should be placed in a nice little box that is their favorite color. The box should be somewhere within the viewing of the parent but where the child is removed from the main area.

Create a place of peace and calm for the student to use their Calm Down kit.

Items in the Calm Down Kit

- Fidget and Sensory toys
- Stress release balloons
- Soft stuffed animal
- Noise canceling headphones
- Cards of Calm (for kids who can read)
- Weighted blanket or vest
- Bubble timer
- Snap and fidget toys
- MP3 Player with music
- Sensory tunnel
- Body Sock
- Bubble Wrap

31

Setting Boundaries for Discipline for School Time and Family Time

Boundary setting and discipline is a big issue when bringing a child home to work and homeschool. Behavior, respectfulness, and a parent's response to it must be adaptable to every situation. Children don't come with directions or on and off switches. Parents are human, and raising children can bring out the best and worst in them.

Discipline is Mental

There are many forms of discipline to consider when raising a child. Use of corporal punishment can only get a parent so far in molding a child, yet keeping their fearlessness intact. Therefore, you must take time to think through discipline before you determine the method. Realize that the military takes men and women from so many different walks of lives and turns them into solder's without putting a hand on them. It's all about building trust, having structure, implementing rewards and consequences. The difference between parenting and building a soldier is, you want your child to have the freedom to speak freely, but respectfully, to understand what authority of a parent means, and to know that there are consequences to every action.

Don't Make Schoolwork the Punishment

Getting the work done is important. However, do not make homeschool work the punishment. That blurs the line of home time and school time. Those tactics don't work when your child is going to traditional school, and they are detrimental to a homeschool.

Steps to Get Your Child to Listen

The tug of war in discipline is a long one between parents and children. With all the many methods to use, select what works for your child. What works for one child may not work for another. Here are some tips to get them to listen:

- Make sure you get your child's attention by looking them in the eye, face to face at their eye level.
- Don't talk until their eyes are on you.
- Repeating yourself is counter-productive; redirect their eyes back to you, and wait until they have calmed down and are focused.
- Be short and direct in your chat with them (1) Don't start off with accusing (2) Start with a question they have to answer (3) Ask them questions to get them to the right answer (4) Then confirm with the parental response.
- Listen to their response.
- Tell them the action and consequence.
- Confirm how they can turn the day around.
- Be consistent.

Know the Difference between Discipline for: Schooling vs Family Time

Many homeschooling parents can't separate the boundaries for discipline when behavior is school related versus family time related. It is necessary to do so, otherwise homeschooling and family time can become something miserable for all parties. Think on what you want to have as your standards for your time for homeschooling. Then consider the difference for your standards for time your child is not doing school. Consider if the child was away from home during the day and you didn't know what had happened during school. That time would be family time. The school time would be the activities that happened during the time the child was doing their schoolwork. A good way to think of it is to separate your roles (seen in Chapter 26) and build from that.

Discipline for Homeschooling

Actions speak louder than words. Create a behavior chart system to avoid arguments and think on actions and consequences.

Before moving the arrow or sticky tab down your chart, see the example of items for chart below:

- Tell the kid specifically why you are moving it down.
- Tell them what to do to redirect actions.

Behavior Chart Example
Move Arrow to Show Your Child their Progression

Outstanding
Great Job
Good Day
Ready to Work
Think About Your Decisions
Turn Around Your Day
Lose A Privilege

Discipline for Family Time

When it came to time off from school, we had different sets of boundaries and expectations. Working hard to not use behavior during family time or school time as a weapon, or backtrack, when disciplining for the out-of-school time is very important.

Do Not Do These:

- Combine discipline for homeschooling behavior with behavior during family time.
- Talk or use behavior during schooling time as ammunition on punishing for family time. (Try to separate the two environments and parental roles)
- Use schoolwork as a weapon or punishment tactic.

Do These:

- Separate home expectations (chores, self-care, respectfulness).
- Use different forms of rewards and redirections for schoolwork time and after-schooling time.

- Create a separate behavior chart for Family Time Discipline

The Family Time chart focuses on different behaviors, and when you move the arrow to the behavior that isn't positive, have a different consequence than for the school day.

Chore Chart Example

This should focus on Task Outside of Schoolwork

**Put a star next to successes
(Break out each task on a separate row, whatever works for your home)**

Woke Up on Time
Finished Morning Chore **(Washed Up, Placed Breakfast on Table, Put Dishes in Sink, Made Up Bed)**
Finished Nightly Chore **(Cleaned Up Play Area, Placed Dinner on Table, Put Dishes in Sink, Took Bath, Brushed Teeth)**

32

Try homeschooling in Summer or Weekends

When deciding to homeschool while working, timing can make or break the goal. It's not for the weak at heart. Homeschooling is challenging and exhausting if you want to be involved in the growth and teaching of your child. Sure, some methods seem hands-off, but even those take time for the parent to facilitate. The best way to see if homeschooling and working can fit into your family's lifestyle is to **just do it**.

Dry Run on Breaks when Child is still in Traditional School

Children that attend a full day of public or private school are usually exhausted by the time they wake up, get to school, attend school, go to aftercare or after school sports, only to come home and have to finish homework. The thought of them getting additional schoolwork usually upsets them. Even so, you can give them a taste of homeschooling by 'practicing' your curriculum on a day during the weekend, during winter, or spring break. Start with curriculum tests that are more fun and interactive to represent learning with you instead of giving them independent work to do.

Summer Homeschooling

The best time to start homeschooling when working is at the end of summer leading into a school year. Starting the first week of August when the school in your state starts in September is a way to test the waters to see if the family can adjust to homeschooling and working. Try to get at least four weeks in before making the decision to stay with homeschooling or to go back to traditional school.

Weekend and Evening Homeschool

Attempt to approach it as if you had to work homeschooling around your work schedule. Consider what your child could do independently or with someone else's help, then how much time you will have available every day for one-on-one time. If you are doing this in evenings and the child is still in school, only do up to 1.5 hours so the child won't be overworked. Do this for up to two days during the week and one day on the weekend. Ask the child how they would feel working independently. Set up the workbox system or the organizing system that you may use in homeschool for their current school homework and the homeschool curriculum you want them to try to see how they manage the change of dynamics.

Curriculum Warm Up

Before purchasing a curriculum, use the time to focus on filling in gaps in learning that your child may have, exploring topics or subjects of interest, learning without workbooks or lectures—make the time fun. For some curriculums that don't seem to offer the ability to do so, contact the curriculum provider; sometimes they offer help you aren't expecting.

When you are ready to actually spend money or time searching for curriculum bargains, buy a few items secondhand to test them and see if they are a good fit for your child's learning style and personality type.

Get used curriculum from:

- Homeschoolclassifieds.com
- Second Harvest Curriculum website
- Good and Acceptable website
- Chegg website
- Thrift Books website
- AbeBooks website
- Yahoo Groups: Used Homeschooling Curriculum

33

After-Schooling for Kids in Traditional School

Kids who attend traditional public, private, or charter schools may need extra help in their subjects where schools fail to solidify the information due to not catering to the child's learning styles. After-schooling is all the additional enrichment schoolwork that parents throw on their kids who spend a full day in public, private, or charter schools. After-schooling is a powerful tool in giving your kid a boost but can also swing in a detrimental direction if the added pressure is overwhelming for the child. Consider using tactics explained in Chapter 32.

Use after-schooling to focus on interests the child is passionate about or to help with improvements in math, reading, and writing. The trick is to make the enrichment fun and not like more of the same of what they do in school.

After-schooling can be enrichment for your accelerated learners. It can be a supplement when the school they attend is underperforming. After-schooling can help improve their grades, allow them to investigate an area they are passionate about, and to review and reinforce what they are learning in school.

After-Schooling use:

- Reinforcement of learning concepts in Math, Reading, Writing, Vocabulary, but do so by using games, interactive software, parental co-learning while reading with them. Teach it in a different method than school. Make it fun.
- Provide challenging work for the learner who is gifted in certain areas and bored in school.
- To focus on child's areas of passionate interest.
- To offer review and extra practice on concepts learned in school.
- To teach and learn a topic in a different way to solidify understanding.

Priorities for the After-schooling Family

It is very important to not overburden the already tired and busy student with more schoolwork that doesn't pinpoint areas where they need help. You want to be cognizant of the time the child spends outside of the home and in school, daycare, or extracurricular activities.

Try to have at least thirty minutes three days out of the seven weekdays for after-schooling time.

What comes first when planning to after-school:

1. *School:* Their obligation to the school that they attend should be first and foremost. This means making it a point to know what their teacher expects of them. Adding accountability to the teacher to inform you as the parent, and then making the child accountable for completing work and letting you know if there is something that they don't understand.
2. *School Homework:* Homework that is assigned by the designated school should be finished first. Parents should always verify the student has completed the work and

should check it. At times, it's the only clue a parent has that the child is struggling.

3. *Playtime:* Time to play and just be a kid should be specifically about being outside, in the air, with other kids, or doing something they love to get the extra energy out of them and to keep them fit and happy.

4. *Extra-Curricular:* Sports and recreational activities (Limit these to a specific season on and a season off.)

5. *After-schooling* should come after they do the above and before any online video game or television time.

Curriculums to Consider

The curriculum should complement what the student is learning in their traditional school. Teaching different methods will only confuse the student and may even cause their grades in the traditional school environment to suffer because of the difference in curriculum.

Considerations in selection:

1. Consider child's ***learning style*** as a basis for selection of after-schooling curriculum.

2. Test child to find ***gaps in education*** in reading, writing, and math that is causing a slip in grades.

3. Consider child's ***personality type*** and how the chosen method works well within their personality.

4. Focus on curriculum that will build skills that are cornerstone to the problem subjects within school

Types of curriculum (listed in Chapter 20) **that is a good complement to a traditional school day**.

1. ***Game Schooling*** is one of the best types as this should involve the entire family and bring the family together for the learning. A weekly game night is a great way to get this in without the child feeling as though they are

being made to do work. You can use different games to build a curriculum. My child loved Minecraft, and I found an online Minecraft class for math and science.

2. **_Topic Scavenger Hunts_** is another fun way to involve the family in learning after school. Use this to make learning fun and to solidify facts. Solving math problems can be a clue, or writing a letter to unlock keys is another way to incorporate play with learning. You would put a scavenger hunt together based on the child's interests and a topics that encourage a search for clues. They complete the hunt by providing the discovered information about the topic to the family.

3. **_Experience-based schooling_** will allow the child to deep-dive into topics by creating or experiencing them through travel, museum visits, creating an experience like learning a song or preparing a dish from a particular period of time.

4. **_Project-based schooling_** allows the child and family to do interesting projects where they build, experiment, and/or create something that teaches the topic at hand. A child can do a project independently and share the findings with the family.

5. **_Movie-based schooling_** could be incorporated into family time as a family movie night where the family watches a documentary, literature transformed to screen, or plays made into a film. Try to use interesting movies, documentaries, and even fiction to build a curriculum. The child can help by selecting the films for viewing with the family.

6. **_Unit-based schooling_** is when the focus is in small chunks where you deep-dive through a subject and can include any of the other methods.

7. **_Unschooling_** is to allow child's curiosity to spark learning by strewing. For example, stacking novels near their bed, have science kits around for them to initiate use, art supplies, documentaries in subjects of their

interest, provide logic puzzles for them to play with, and basically create an environment for them to want to dive deeper into their own initiated learning.

Car schooling

When you are carting kids to activities, they can get in some reinforcement with fun and interactive curriculums in the car. Creating the workbox method but moving the items from a drawer set to a colorful car desk that allows the child to work or do something fun while you are riding from one location to another. It's a great way to keep siblings busy when taking another child to a sport practice or recreational event.

Ways to Persuade Child into Discovery

Sometimes placement and enticement of interesting materials is the way to go when persuading a child who was in school all day to want to do more.

- Strewing is a method used for Unschoolers that means the parent will strategically place and leave items of interest about the home to 'spark' the desire in the child to dive in. Leaving books that appeal to their interest, science kits on the living room table, a markable scavenger hunting map on the wall, art supplies, or puzzles.
- Having themed nights of learning where the child and family can interact and solidify relationships.
- Games and field trips of discovery help to ignite interest.
- Camps can also offer focused learning and complementary education while also being fun.

Homeschooling After School

After-schooling homeschooling is another popular way to get the family used to a homeschooling environment (see Chapter 32). In many cases, people do a version of homeschooling but after school and during the summers or long breaks as a way to supplement their child's education. For example, taking kids to music lessons, private tutor sessions, STEM clubs, debate clubs—all which add to their kid's enrichment. In reality they are doing some form of after-schooling. Many kids are in many educational enrichment programs after school (Mine were in Kumon and Reading Camps.) that take up more time than if their parent just incorporated homeschooling principles and environment in their homes.

The benefit of being an after-schooling and homeschooling family is that the child gets the benefits of both environments. As long as the homeschooling doesn't diminish the skills and growth of their traditional day school.

Homeschooling After school Focus Areas to Complement School

- Create an environment that makes kids want to dig deeper into topics and encourage playing and learning.
- Make curriculum complement what they are learning in school: if they are learning common core math, teach and reinforce that math curriculum during after-schooling.
- Get a copy of the textbooks used in school and have tutor work by identifying gaps and filling in gaps in areas noted from assessment test.
- Enforce study, memorization, and speed-reading skills.
- Teach effective note-taking skills.
- Teach logic skills.
- Teach test taking skills.
- Teach to write in cursive.

SECTION TWO

DAY TO DAY
WORKING
AND
HOMESCHOOLING

Introduction

Getting through the first year of homeschooling while working offers many challenges. This section will focus on some of the trials that most homeschooling and working parents face and how one can mitigate or prepare for them. Read this section first to identify the signs of these in homeschool so they can be easily rectified.

Starting the transition to homeschooling by de-schooling is a must. Then realize that everyday isn't going to be perfect. Kids sometimes don't want to do their work. Parents who work all day don't always want to come home to tackle one-on-one instruction time or checking work. Also, understand that every bad behavior challenge or coping mechanism they used at school that you may not have known about will show up in homeschool. This is a life journey of molding and shaping an adult, and it doesn't come easily. Remember, nothing worth having comes easy.

Here are some overall tips to consider when reviewing this section:

- Know the difference between there being a homeschooling problem and a discipline problem.

- Homeschooling changes every day, so stay positive and own your flexibility and control over schooling.
- No school is perfect – and yours doesn't have to be either.
- You are combining living with schooling; it will look different than traditional school.
- Get organized – it will help with your sanity. Get everyone to pitch in.
- Kids have a voice too; constant communication with them will make this work.
- Carve out time specifically for one-on-one with your child, and make it non-negotiable. So turn off phones, TV, and outside interruptions.
- Change it up. You can if you want; you are the boss.
- Give yourself and your kids breaks when you need it, and ramp up when you are refreshed.
- By all means, focus on your relationship with your child first and foremost.

34

Know that it won't be Roses and Rainbows

Starting the new year of homeschooling gives parents hope and purpose. That's a great feeling, and it's warranted because homeschooling has the potential of positively changing so many things in a household. However, be realistic and know that change and growth doesn't come easily.

These are some things to be prepared for so when you see them pop up in homeschool, you will realize that you are not alone, that this was something typical and that you can work around it in a way that fits your family dynamic.

Common challenges of homeschooling the first year:

- Confusing the true cause of discontent and discourse in homeschooling with there being a problem with discipline.
- Kids display habits and behaviors that parents weren't aware of previous to homeschooling.
- Kids get unmotivated, bored, and depressed because they miss the active chaos of the school environment.

- Parents and kids feel isolated and have no support or 'tribe' to give them friends or like-minded peers.
- Overwhelmed schedule for a parent, child frustrated because they aren't getting the educational support, they were used to in previous school environment.
- Parental burnout from overambitious planning and management of home and kids' education.
- Imitating a traditional schooling environment at home and confusion of roles as parent and child.
- Parents feeling as though they aren't able to teach their child or find a curriculum that works.
- Desiring to quit and just go back to the freedom of letting someone else educate and facilitate education for the child, basically get their free childcare back from a traditional school educational path.
- Parents' disagreement on aspects of homeschooling.
- Family dynamic changes as one spouse changes job, the marriage aspects change, schedule changes.
- Over-scheduling of homeschooling activities.

Ways to mitigate challenges:

- It will be a journey of ups and downs. Remember, not every day in a traditional school environment was good. Many challenges children faced are hidden from the parent until it's late to mitigate.
- Make time to just play and connect with your kid.
- Give the child a voice in their homeschool journey.
- Take a break and re-evaluate before making any decisions on how to fix the problem.
- Remember, focus on the bare minimum for a period to tether over-ambitious homeschooling when parent or child is feeling overwhelmed (see Chapter 17: What is the Least My Child Needs to Learn for Educational Success)
- You are in control of the homeschool. Remember that, and know if you need help, you can get it. Many

Facebook forums, blog posts, and coaching help are available.

- Self-care for the children and adults should introduce methods or ways to relax and rejuvenate.
- Take care of relationships and make the time not spent on actual homeschooling or instruction about something else. Don't make every single part of the day revolve around homeschooling.
- Get a life, a hobby, an outlet that refocuses attention off getting schoolwork done.
- Hire out the difficult subjects.
- Give yourself permission to change homeschooling style, curriculum, and schedule and take a break in between for a fresh start.

Keeping Your Cool as a Parent and Discipline

If the parent isn't balanced, then the kids won't be. Don't let them get you off kilter or upset. Take a break, breathe, and think of a way to redirect the trend or behavior you all are facing. Sometimes, parents will lose their tempers. Kids need to realize that parents aren't perfect either. Show them how to turn it around. You are human, and they have to learn from you how to recover when they lose their temper, and they observe this by how you recover when you have acted in a manner that wasn't favorable.

Discipline regarding your reactions to stress and your responses to your child's behavior can make or break a parent's ability to notice when homeschooling and working is not the problem – but the parent's reaction to the stress they've created for themselves is the issue. Sometimes, we are our own enemies and cause ourselves the most stress by setting unrealistic expectations. We decide how we are going to react to our environment. Remember that, and change your internalization of a bad day or even school year. Learn from your mistakes, step away from them and approach them differently. Lack of discipline sometimes is the main reason why a homeschool fails.

- Spelling out the actions and consequences in advance keeps you as the parent from getting emotionally agitated at the child's behavior.
- Be consistent, don't falter when addressing the behavior with a warning, and after warning, if it happens again, the child gets the corrective redirection, consequence, or reward for improvement.
- Step away from the situation after the initial warning to collect your emotions if needed. Try not to respond in anger. Apologize if you do; kids need to see that parents are human, also, and make mistakes. Act out how you would have them respond to being angry.
- Do not argue with child, but explain why they are being redirected, given a consequence or reward. Have them repeat what was stated. Ask them questions that lead them to the corrective action.

35

Before You Start: De-schooling is a MUST!

The worst mistake made when transitioning to homeschooling is to withdraw a child from school and immediately throw curriculum at them and start homeschooling. It is a recipe for disaster that festers and can make the child and parent give up on the idea of homeschooling completely.

The de-schooling period is a time the child needs to adapt to the change from a rigorous, structured, chaotic environment to whatever environment or style of homeschool that the parent decides to implement. Basically, it's a month or two months of just not doing anything school related until the child is so bored, they are ready to get to work. It's the time off that can re-spark a child's desire and interest in learning. Mainly, it's time where you and your child work on building a deeper relationship and appreciation for each other without the constraints of school.

Taking a Break from Traditional School Thinking

Before jumping into the de-schooling stages, which are a more purposeful transition from thinking in a traditional school structured model to a homeschooling unstructured model, everyone needs to take a vacation from just thinking about school. Use some time to work on and build your relationship with your child to establish bonding that may have lost when the busy schedules of public or private school, working, sports, and stuff pushed you further away from each other.

- Take a vacation from the rat race of waking up, getting dressed, and going to school. Just let your child sleep in until they wake up on their own.
- Slowly focus on building the relationship between parent and child by playing with your child.
- Create experiences which you do with your child that teach life skills like setting the table, cleaning the home, preparing meals together, creating a piece of art, having a slumber party.
- Play games for fun, watch movies, read a book together, decorate the home together.
- Have your child talk about themselves, engage them in conversations, hang out, have a spa day, a hiking adventure, or even a small window-shopping break.

Stages of De-schooling

These are the stages where you rewire your way of thinking about educating, learning, and understanding the freedom your family has with homeschooling.

Stage 1: *Rewire concept of thinking about education*: Focus on immersion learning: learning through environment and curiosity. (An example is a school that teaches completely in French, and the child learns the language and culture just because they are absorbing from the environment.) After the vacation period, accept boredom from your child. Boredom will usually result in them being open to diving into a new concept of learning.

- Both child and parent point out ways learning happens

outside of the traditional classroom. Take time to experience them.

- Games, projects, movies, adventures that include walking, and plays.
- Ensure the family lets the child select books of interest and the entire family reads the book out loud together, creating a platform for discussion.
- Explore together the power of research, and discuss with child their interests, and search for information about it, ways to experience it, and chat about it.

Stage 2: *Identify areas of interest.* After both the child and parent are used to the concept that learning can happen in many forms, from many places, and can identify times they are learning without a typical school structure, it's time to allow child to *deep-dive into areas of interest.* Also, sparking those areas by exposing them to topics, adventures, and seeking of interesting possibilities. Follow some of the steps in *LM Preston's books Building Your Empowered Steps* to discover new interest and possibilities to explore.

- Allow the imagination spawned by boredom to spark interest-driven questions and experiences.
- Have open conversations with your child by using the game Letz Talk. (There are different ages for these card conversation starters.)
- Focus on experiencing learning and make it a student-driven activity focused on what they are curious about.
- Use the strewing method from unschooling style to creatively place books, experiment sets, games, or puzzles around the house to pique their curiosity.

Stage 3: *You and child are a learning team.* The final stage is where parent and child recognize that they are a team in the exploration of learning and that learning can come from many places.

- Child and parent have easy-going discussions about their child's curious interests.
- Both parent and child recognize learning and educating taking place in everyday activities.
- Understand that play and interaction with family, environment, and others can spark curiosity and learning.

Summing up of Tips to Remember When Deschooling

De-schooling is a mindset change about education. It's giving yourself and your child time to bond, realizing the freedom and flexibility you are granted through homeschooling, and realizing how it fits into your family.

The takeaways should be:

- Learning is the focus not teaching.
- Learning comes in many different forms.
- Sitting at a desk, hearing a lecture, taking notes, finishing workbooks isn't the only way to learn.

36

Daily and Weekly Capture for Documentation

Keeping notes of what the child is doing on a daily and weekly basis makes the process with documentation reviews needed by some states much easier. Now that you know that learning takes place in the most unusual places and times, you know what to document and realize that you can fill up your child's notebook with constant learning; even when you took those hours your kid spent playing video games for useless play, you can break down the skills they've learned from that activity into a documentable educational source and curriculum.

Documentation Notebook

The easiest method is to use a large notebook to keep all learning-focused information in for quick recall when needed. Using a five-inch three-ring binder for each year is sufficient. Separate the binder, and use clear plastic paper sheet covers to keep papers in groups per purpose and topic. See Chapter 6: Requirements for Homeschool for the binder divider labeling tips.

Learning Happens Everywhere–
Learn How to Capture It

Practice finding lessons that are learned in every single thing your child does throughout their day.

- Keep a daily log or notebook
- Activities they are involved in, try capturing those activities by subjects:
- *Reading*: Read closed-caption television words for anime cartoon, read a script for a play child is participating in, read game cards from a board game family played today. Read Life of Fred math books.
- *Math*: Played games Yahtzee, Dice, Uno, and Monopoly. Read Life of Fred math reading books.
- *Science*: Completed family friendly science experiments, geocaching hike. Watch a documentary on wildlife. Skateboarded, made goop, collected rocks, trained dog, recorded the weather, star gazed.
- *Technology*: Played Minecraft and Kingdom Hearts. Created YouTube video and edited it.
- *History*: Watched movies on the Wild West and black Wall Street.

Traditional Learning Sources for Documentation

Most curriculums will have a format to test or verify a child's recall of the subjects, so keeping samples of the major points helps to show the child's progression.

Samples of each subject area's level of accomplishment is usually sufficient.

- Quizzes, tests, papers, projects
- Handwriting work
- Generated reports from curriculums used

- Pictures of the child completing some activities from the list above in the learning happens everywhere section

Example: Excel Spreadsheet to Log Learning by subject

Learning Log	Math	Writing	Reading	Logic	Science	Geoghraphy	Art	Language
Watched Japanese Cartoon (reading caption)			x					x
Played Minecraft	x			x	x		x	
Made Cookies From Recipe	x	x	x				x	
Watched Discovery Channel Animal Planet					x	x		
Played Pokeman Go	x			x		x		
Played Scrabble			x					x

37

Manage Distractions for Your Child

It is true that some distractions can be learning tools, but learning to be creative without those items is a great discovery opportunity in itself. Parents even have a difficult time being able to unplug and actually control the influences and sources that affect our moods, motivations, and abilities to think creatively.

With homeschooling and working, it is rather difficult to police distractions all the time, especially if the child needs these items to do their work, to communicate with a parent that is outside of the home, or to just fill the empty space and have background noise to keep them grounded and working.

Using Tools to Manage Distractions

Computer and cellphone use is a major distraction for most kids. Having tools in place to limit type of use is best. Also, if the child isn't getting anything done because they are using the devices, these actions can help manage use:

- State the rules for use of electronics.
- Use applications that will automatically shut off and start

computer and cellphone capability for hours of allowed use.

- Also, use apps and tools that will allow you as the parent to view all of the actions of your child on their computer. These are a few we have used:
- Splashtop – we used as a family to view our child's computer use, screen share, and search, interactions
- Mobilewatchdog
- NetNanny
- Qustodio
- Zift
- Kidlogger

Use Chart for Notification of Use Rules

Have a chart to display the time ranges and circumstances for using items of distraction. Assess what works best for your home-schooling style, your household, and your child. Realize that kids will challenge this occasionally, so creating a visual reminder to all makes this reasonably effective.

Keep Cellphones, TVs, and Video Games Out in the Open

Having a cellphone and video games with applications on them that could endanger a child is a frustration many parents face daily. We opted to get our children flip phones that allowed calls and texting, but no pictures and no applications where they could have private chats. It was from experience that we realized that kids are curious, and the available applications can exploit them through that.

Video games also pose some problems since they can give them access to adult websites without parents being able to track. Video games and online play can entice kids to steal parent's credit card information for games. The payment feature has been part of the recent trend of kids spending upwards of thousands of dollars on video games before the parent discovers the problem. In addition, games now have live play where children communicate with grown adults who can groom them to gain personal information.

The reasons to monitor these devices are many, and parents should be aware of this, especially if the child is home alone at times.

- Don't allow kids to use headphones and microphones to talk to people they don't know (especially if you aren't present).
- Keep all gaming to family traffic areas.
- Stay in the room while your kids are playing.
- Disconnect access to internet to purchase games.
- Purchase software that monitors use at the server level.
- Give them a rechargeable credit card to use for game play purchases, and add to it based on their behavior.
- Have them talk to you about their game, and learn what they are doing online.

38

Single-parents and Homeschooling

As a child of a single-parent, I realize that it's a struggle to parent alone. As a single-parent, you have the freedom of being able to raise the child without as much day-to-day input from a parent that may not have the same ideals. With that said, as a child of a single mother, I valued the focus gained from having her undivided attention and protection.

As a single and homeschooling parent, you face challenges that may stand in the way, but like anything, being creative, networking, and keeping a positive mindset, you can find your own way to implement the direction of your family. Giving your child the ability to take on more responsibility will only help them. When my mother worked, I stayed home with my brother, and I knew that having dinner cooked and the house cleaned made it easier for her to focus on us after work. Your child will grow in maturity by taking on more responsibility.

For a single-parent, homeschooling does give flexibility that a traditional schooling environment doesn't give. The schedule of traditional school compared to homeschooling shows that with homeschooling, the parent is in control of the child's schedule and learning journey (see Chapter 8 for comparisons of both). Homeschooling (even after-schooling) can give a single-parent the ability to boost their child's education path with a single income.

Deciding How to Approach Homeschooling as a Single-parent

The most difficult part of executing homeschooling as a single-parent is childcare. Not having a spouse means that everything resides on one person's shoulders. Questions to think through before deciding to homeschool as a single-parent:

- What are the ages of my children? Maturity? Hours of childcare needed. Hours they can be home alone.
- What sacrifices can we make as a family to homeschool? Salary? Career choice? Money?
- Is the other parent on board? Can they help? Will they sue for custody? Will they fight this?
- Do I have a network of family and friends that can help with childcare?
- Do I have the ability to pay for childcare if I'm at work?
- Can I convince my current employer to allow work from home?
- If change of career cuts pay, can I still maintain my household on that budget?
- What is it I'd like to accomplish by homeschooling? Is there any other way I can accomplish that goal? Can after-schooling help?
- You aren't a typical homeschooler. Are you comfortable thinking about your homeschool differently than most?
- Can you open and run a business from home that affords flexibility? If so, how long will it take for business to be profitable enough to maintain my household?
- Can you change career or work multiple part-time jobs to give flexibility needed to cover childcare?
- Are you willing to go back to school yourself, get

scholarships, financial aid that can support your child and yourself while homeschooling?

After considering the above, the biggest hurdle is deciding how to attack childcare, how to have enough income to sustain household, how to educate your child and still get everything done. Know that it is a challenge that you can take on if you plan for these things and have a backup plan for them, also.

Childcare Considerations

Networking with other parents in the same situation can really help. My own parent did trade-off childcare with her sisters and a best friend who was also single and raising kids alone. In those situations, you should have more than one in the network to ensure that if anything changes, someone can step in for trading childcare.

See Chapter 11 for list of options. Additional options for single-parents:

- Combine different jobs to make income and build in flexibility.
- Find work-from-home opportunities for work and your own business.
- Cut cost of living expenses to afford you the opportunity to be home more with your child.
- Think outside the box, open a daycare, offer childcare.
- Work hours where it's easier for family member, friends, or childcare providers to be more available to babysit. (For example, working weekends and nights makes it easier to find a babysitter for your child.)
- Find information and support systems of working parents, entrepreneurships, and ways to live frugally to help you customize your lifestyle to support homeschooling.
- Network with other parents that work for childcare Co-op.

- Welfare, request childcare assistance or Up Child support.
- Get another parent to pay for childcare.
- If kids are old enough, have them stay home until childcare comes.
- See if child can go to work with you.
- Change career to work less hours, pay for a nanny or childcare, or accommodate a schedule that is easier to find childcare. (It's usually easier to find mid-shift or overnight childcare than during the day.)
- Child can stay at private daycare home.
- YMCA is a great consideration as well as other gyms that offer up to two hours of childcare.
- Roommate with another single-parent or parents for help with the kids.
- If going back to school to change career, find schools that have free and onsite childcare that take subsidies
- If in the military, request assistance for childcare as single-parent.
- Consider applying for scholarships from the United Way and 2-1-1 programs that help with childcare for working parents.
- Find help with the Human Services Childcare Assistant Programs (CCAP) that helps low income homes find childcare.
- Contact ChildCareAware.org or call **1-800-424-2246.**

Career Change Considerations

Deciding to homeschool while single and working can inspire a career change if the opportunity is available. Taking time to transition life for the things we want to accomplish shows children that anything is possible. In my household, my mother as a single-parent changed careers often to support us. Working at hotels allowed us to stay with her when she was at work. Also, working as a mortician's assistant helped with childcare because she could work evenings and be home with us during the day. Finding opportunities that allow flexibility is a creative approach. Going back to school or training to transition careers or to owning your own business is something that can be planned in advance of homeschooling while single and working. Finding companies that have childcare included in the work environment is wonderful, so working at a childcare center could be optimum.

Building a Support Group

In the homeschooling community, working parents and single-parents aren't the norm. In this, building a community and group of others in a like situation is a challenge. The best place to find others in a similar situation is through local groups that aren't homeschool affiliated, co-workers, relatives, and other working or divorced parental support groups. Use those resources to build your own support group. Locate groups on Facebook to find other like-minded pioneers in educating their kids. As a single-parent, building a support system is a must. Typically, you don't have time for extra, but make the time to feed your level of positivity and find somewhere to get ideas, to vent, redirect, network, ask for help, and more.

Realistic Focus and Sacrifice

When taking on raising kids alone, fun time, self-care time, and any time is limited. Having a schedule for learning means involving the kids in the adventure. Groom your kids to be an active participant in their learning, family house cleaning, cooking, and voicing what they need for support. It's a team effort, and getting kids to pitch in is optimal. Also, there is little time for yourself, but you have to make the time for yourself. If the parent isn't healthy, rested, and renewed, then everything will fall apart. You deserve a moment; take it, it's important to your family. Ask for help, take help, and know that kids will appreciate the sacrifices you made when they are old enough to raise their own kids, but at the end of the day, building a loving relationship with them now is priceless.

Try After-schooling

If you find that taking on a quest to find off hours childcare is not working, or changing career and focus doesn't fit, there is still a way to have the homeschooling experience with your child. After-schooling can offer this and, if done in fun ways, will show growth in your child's learning and will deepen the relationship with the single-parent. See more on After-schooling in Chapter 33.

Using Less Restrictive Curriculum and Focus Time on the Core Subjects

As a single-parent, using curriculums that require the least amount of one-on-one time is best. Use the time you have to spend with your child focused on reading, reading comprehension, writing, and math. All other subjects can be done by finding their learning in various places besides a textbook, workbook, or traditional curriculum (see Chapter 36 for more examples).

39

Ease into it

Many make the horrible mistake of diving headfirst into a full day of homeschooling when they start their homeschooling season. Please do not make that mistake. The approach to doing so below is what has worked for our family and many others.

Prep the Day Before

Depending on the schedule, the preparation Sunday or night before makes life less stressful on the day of homeschooling. Meal prep, lesson prep, and getting the house ready for school makes all the difference in how easy the week goes. Put out clothes, and do a quick walkthrough with kids and other educators, and review rules, quotes, and school goals.

The First Week of Homeschooling

The first week should begin with a picture of your new student. You will be surprised how much your kids grow in a year. Here are tips for your first week.

- Begin reciting school rules with students.
- Walk them through their schedule for the day (should be visible to them).
- Walk them through the workbox method (see chapter) and the expectations for the week.
- Have a school supply scavenger hunt, trade exchange with other students.
- Start with only three subjects (for example: Math, Reading, Writing).
- Do something fun each day, either a game, movie, project.
- Give them ownership of their binder, workbox set, folders, and work areas by letting them do an activity to decorate them that first week.
- If you are present, set timer for their work. If they are working alone, tell them how much time they have to finish a particular workbox # and subject.
- Have their lunch and snacks prepared so when they finish three subjects, they can independently get their food and have lunch.
- End the day with some family bonding time.

Once you have had a successful week where three subjects a day are completed, evaluate how long it took the children to finish, how much interaction they needed, how successful they were at their lessons, then plan to either add on two additional classes or to do another mild week.

Before You Add on More Work

After each week, take time to make sure the children are comfortable with the amount of work, the curriculum, the organization of the room, and the rules of your homeschool before planning for the next week. When they are finishing their tasks in a reasonable time (This changes every week depending on child's attentiveness and ability to understand new curriculum work.) Consider increasing work by two classes, or making the work less school-at-home, and more interesting like the other curriculum and styles mentioned in Chapter 20.

- Evaluate how well kids worked independently and note what to do to reinforce.
- Give them ownership of their binder, folders and work areas by letting them do an activity to decorate them that first week.

40

Start by Filling in Learning Gaps

The first year most parents take their kids out of school to home-school them is overwhelming. The common issue is finding that your child has some educational gaps that make moving forward in reading, writing, and math difficult.

Expect to have those latencies, and plan to tackle those gaps the first year of homeschooling. The importance of filling in the gaps is to reset the foundation for learning that is going to be built before going forward. If it's not done, it's pretty difficult for some kids to work independently because they get frustrated at not being able to pick up new concepts that build on one another.

The benefit of homeschooling is that there is no rush. You have time to build a firm foundation. Don't waste that opportunity, because your child could falter later. Focus on those areas that may have been glossed over, rushed, or even skipped in traditional schools. With homeschooling, the child has nothing to prove, no grades, no other students; it's just about helping themselves to be successful.

Reading and Comprehension Foundations

If your child can read and comprehend, they can teach themselves many things independently. The core ability to read feeds into all other courses and career paths. The child should learn to read well and hopefully fast. Small children can't teach themselves to read alone; they need help. The older they get, motivation from a parent reading with them out loud makes a huge difference. Testing comprehension and specifically reading for comprehension should be part of the building blocks to reading. Reading is a foundation subject that should be mastered. Taking shortcuts by having them only use audiobooks, visual books, or movies is a long-term detriment to the student. Take the time to effectively build this skill, and the student will soar going forward. Using audio books, visual books, and movies are supplementary for reading and comprehension, but building the foundation from learning phonetically, then memorizing sight words, will lend greater benefits to these tools as the student progresses in their comprehension of words, wordplay, and more.

Writing Foundations

Writing with the use of proper grammar is a strong tool in all coursework and many careers. It's a skill that many don't do well, but if a child knows how to express themselves in writing, to edit their work, to point out grammatical errors, and to spell, they will consistently be ahead of the game in education.

Math Is Constant Review

Math has always been a long-haul subject that is repeated and built on for eight to twelve years of a student's academic career. Take no short cuts with it except when the student knows the core math concepts backwards and forwards.

Students that don't feel confidence in their basic math skills may struggle with the concept of it their entire lives. Some will not even pursue careers that they think have a strong math requirement. Colleges prepare for students with these gaps by having remedial courses, tutors on hand, and even in-placement testing. You can use the flexibility in your schedule to repair damage and rebuild a love of learning math.

If you follow your child through middle school and really observe the curriculum, you will find that 6th, 7th, and 8th grades basically repeat the same concepts and are totally focused on mastering them prior to starting pre-algebra. So, if your child has been working on the same math concept for two years, don't despair, that is normal and typical. Therefore, using one year to work on gaps won't hurt and the student can accelerate learning after the foundation is firm.

Approaches

Rebuilding the child's foundation starts with understanding the unique challenges the child faces. The age of the child, their maturity, and finding a method that works may take some trial and error.

Move forward while working in remediation: This approach can work with a child that can do the basics but may be fuzzy on some of the concepts. For example, my son was comfortable with addition, subtraction, division, and multiplication but couldn't understand or complete fractions or decimals.

This method works well if done before the student starts pre-algebra. We started with the 4th grade curriculum but added daily math drills where, once he mastered a basic concept, we moved up to the next. We used xtramath.org and ctcmath.com for remedial practices and reinforcements; however, there are numerous choices available.

If the student doesn't know these skills (up to 8th grade basic math) repeat basic math with remediation until they are comfortable and tested with an improvement of gaps.

Substitute method: If the child can move forward in concept but still needs to address the gap, using another substitute for the missing skill can help. For instance, if the child can do math, but it just takes them a while, using a calculator or abacas or math chart to speed them up can help.

If the child doesn't like writing, they can do copy work or learn to type. If their reading is slow, they can listen to audio books, have parents read to them, or use a reader.

Even though tools can help them move forward, it's best to make sure they are using basic methods to solidify the topic.

Skip it to cover topics needed to move them onward: When one task, like writing or reading fast, is slowing the child down, and you decide to move them forward, see what you can skip or a skill they can pick up as they go. For example, spelling was a subject my son didn't like, so we used spell check often, and I would have him write down the word for practice later.

41

The Importance of Playing with Your Kids

Children have a gift that parents tend to forget to use once they grow up and have responsibilities. Playfulness and silliness are a big stress reliever and also a great bonding tool for parents and kids.

Playtime should be interactive for parents with kids of all ages, even teen years.

Purpose of Play

Cultivation of the relationships takes work, and building a lasting open and honest one with your kids requires interaction outside of the confines of homeschooling, chores, and discipline. The benefits are bountiful.

- Solidifies relationship with parent and child
- Makes child feel more comfortable talking to parents about what is on their minds
- Builds kids' social skills
- Makes them creative
- Cultivates strategy, patience, and competitiveness
- Reduces stress for a parent and child

- You as a parent, rediscover the benefits of playing just because.

Silly Games Kids Will Play

Search for games that you and your kids can play together. Remember all those games played outside that made you love staying outside, then do those games with your kids. Playing is a must-do and should be part of every homeschool or after-schooling parents bonding time with their kids. See some examples:

- **Tag:** Tag is a fun game; they made a movie out of it. One person is *it*, and that person runs and catches another, who then it becomes the hunter for victims to tag.
- **Hide and Seek:** My oldest kids still love to play this. One person is designated to find the other people, and they count while other people hide.
- **Hop Scotch:** Find the hopscotch pattern online, draw it with chalk outside, using a stone or bottle cap to mark place, then hop to the spot.
- **Traffic Cop:** Stand a distance from the traffic cop who calls *red light, green light, yellow light* until someone messes up.
- **Simon Says:** Player that is Simon directs everyone in following directions. Those who don't lose.
- **Street Art:** There is nothing like colored chalk and imagination. Doing this outside is fun, and the clean-up using the water hose is another fun part of it all.
- **Sock Wrestling:** Play on carpet or padded floor and wrestle. The first person to take off the other person's sock wins.
- **Plastic Cup Challenges:** Play several tournament games this way. The first to build a pyramid and take it down wins. Tossing cotton balls into a cup sitting on top

of one's head. Blow their cup across the table before anyone else does, and more.

- **Capture the Flag:** If you have a big family and like playing outside, set the border, break into teams, plant flag out of other team's sight, and create a jail. The offensive team tries to get flag, and defense tags and catches and puts them in jail, and offense team saves them by tagging the captured player and running back with them.
- **Double Dutch:** Using two large ropes, swing inward and try to jump both.
- **Marbles:** Takes two players. Draw circle and take turns trying to flick marble to knock out the other player's marbles.
- **Sock Wars:** Chase each other with balled-up socks and person with most hits loses. (Parents, let kids win sometimes.)
- **I AM:** Each player will select a person to impersonate and the other players will try to guess that person.
- **Musical Chairs:** Set up chairs in a line, someone play the music, everyone walks around the chair (except the person playing the music) when the music stops, all sit down. (one less chair than people)
- **Board Games:** Some fun family games are Uno, Sequence, Apples to Apples and more. Have the kids pick the games.

Play some of their Video Games With them

Using family game time to understand and get acquainted with something your kid likes to do makes it important in letting them know you are interested in their interests. You don't have to like it, be good at it, or love it. Just enjoy the moment with them, and use it as a means to open communication with them.

42

Weekly Scheduling and Planning

Even though you've completed your rough yearly schedule, it's best to put aside time to update your weekly schedule. Select the day that makes sense for you to do this with your family. There are several quick techniques, such as using a dry erase board to create the schedule, using google docs to do it which makes it shareable, or using an excel spreadsheet to work on it as the week ends. (see Chapter 22 for types of schedules and Appendix A to G)

Set a Time and Place for Scheduling

Selecting a central place to do scheduling and planning for the coming homeschooling and working week is important. Being where the people are is a big help in getting everyone to buy in and give input to the schedule. Sometimes having a draft for the week helps when there is a dry erase board present and easily accessible for the family to update with weekly changes.

Collaborating everyone's Obligations

Scheduling for the week should have the input of the entire

household. Getting the family used to reporting their coming events, pop-up activities, and obligations is a must. Use online calendars, a dry erase board, and cellphone apps to send schedule reminders and for use to communicate schedule changes. It's best to have one central place that is the main schedule for the family. Teens can be taught that if they don't update the calendar, their event or plans will not be a priority.

Decide How Many Days of School to have for the Week

Every week, do an assessment of how many days of active schooling is planned. The time the parent and child are working together. That includes time that you as the parent will be spending with the child, time the child will be working independently, or time another educator will be working with the child. Also, consider topics and lessons for the week that can be dropped, combined, or added later in order to keep the student moving forward.

Keep in mind the bare minimum of one-on-one time that's required of the parent should at least include Math, Writing and Reading.

- Have hard set plan for core subjects Math, Reading, Writing, Grammar, and Vocabulary – make those one-on-one time.
- If you only have two hours a day (1) Use time to make sure child understands lesson requirements, (2) Independent time for them to do the actual work, (3) Time to sit with them while they review answers, (4) Split each subject into thirty minutes of one-on-one time.
- Math should be daily, even if only a five-minute drill for practice. Math format should at least include (1) Day 1 explanation of one to two topics and walk-through of the rules to complete. Child writes rules where they can be seen, do practice problems, (2) Day 1 through 5, child practices problems with the rules, checks their own work,

goes to parent for help. Also completes five-minute drill of previous topics. Parent reviews their work, (3) Day 5, parent one-on-one to test child's understanding of the topic for the week.

- Writing rules should be visible for child. (1) Include writing for child's review of each topic, (2) Grammar review three days a week, (3) Teach child to correct their work, (4) Parent read, edit child's writing at least one day a week.
- Reading can be done independently, but parent should have: (1) Read aloud time with child, (2) Reading comprehension review one-on-one time.
- Mix in non-traditional forms of instruction that child is learning without books or writing. Plan some for each week to cover topics or subjects that as a working parent you don't have the time to review with them.

Include Your Child in the Planning

While planning, ask the child what they want to accomplish that week. They usually are very willing to respond honestly with how they are feeling about their work, what they want to accomplish, and if there are topics they may want to work on longer.

Do not overbook

Over extending the schedule when trying to successfully home-school and work is common. The key is not to overdo it and learn the power of the word, *No*. When working and homeschooling, it is very difficult to add in tons of sports, church obligations, kid home-school meet-ups, and more. Use weekends, nights, and a combination of schooling methods to free up time to do anything other than working and schooling together as a family.

Be Prepared That It Will Change Through the Week

There is a saying about the best laid plans—sometimes they fail. Plan flexibility into the schedule so that if a kid doesn't want to do their work, or you have a chaotic week at work, the schedule can be thrown out and whatever is done is a positive.

If Sending the Child to Babysitter or Family Member

When you are expecting someone else to instruct the child, make sure they are comfortable with taking on that activity. If you find the person is better as a babysitter, have them do fun activities: a project-based, game-based, movie-based, or experience-based curriculum item with the child. Don't put too many high expectations on the child and the other adult to do workbook style instruction if that isn't their strength. Adjust your schedule and curriculum lessons accordingly.

43

Daily Prioritization

Priorities are something that a homeschooling and working parent can't take for granted. These must be understood and communicated between the co-educator and the parent scheduling the week. Don't let activities that aren't in line with the goals of the homeschool become a priority over building a great relationship with your child, educating them, and finding a moment for self-rejuvenation. If an activity comes up that doesn't fit or distracts, really weigh if it's important enough to do so.

Do A Quick Review of The Day's Priorities with Everyone

First thing in the morning or when your children wake up, go over verbally what is the most important task to finish for the day and when it is expected to be done. Also, go over your school mantra or rule review. This can be done by a phone call, video call, or in-person.

Multi-tasking can be a Life Saver

Look over your curriculum, and see what you can combine. As a parent, you can be at work, but also find time to check your child's progress on your work breaks or lunch hours. Mixing chore time with learning time is possible with posters based on topics in the areas the kids are working. Playing music that has addition or multiplication facts on while driving to an errand is a way of multitasking learning in with other task.

Toss Out Activities or Actions That Waste Time

The time-sucks that waste time during the day should be alleviated. If kids are spending time taking multiple bathroom breaks, fixing breakfast or lunch, and playing on their phones, find methods to remove those. Using a timer makes a big difference when scheduling tasks. Also, as a parent, giving up television, cutting off your phone, and focusing only on your kid during the time of day you are instructing is important. Asking them to give up an activity that you can't give up yourself makes it harder to get them to focus.

Squeeze in Learning during Wasted Time

When running errands or sitting at a one child's sport practice, use the time to do quick work with the other children. Take those in-between moments and teach by pointing out things to your child, having discussions, going over flashcards, playing a learning game on your phone with them, using the sometimes 'dead time' to bond and do some learning together.

Take A Breather – Everyone Needs Fresh Air

If you see the kids stare off in space, have meltdowns, or just seem like they aren't interested, change gears and go outside. Step away from the work. Everyone has those moments, and taking a breather and break outside of the house if possible is the best way to get the creative minds back on task. Remember, learning comes in many, many forms.

Delegate When Possible

Build a support network of friends and family, even for purchase services that will help relieve the stress on yourself and family. Give the kids more responsibility. Have them teach the younger kids what they already have been taught. The best way to test what one knows is to have them re-teach it. Hire out tasks that can't seem to get accomplished, like cleaning the home, washing clothes, mowing the lawn, even tutoring the kids. If you are a homeschooling and working parent, use some of the resources to make your day move more smoothly.

Enforce the Boundaries

This is a challenge but has to be done. Making a note of your boundaries and your homeschool boundaries is important. Those boundaries may mean that there are activities that your family can't support, participate in, or manage during the times that you are doing school-focused work. If the child needs to work on math, then have them do it before other activities. If socialization is more important to your family, the math lesson waits for when there is an opportunity for the children to interact with longtime friends.

Flexibility

Rigid schedules will surely be shattered often and cause everyone to be overly stressed at the end of the day. Type A personalities really have a challenge with being flexible. It can help in keeping people organized, but there has to be some room for constant change as work schedules change, children's learning objectives and maturity changes, and family dynamics change. If something doesn't get done, adjust the schedule and do it on the weekend, or combine the lesson with the next day.

Do Not Let Stress of Change Bring You or Child Down

Know the signs for depression, overbooking, and unrealistic expectations that show up in your homeschool day. At that point where the child or parent is feeling sad or anxious about homeschooling, remember that there is freedom in the choice and time to make up work. Go over the signs that led your child or yourself to the moment when you are stressed in your freedom in homeschooling. Review those points and address them.

Review the Day

Your children, co-teacher, or spouse should weigh in on the review of the day. It's a way to be able to better accommodate everyone. Homeschooling should be fluid when a parent is working and homeschooling. Take the time to review the day. Note what went well and what didn't. Then try to work towards a way to improve every day.

Self-Care Quick 30 Minutes

Don't become enslaved by the schedule. Make sure you and the co-teacher give each other a break of at least thirty minutes to just relax. That is the time you do whatever you want without the kids interjecting. It should not be your bedtime or shower time; it's time spent doing something to release the tension of the day. Groom your kids to respect that time. Put a sign on your bedroom door, your office door, or on the door leading to your porch that it's thirty minutes of parent time. Make it a priority. Even if the release comes with a thirty-minute nap the moment you get home from work.

44

Accountability for Your Child

Accountability is a great tool in creating an independent learner. However, kids are so different and the point of teaching and investing in a child is to make sure they are benefiting from the experience of learning. Educational neglect is a red flag for children today, both in traditional educational programs and in home-schooling programs. No matter what style or method that is used to teach, eventually the child will go mainstream in an environment that uses testing and other tools to evaluate a person's abilities. Testing is something used to get into most colleges, to pass a trade school program, to get a job, to continue to keep a job. Testing and accountability of level of understanding should be part of every homeschool in order to prepare the child for whatever may come.

You want to inject accountability into homeschooling without it being overbearing and stressful. Find the methods that work for the schedule and your child's learning style and it will be a positive evaluation of the student's growth, ability to stay on task, effectiveness of curriculum chosen and planning for the next year.

Daily or Weekly Checking of Work Assigned

Checking your child's work daily or at least weekly is one of the most diligent tasks a homeschooling parent has to make sure their child is progressing through material. Although children have a great capacity for self-motivation, many people, even adults need that consistent level of accountability. For example, most people start with great expectations about losing weight, but until someone else is looking at the scale, cheating on a diet or life change is easy. Expecting a child to thrive without checking their progress can be a detriment to their overall progress. However, recovery can be quickly gained by taking the time to check on the child. Children do enjoy and thrive knowing that someone is appreciating their progress and growth.

Weekly Chat

No matter what curriculum or style of homeschooling is done, sitting down and having an interactive communication session with your child regarding the subjects or topics they are learning about fosters solidification of the information. It also helps parents note the areas where there is a lack of understanding, or that the child may need re-direction to be able to successfully grasp a topic or subject. Doing this weekly makes sure that the child's growth or hindrance of growth isn't going unnoticed for too long. This should be a series of casual questions of interest you have about the topics of the week, the curriculum, the student's interest in the topic, and their take-a-ways from the week or day.

Tests & Quizzes that the Child Goes Over with You, And the Search and Discussion of Answers Later

Have your child do a weekly quiz, give it their best shot, and then sit with them while they research and find the answers to the questions, they got wrong. Checking through their quizzes with a parent helps to identify areas that the child may not be grasping. Also, building up quizzes to ultimately have a test on a grouped set of topics allows for verification that the child is actually grasping, thinking on, interested in the topic.

Weekly Family Presentations

Weekly family presentations will not only provide accountability but will also provide the child a way to show off what they've learned. Know the topic areas of the discussion. Have the child build presentations on each portion of their assigned lessons for the week or month. Then have the child speak on the subject where parents can ask questions that the child answers or notes that they will have to do further research to get an answer for the audience.

Projects and Experiments

Projects are another good expression of learning for a topic. Doing projects with your children makes the moment fun and assists in solidifying the information since they are working through what they learned. Experimentation is great for many subjects that include science, math, physics, and English. A project can be any kind of expression on the subject matter the child wants to share. Have them walk through the project as sharing is another way to solidify learning.

Note booking or Lap book Walkthrough

Your child can build a Notebook or Lap book of their learning interpretations and experiences with a particular topic. Once they have finished that topic exploration, sharing their Notebook or Lap book with the family is a great way of recall and accountability.

- Note booking: Faster than Lap booking in it doesn't require as much hands-on crafting or elaborate design for a child to creatively express what they learned from a lesson. This form of expressive sharing is best for older students that can write well.

- Lap book: The Lap book is a scrapbook of artsy, colorful ways to show what the child has learned or is learning. It's like a few mini-projects on a poster board that is folded and unfolded to reveal the progression of the lesson learned. It is a tool of expression for a student that doesn't write well or who enjoys more expressive hands-on designs to show what they have learned.

Standardized Test

Standardized tests, as mentioned in Chapter 16, are a great way to evaluate your child's growth for the school year. Administering the test at the beginning, middle, and again at the end of the year can give a good indication of the child's progress on the main topics required by schools for the year. Use as a good measurement of the child's abilities, especially if you are planning on sending the child back to traditional school at some point.

Ask Them to Explain the Steps

Explaining how they got their answers or solutions makes them consider their process for understanding. It also allows parents to learn how their child comprehends the topic. This works especially well with math and other structured topics.

Weekly Work Review

A weekly work review is a parent and child work walkthrough. Have the child explain what they did in each assignment or on each topic for the week. Let them show what they didn't like, what they enjoyed learning, and tell whether they want to further explore the topic and what they completed for the week. The review is child-driven and one-on-one.

Yes, a Homeschooler Will Cheat on Tests given at home

If you are using a curriculum that has a teacher's answer book, keep the information out of reach of the child unless you want them to access it to check their own work. Even so, parents should be involved with checking the child's work with them. Children may feel the need to succeed or think that testing is something they have to pass in homeschool, but redirect their thinking and allow them to retake quizzes or tests as many times as they need to until they learn the information. Reinforce the concept that it's not about getting a perfect score; it's about making sure they are getting the best out of the curriculum. And if they need more time or help, the test will assist the parent-teacher in giving them more time with the topic. This should only be the case in core subjects, though. If a child isn't grasping a concept that isn't a building concept, and they get a bad grade on the test, you can teach the topic in another way or skip it and continue.

Do the Class with Them, or Have Tutor Do the Checkup

Some topics are hard to understand the first time. In some cases, doing the coursework with your child helps them to grasp the information. It also assists in pinpointing the issue in their learning. Having a tutor to help can also be a tool to validate the child's learning on a topic or subject. Also, doing the course with them will help you identify where the topic is hard to understand or the curriculum is failing in some way.

They Can Create a Portfolio of Their Work

A portfolio of their work is helpful in seeing a progression of a student in a specific subject. Writing journals, art portfolios, math project sheets, logic activities, and papers can be kept in a portfolio that is shared with family members on a monthly basis.

Write a Paper on A Specific Topic

On many topics, writing a paper, providing the topic research, solidifies the subject and is a way to give a child accountability in their learning. It is best reinforced when the child reads their paper out loud, or allows parents to read and ask questions on the specific subject to continue their interest and understanding of the topic. This works best when assessing a student's understanding of a group of collective topics or lessons as a subject wrap-up.

Sign Off When Done

When children know that someone will be signing off or checking to make sure their work is done, they will make it a point to finish it. The sign off can be where all can see and when they earn their reward for a job well done.

45

Life Skills to Incorporate

While you have the opportunity, teaching your child life skills in an integrated method of responsibility and experience can go a long way. Think on things you wished you'd known how to do when you graduated from high school and add them into your child's curriculum. Also, consider skills you are using at your current job or that are used in a career your child may want to explore. Homeschooled kids are considered in some circles to be odd, or not adjusted to mainstream peer groups, but don't let that be the guide for what you want to teach your child. Base their skills on how they will benefit beyond primary school. Make some of these tasks a weekly project that the child either completes with someone or researches.

How to Communicate Well

Communication and networking are beneficial tools for all kids to cultivate. This includes knowing how to do so verbally, written, and even with their body language. This is best taught by actively participating in debate teams, role-playing, and in some online curriculums.

- Public speaking with presentations
- Conducting a business call or professional call about an issue like a bill, a class, fixing an item, inquiry
- Writing business professional letters
- How to control body impulses in meetings, in interviews, during presentations, in quiet places, when sharing space with others

How to Read Body Language

Children rarely understand the importance of understanding body language, and it can help so much if taught before they leave school. Body language in most traditional schools is learned by trial and error, but in homeschooling, finding opportunities for kids to be outside of their home environment is a good way to hone this skill. Camps, peer groups, and even online courses teach interpersonal communication.

Cooking

Teaching your children to cook can free up loads of time for the parents who have to work and cook and clean up behind their kids. It is a great family bonding activity and is a very important skill for young people who will someday be on their own.

Household Maintenance

Taking care of the home skills should include cleaning, washing clothes, and fixing minor items around the house. Changing lightbulbs, fire alarm batteries, painting, pest control, and more are needed for young people who will move into their own homes and should know the responsibilities involved in doing so.

Car Maintenance

Kids that are driving age should know how to do minor repairs to their cars. Changing a tire, assessing a battery health, oil or fluid changes are important. Also, if your child plans on driving, they need to know what to do when the car breaks down, if they get a traffic ticket, or an accident happens. These are scenarios you want to review with your child prior to them getting a license to drive.

Budget and Manage Their Money

Most kids go to college without ever learning how to make a budget, stick to their budget, open a bank account, write checks, pay a bill, save for the future, or invest in the stock market. Build this into your curriculum. It is as easy as having them sit with you while you do these things, taking them to the bank with you, going over the family budgeting and savings methods.

Pitfalls of Alcohol, Drugs, and Pre-marital Sex

You would be shocked by the number of young people who don't know how to protect themselves from abuse of alcohol, drugs, or sex addictions. Unhealthy relationships and aggressive manipulation by others are another thing you want to prepare your child to identify in advance. When going to college, the military, or workplace, many young people are faced with these challenges head-on. Having ongoing conversations, educating them on how kids are lured by a predator and role-play can facilitate their handling of uncomfortable situations.

How to Check Credit and Dispute It

A new college student or adult may have a bill appear on the credit report that isn't correct, or a charge is applied to a cellphone bill or rental cost that is wrong. New adults should know how to check their credit yearly using free credit check methods and to dispute any items on the report. Also, they should be able to dispute incorrect charges in person and in writing.

How to Negotiate Sales for Cars, Houses, and Other Items

The purchase of a first car, a first house, a boat, motorcycle, or computer are big ticket items that young people should learn how to negotiate the best possible price for while understanding the importance of doing their research before purchasing.

How to React If Stopped by Police for Traffic Violation or Car Accidents

They don't teach how to respond to police interaction in driver's ed. Your child should know to respond to police when stopped. Making sure all information needed for the car is in easy reach and knowing what information to collect for an accident will save them time and worry if faced with these situations.

46

Delegation of Chores

Children build a sense of character and accomplishment when they have their own jobs and place in the family. Learning how a household runs by actually participating is an invaluable skill. For a working and homeschooling parent, their kids' help is priceless. Many parents try to do everything themselves, and unfortunately, they get burnt out. Besides having the kids do chores, some chores are also great to hire out. Making sure no one gets overwhelmed with keeping up the household will make or break the success of a working and homeschool environment.

Have Each Child Responsible for a Specific Chore

Many parents complain that their child doesn't do a good job or a complete job on their chores. One reason they don't is because they weren't taught how to do it completely, and they don't do it enough to commit the expectations to memory. Having the child do the specific chore for a long period of time leaves out the question of who didn't do the work, why they didn't do it correctly, and who needs to do what.

Everyone has a Job

No one is too small to have a job. Make the job specific to the child's age, and it gives everyone a task and responsibility. This makes everyone feel as though they are working together as a team to do the big job of taking care of the home.

Daily jobs should include:

- Make up bed
- Pick up items off the floor (use a bin, bucket, basket, or box) in main rooms
- Put away items in the pick-up bin
- Wipe, rinse, load dishwasher
- Wipe kitchen sink
- Wipe down surfaces
- Sweep the floor

Teach to Clean as They Go with Oversight to Get Them to do it Right

This is a major issue in most homes, especially when it comes to the kitchen and common rooms. Kids hate doing dishes because they pile up all day long. It's best to teach them to clean the table and the dish once they finish a meal. Teach to put away their items after use. Once the child does it consistently, it becomes a habit. It makes for a less messy home and chores that are manageable.

Kids will not work to the quality that parents expect when cleaning if they aren't accountable or rewarded for the efforts. This can change if the child knows that they will be walked through the task, or the task will be inspected, or they can't move onto something fun until the task is done. After they learn the expectations, periodic checkups while completing the task are helpful.

Speed It Up – Speed Cleaning Fun

Set the timer, get a bin for each room, and race to see who fills up the room's bin with all the items on the floor, tables, and shelves that don't belong. If the bins are stackable and colorful for the room, you can leave them in the room until the weekend or another time when you can put those items away. Also, you can have someone different be timed to do the putting away of the items in the bins, bucket, or box.

Use speed it up cleaning to:

- Pick up items that show clutter
- Dust and clean surfaces
- Do quick sweep up or vacuum of room
- Put items away in bin, bucket or box where misplaced items were put in per room
- Wipe, rinse and load dishwasher

Do It to Music

For younger kids, having a cleanup song is a great motivator. Create a song while cleaning to sing with them. Older kids just want to play music and it makes the time go faster. Use music that they like, and that reinforces their focus to the completion of the task. Sometimes playing the same songs can work as an internal timer for the kids to clean up faster.

Set the Time of Day to do Chores

In most cases, routine times for cleaning up makes it a task that will be completed without argument or question. It keeps the kids on schedule and makes cleaning part of the typical day's activities.

Have One Day and Time a Week for Overhaul Cleaning

Setting a day of the week for overall cleaning makes the task easy to accomplish. Make that time of the week the one time when everyone is expected to be home, and if they aren't, they have to finish their chore or task the day before the designated time of the week.

Job Rotation every thirty days or more

Rotation of duties every thirty days gives the child the chance to learn the expectation of every aspect of maintaining the home and doing a job well. After thirty or more days, you can give the children a lottery or have them pick out of a hat the chore they will be taking over. It makes it fun, and when they start their new task, have the previous owner of the task teach them how to do their new chore with parental supervision to make sure that all tasks are completed to satisfaction.

Reward and Consequences

The great motivator for kids to complete tasks is to give them a reward and a consequence if the task isn't done. Find the right reward for completed tasks. Consequences for lack of work should be spelled out in order to deter your child from not completing the tasks. Sometimes a consequence is having your parent watch and direct you through fixing the problems with the chore.

47

Meal Prep and Who's Putting Dinner on the Table

Eating and feeding a family can be an extensive job. Especially if kids have different diets and tastes than the parent. When both parents are working in or outside of the home it is even more difficult to make sure that there is a healthy dinner waiting for the kids or available for the family while having a hectic schedule. Prepping meals at home can save the family time and money. Therefore, consider methods to prepare most meals at home to take with you or to eat in house.

The Easiest Cooking Methods for Meals

Finding ways to cook it fast, hands off, and something that the kids can get started is the best options for working parents. The crockpot, Crockpot Express, Instant pot, George Foreman grill, the oven, or fresh fixed meals are the best options for a busy family. There are also options that kids can prep while the parent is on the way home, or they can cook while parents are working.

No Time to Prep – Meal Prepping

Meal prepping is great when you have the time to do it. Try to make the time to meal prep at least once a month. If you have that one month that you can't prep, then go with already prepped meals.
Buy Pre-Prepped Meals from local stores:

- Pre-Frozen prepped meals from the store
- Fresh and Veggie prepped meals at the grocery store
- Pre-prepped fresh meals at the grocery or discount stores
- Restaurants also offer prepped meals that can be frozen or refrigerated.
- Meal Prepped businesses like Let's Dish (a meal prep business)

Quick put together prep: Try to do it on Sunday; put each meal into gallon freezer bag for toss into over, crockpot, or grill.

- Search for multiple recipes with your meat choices for the week.
- Use pre-seasoned meat from store.
- Toss in store prepped mixed veggie.
- Pick a starch of the day rice, pasta, potato type.
- Mix and match for dinner each night.

Family Favorites quick prep:

- When you prepare it, cook enough for two meals.
- Then freeze or refrigerate for meal on later day or the next week.
- Prepare it a different way.

For example: We like tacos. I make the taco meat and we have (1) Tacos on Monday (2) Mexican Salad on Tuesday (3) Cheesy Mac with Taco Meat on Wednesday (4) Chicken wraps Thursday (5) Chicken and Rice and Veggies on Friday (6) Barbecue Chicken pizza on Saturday

Menu Planning

The easiest way is to plan meals that complement each other and have similar ingredients that are prepped and seasoned different ways. Take a family poll on what meals are their favorite, that they wouldn't mind having every other week, then build a two-week menu for prepping. Also, for those days where no one is fixing dinner, buy a few store-prepped meals that kids can heat up. Don't forget to meal prep for all three meals, and if dinner is one meal likely to eat at home, make sure those are prepped for quick use. Add some grab-and-go meals that the family can take with them. Fresh veggie and fruit snacks that can be used for munchies should be planned also to make meals more streamlined.

- Two-week meal prep for freezer and refrigerator meals
- Build four two-week meal plans that can be rotated for months; note the family favorites that can be repeated every two weeks.
- Plan meals that build on each other, and have similar main ingredients that will lower the cost of the grocery bill.
- Mix up meals with crockpot, oven, or meals that don't have to be cooked.
- Menu prep for snacks
- Grab-and-go meals
- Have a plan for leftovers. They can be put into a new meal or munched on for lunch or snacks.
- Label the meals with cooking directions, person who is going to cook it, and expiration dates.
- Consider cooking methods that are the fastest, easiest, and that the kids can do with minimum supervision.

Budgeting and Shopping

When planning the menu, make sure to budget the cost of each of the items. Build menus that have the staples that the family enjoys but are within the budget. Look for various ways to prep the same items such as chicken, beef, turkey, or fish. Don't budget only for dinner; budget for all meals, snacks, and even eating out. Make the shopping day be list-driven, and if that means not taking the kids with you, then go it alone. Unless you truly left an important item off the list, don't pick it up on the meal prep trip. When you are comfortable meal planning and budgeting, you can save more money by stocking items, buying them in bulk, rotating menu plans, creating meals around cleaning out the pantry or freezer, and pre-order shopping lists are offered at some grocery stores and even online.

Meal Prep with Entire Family

Getting the kids involved in meal prep is a learning experience for them as well as giving the parents help. The kids can be involved in the meal planning, prepping, and serving. Especially older kids who can take over the responsibility of cooking and meal planning for you. It also allows them ownership in the task and the meals shared. It can be even considered a school course in home economics, math for measurements, and even chemistry.

Have the Kids Cook Tonight

Kids can cook and prep a meal at all ages. The method and tools should be age appropriate. When meals have been planned and pre-prepped, they are so easy to get kids to help prep them for the day. These make grab-and-go for sports or outside activities simple, and it is easy to call ahead to tell the child to put dinner in the oven, in the instant pot, the microwave, or even the in-house grill. Teach them how to use each by walking them through meal preparation but allowing them to do the task. Then, when they are comfortable, have them explain how they are cooking the meal. Some fun ideas are to have your own version of home chef and videotape them explaining how to cook the meal of choice.

The Meals That Cook Themselves - Practically

The crockpot and instant pot meals are the absolute lifesaver for a busy family. It's a dump-it and forget-it type of cooking that makes it easy for kids to do. These meals practically cook themselves, and finding several cookbooks or recipe websites will share many of these meals that will make meal prep easy and cooking a breeze. These are very easy meals for young children to prep and cook for the family.

48

Socialization for Your Child

Socialization is one of the main issues that many homeschooling and especially working parents battle with when considering home-schooling. It's the main topic of conversation when people ask about your homeschooling and working decisions. This is an easy fix, but realistically, socialization doesn't happen spontaneously for every child in a traditional school system.

Seek Activities Where Kids See the Same Kids Often

Taking the time to seek out activities, hobbies, and interests that involve other children and meet on a regular basis builds long-term friendships. Scouts, 4-H, dance, after school camps, and robotics clubs are some examples. Seek activities that can grow with your child. Try many groups to see which ones are more accepting of your child and that your child enjoys. Then, use those environments to invite kids to play-dates, get-togethers, or even your child's birthday parties.

Use Traditional After-School and Before-School Programs

Who says your child has to be in a traditional school to benefit from the various fun and exciting after- and before-school programs? They are usually freely open to anyone that can pay for it. Enrolling your child in an aftercare program can be a way of keeping them connected to kids their age while having the best part of a school day: the fun part. This includes homecare, private centers, and even a local martial arts school. Also, some after school programs will include 'homework' help, and that can be used to also help them with work that they have as part of their curriculum.

Recreational Sports Activities
Parks and Recreation or County Youth Programs

Sports and other public recreation after school and weekend programs can be a lifesaver for kids. Also, they may offer a break for parents. It's another great way to meet parents where childcare tradeoffs can be made and carpooling to sports events can be done. Another bonding option is for parents to volunteer as coaches, team moms, or team support.

Pick up Weekly Flyers from Local Public Schools

The local schools, library, and recreation centers usually have tons of books and flyers on kid-focused activities, resources, and things to do. These can be taken advantage of by homeschoolers for networking, building friends, meeting new people, and having some fun while learning about their local community. It's usually a missed resource for homeschoolers who haven't had their kid in traditional schools. Take the time to drop in and grab or request community flyers. It is easy, and most schools are helpful in giving them to parents.

Summer Camps, Spring Camps, and Winter Camps

Camps can be found open for the summer, winter breaks, and

spring breaks. Also, camps for the weekend are sponsored by private and government-based programs. Many camps have scholarship programs, and students may be able to attend for free.

Library Programs

Places with a large homeschooling community will have libraries which have homeschool-focused programs. The evening and weekend programs are usually free. These programs can offer great outlets for kids.

Group Lessons for Music, the Arts, or Child's interest

A nearby orchestra, choir, drama club, or dance club will be a great way for your child to participate and learn something new while building relationships with kids that they meet every week.

Museums and Zoo Programs

Museums and zoos have onsite camp programs and activities focused on kids. These programs are on weekends, afternoons, and sometimes during the week. The fee is usually reasonable and sometimes free. They also have scholarship programs.

Homeschool Organizations and Co-ops

Homeschool organizations and cooperatives are where homeschooling families get together, have courses, and plan events. These are usually during the day and week, but sometimes have activities on the weekend, which is convenient for working homeschooling parents. A limited number of working parents participate since these groups do require a parent volunteer in some capacity, and leaving the child isn't possible in most cases.

Tutorials

Tutorials work well for working and homeschooling parents. They are similar to Homeschool Co-ops since they are full days of classes but are paid, and parents aren't required to participate actively during the day. They have semester sessions, usually for the typical school year. The child would attend two to three days a week. The course offerings can be graded or not graded as per the parent's wishes. They aren't the same as a private or traditional school. The teachers can be degreed or not, so take the time to research the tutorial and their rules as they are all different and not regulated.

Join 4-H Groups

4-H is a mainstream program that is a community supported agriculture-based program where kids get mentorship and support to learn to be leaders. All states have programs like this. This program allows kids to work at their own pace, in groups, and can follow them from elementary to high school. These are after school programs that allow homeschoolers to participate.

Create Your Own Kids Meet-up Group, or Coach a Sport

As a homeschooling and working parent, time is crunched, and many of the homeschooling group activities aren't convenient. In that case, have your kid play recreational sports, and be the coach, team mom, or somehow involved in the team. That way you can plan team-building parties and get-togethers that help build relationships for your child. The other option is to create a monthly game night or day for the kids to come and hang out at your home. Do it consistently, and even trade off with other parents to give children bonding time.

Encourage them to Volunteer or Work Part-Time

As kids become teenagers, many of the recreation programs go to high school. Volunteering to help at schools, libraries, after school programs, and more can help a teenager build friendships. Other high school students work jobs, and it's possible for them to build relationships in those environments.

Working and homeschooling isn't easy. There are times where you feel like you are not making progress, the house is a mess, and it's all for nothing. Well, kids feel this way too, and when they do, take a step back. Realize that there will be bad days. Life happens more vividly when your child can't get away from home. Behaviors that go unnoticed at school become more apparent the more time parents and kids spend together. Also, understand that even as adults, when we are at work, we don't want to be there. Bad days come and go, but when they pile onto one another, you may need to work more diligently to find the root cause and address it.

Know the Signs

The point of homeschooling should be to get to know your kid. Learn the signs, and plot in your memory when they are getting frustrated. Keep a notebook to help remind you of small nuisances of your child's behavior triggers. You can create a chart where your child can move an emotion to the top that shows how they feel that day or hour. The chart is a way for them to communicate without words. These signs should also be something to take note of about yourself or your partner in teaching. If no work is getting done, the child is disagreeable, or teacher/parent doesn't want to be there, then these are clear issues that need to be mitigated.

Plan How to Mediate the Challenge

The main issue is understanding what went wrong. Evaluate your expectations as a parent then how your child reacted to the circumstances of the day. After you've taken a time out, try several different solutions like redirecting the child to take a nap, or do an interactive activity. Ask them what they would rather be doing, and negotiate for the options with the intention of getting back on task.

When Parent is Too Tired or Irritable

A bad day can be totally parent-inspired also. If the parent teacher is feeling overwhelmed, it flows downward to the kids. Some homeschooling parents suffer depression due to lack of external adult interaction, overly inflated expectations of their homeschooling results, or overbooking. Notice when tasks and expectations are unrealistic. For example, if you work full time outside of the home, you can't have a 3 to 4-hour day of instruction for 5 days a week and expect to not become burned out within a few weeks. Re-evaluate expectations against what is realistically being accomplished, and lower those expectations in order to truly see the success.

Don't take it Personal

Having a day, or even a week, where the obstacles pile up and it seems as though there are no successes, let it go. Don't take it personal. Realize that even if the kids were in regular school all day, both of you would probably have weeks like this only neither of you would be able to evaluate why or how to fix the root of the problem.

Fill in Idle time

When the kids don't feel inspired, make up the slack by filling in the idle time with interactive learning you can do with them on the go. Play a quick drill or card game with them. Initiate conversation around topics they are passionate about. Color or draw with them. Listen to an audio book together. And do whatever you can to squeeze in a bonding activity to redirect the negative effects of a bad day.

Realize the Physical, Mental, Emotional, and Growth Changes can Impact Child's Responses

Kids are ever-changing little beings, and it's hard for parents to keep up with the hormonal, intellectual, and physical changes that seem to happen every day with them. Once you believe you have your kid figured out and have reached a rhythm, those little people change again. This means you have to be aware of the key changes in their physiological makeup that can initiate mood swings, boredom, depression, defiance, fatigue, and aggression. To further challenge parents is the fact that males and females respond to these body changes differently. Children change physically, cognitively, and socially. When you know that they are having hormonal changes that spurn reactions in their body that they don't understand, you can judge their responses based on their change in development. Taking the time to understand those changes can make it easier to know how to transition your homeschool to be flexible enough to positively respond to them.

Tip List for Bad Days

Use activities, redirections, and methods that help in overcoming those bad days. I've put together a quick list to consider for those times. Also, create your own list for when you've successfully turned around the day or week for a positive outcome.

- Give your child ownership in deciding what would make

them more productive, happy, and interested in turning their day around.

- Redirect to a task or activity or method of learning (or not) that they prefer, with the agreement on how and when to take up the previous activity (or not).
- Get out and get physically fit. Taking a walk, a run—playing outside or somewhere besides in the home can breathe life into a bad day.
- Take school out of the house, and do it somewhere else.
- Take a nap – everyone.
- Give self-care to both parent and child. Kids need self-care, too.
- Share a hug, sing a song, play and be goofy.
- Play games, watch a fun movie, do a craft.
- Visit friends.
- Cook something together.
- Change the curriculum to meet the child's style of learning.
- Don't stress – everyone has a bad day. Give yourself and your kid the day off.
- Deal with and re-direct the major distraction initially. Then, work on the underlying issues of the day.

Multiple Kids-Dealing and Sibling Rivalry

Teaching multiple children in a homeschool setting has some benefits. The main benefit of a sibling is they can motivate, teach, share information, and give another perspective to the multiple-aged students participating in homeschool. There is even an opportunity to combine teaching several subjects to all the children at once. Also, they are socializing even though it's with a sibling or two.

Having multiple children being homeschooled is also a challenge. Siblings have been arguing, fighting, and disagreeing from the beginning of time. Every parent or caregiver of more than one child has to manage sibling rivalry. The key is that they are raised to be each other's support system, refuge, and friend. This is work, takes time, and requires understanding of each other's boundaries. It doesn't end when they grow up; they will always have the challenge of working on their sibling relationship. Try to give them the tools while they are still at home.

Combining Several Subjects to Teach Multiple Aged Students at One Time

When you are homeschooling and working and time is a

premium, finding curriculums that allow you to combine teaching one topic to multiple aged children is the best use of time. Several curriculums are good for this (Tapestry of Grace, My Father's World, Charlotte Mason, and Classical Conversations), but be mindful of the children's learning styles.

Another option is to combine subjects like History, Science, and Languages into one class and curriculum level for all the students. This may mean changing the curriculum in some areas to appeal to the younger or older student.

Goals to Cultivate Sibling Relationships into Positive Relationships

As you are seeking to build a list of rules and principles for your kids' sibling relationships, keep in mind that ultimately, the desire for siblings to build supportive, long lasting positive relationships with each other is the goal. Here are some example goals in sibling relationship building guidelines.

1. Be supportive of your sibling.
2. Make sibling a priority over friends.
3. Continue healthy communication.
4. Look out for your sibling without selfish intent.
5. Be there when they need you.
6. Forgive each other.

Have Rules Posted

Having rules that are well thought out and specific to your goals for your children's sibling relationships should be placed where the kids can see them. They will know what it is expected and the consequences for those behaviors. Stating all the obvious sibling issues and challenges saves the parent from repeating, changing focus, debating the consequence in front of the kids, and basically derailing the lesson in working to strengthen these sibling relationships.

Make a reward system for positive days and actions, but also make it clear what the consequences will be.

- **No Hitting** > Have a Reward > A Consequence
- **No Bullying** > Have a Reward > A Consequence
- **Teasing** > Have a Reward > A Consequence
- **Lying** > Have a Reward > A Consequence
- **Throwing a Tantrum** > Have a Reward > A Consequence
- **Screaming or Yelling** > Have a Reward > A Consequence
- **Being a Bad Sport** > Have a Reward > A Consequence
- **Mess with Someone's Things** > Have a Reward > A Consequence
- **Tattling** > Have a Reward > A Consequence
- **Not Treating Each Other with Respect** > Have a Reward > A Consequence
- **Apologize** > Have a Reward > A Consequence
- **Hug and Make Up** > Have a Reward > A Consequence
- **Accept Apology** > Have a Reward > A Consequence
- **Shake hands on it** > Have a Reward > A Consequence
- **Start over again** > Have a Reward > A Consequence

Encourage Team Work

Siblings will be in our lives always, and it is the best and first opportunity to build a friendship. Realizing that they are both different, yet working as a team, is a good way to build their relationships.

Time apart is needed with Outlets for Aggression or Boredom

Siblings need, and should have, a break from one another. At those times, give each child a different outlet than the other so that they can have the space to do things on their own. Sports, clubs, activities with other recreational groups where their sibling isn't present are great ways to give each child the space they need from the other while releasing any extra energy.

Evaluate where it's coming from

Consistent sibling rivalry may have a deeper cause. Take the time to understand where it's coming from. Does the child need attention? Are they being bullied by another child or sibling? Is there a deeper emotional challenge? Take the time to talk them through these conflicts, get them to answer without telling them what the solution could be, and take time to address serious disagreements.

Make them all responsible

Giving siblings responsibility for watching, caring, feeding, or even teaching another sibling is a great idea only if and when that sibling is ready to do so. Sometimes, payment can make an older sibling desire to be responsible for their younger siblings in some ways. When they are given those responsibilities, outline the expectations, and inform the younger or other siblings of how to respect the rules given to both. If you have rules established for sibling engagement, then easing a more responsible sibling into the leadership role will be a great transition and learning experience.

Explaining When Telling is not the same as Tattling

Don't allow siblings to make tattling a weapon. There is a difference in telling in order to make sure a sibling is safe and tattling to get the sibling in trouble on purpose. Make it obvious and understandable to your children that there is a time, place, and a reason to tell your parents when your sibling is misbehaving. It has to be done in the right spirit and tone, not for their own personal gratification.

Tattling is: Purposefully trying to get sibling into trouble; the act reported is harmless or done by accident, and is a dilemma that can solve itself.

Telling is: Done to make sure your sibling stays safe or gets help, done with true concern for sibling safety, is important, and needs help from an adult.

They May Never Agree – But in the End Will Always be there

There is never a blissful relationship created that didn't have challenges and struggles along that way. Don't have unrealistic expectations for sibling relationships. There may be cases where certain personality types just won't be able to get along without discourse. Siblings may simply be disagreeable. Even in those tense relationships, they should garner respect for the fact that a sibling should always be there for them. It is important to connect on the level of being family to one another, even when you don't get along. That is something that has to be taught. If you have taught your kids to help one another, to be fair with one another, and to be there for each other, then that is a valuable feat.

51

Child Is Overwhelmed or won't do Work

Getting overwhelmed happens to kids that are in traditional school, private school, and even homeschooled. There will be a time when your kid just doesn't want to do work. They could have gotten off to a great start but every day desired to do less and less. In some cases, kids keep rising to the occasion. Whatever you give to them, they do it and well. Then, all of a sudden, they crash, have tantrums, and start underperforming.

Realize that you own the power and ability to teach as often, in whatever method, and to give more, or less as needed. The end game is far ahead; focus on building relationships with your children that will last a lifetime, not badgering them to consistently finish a school assignment.

Revitalizing Their Attentiveness through Movement

Movement is a way to jumpstart a child's body into the thirst for more, or it can use up all the excess energy that they need to release in order to relax and focus.

Types of Attentiveness:

- **Sustained Attentiveness**: Being able to stay focused on a specific activity while not becoming distracted.
- **Selective Attentiveness**: Being able to concentrate on only one of many stimuli in the environment.
- **Divided Attentiveness**: It's not typical and hard to do for most people. This person can focus on more than one stimulus at a time and can respond to them fully.
- **Alternating Attentiveness**: Even though it's similar to divided attention, it is switching focus between one area of focus and another. This leaves the possibility that something could be missed.
- **Visual Attentiveness**: It's a visually focused attentiveness that one's eyesight focuses on one item with a pinpoint focus while blurring out the surrounding distractions.
- **Auditory Attentiveness**: The ability to focus hearing on one particular sound while muting the distractions around.

Get Moving to Improve Attentiveness:

Use this method to redirect your child, give them a boost of mental alertness, and get their excess energy out of their bodies.

- **Use bucket of Re-direction:** Use a bucket or hat to hold various movement inspired Simon-says type directions. Also, you can purchase physical activity cards, which are easy to find online or create yourself for your child.
- **How to Use It**: Get the child to: (1) Request to pull an activity out of the bucket if they are bored, but state why, (2) Set the timer of five minutes, (3) Select an exercise or other type of activity out of the bucket, (4) Do the activity and redirect.

When Tears Fall, Tantrums Abound – Cease Work Now

When your child comes to a screeching halt in work and shows physical signs of frustration, stop work, and take a break. Doing this here and there is all right, but do so with effort in finding the root cause of these meltdowns or refusal to work. It can cue you to see the need for an adjustment to the environment, curriculum, or circumstances that are working against your child's success.

Communicate with Them

Communication is key for understanding your kids and their stage of development. Each child is different, and a parent's best tool to assist their children to grow to be healthy emotionally is by communicating with them. This can be done in games, hangout sessions, relaxing at home, and playing with them. This builds the bond and makes it easy for your kids to talk about what upsets them. Two games that are good at starting conversations are Letz Talk and Totem.

Take Time to Understand the Triggers

Children usually have a core reason for checking out of the learning process. Take the time to evaluate their reasons. Make those observations over time. Don't rush to judge, but think, observe, and ask questions. Then, talk to your child and ask them what is bothering them, how they would like it fixed, and come to an agreement. This is a process of trust and understanding that is ever-changing when raising children.

Also, take the time to get their vision, eyes, hearing and grade level understanding checked. Doing these things will point out some unforeseen problems.

Make time for Relaxation

Making time to relax and re-adjust is important for both parents and children. Often parents forget that kids are going through so many physical, mental, emotional, and hormonal changes that affect the way they respond. Kids feed off the emotions of their parents. They haven't learned how to express themselves or how to react in situations of stress in a way that is best for their personalities and self-care. Take time to teach them those tools, and do it together.

Teach and Train Time Management

Time management is a skill that many adults seek to manage in their lives and hectic days. If children are taught time management skills, study skills, and techniques to manage their goals, they will improve and feel less overwhelmed. When there is evidence of the child shutting down, make this part of your curriculum, and refresh these skills consistently.

Address Learning Shut Down

We all shutdown at times. When this happens there is always a reason. Lack of motivation or enthusiasm to finish work is a symptom sometimes of the child testing their boundaries set by their parent's expectations. Most of the causes stem from lack of understanding, frustration with the topic, boredom with topic or method, which all equal a feeling of being overwhelmed. As the parent, you have to trust yourself to understand the triggers for your child. Take the time to sit with them and walk them through their work. Ask many questions in a casual non-aggressive manner to get your child to open up and share why they are frustrated or unmotivated. Understand that children don't always know why they feel unmotivated. Changing the method of teaching can sometimes get kids back on track.

If it's just the Way They are Wired

We are all very different. Some people are overachievers. Some are self-motivated. Some have lots of extra energy. And some people are okay doing the minimum. If your child is okay doing the minimum, accept that about them and realize getting more out of them will be a continuous challenge. For kids that are wired to be active, try using a timer to get them on task. Train them to stick to a schedule. Be watchful of things or even people who motivate them. Accept them for who they are, and find the positives to their relaxed nature.

Lighten the Load – Scale Down to the Basics

There isn't always enough time in the day to spend in face-to-face instruction time with your child. If you are only available two hours a day, only schedule subjects for half of that time then cut down the subject focus time or focus on only two topics a day. Eliminate less critical topics and subjects to just focus on the core subjects that make learning the other topics easier. Then, add on only when student is able to positively handle the current load. Space out the adding on to get the student accustomed to the load. If you want to squeeze in learning, try some of the less traditional forms of learning. Also, remember, learning happens everywhere.

Redirect Learning to A Different Form of Instruction

When what you are doing isn't working, getting the work done, or it's causing distress, take a moment to relax then start in a new direction. This can be as simple as changing the curriculum, or they may even need accountability and teaching by someone in person or online or with manipulatives (hands-on learning tools) for a time period. Realize that kids learn differently at different stages of development as well as for various subjects.

Face Time on the Bare Minimum – Math, Writing, Reading

Taking it to the bare minimum sometimes gives everyone a break. Parental face time with working parents is at a premium, and to make the time count, have structured or unstructured focused time only on the '3 R's in education' which is Reading, Writing and Arithmetic. Writing can be done two to three times a week, reading two times a week with comprehension exercises, and math at least four times a week. All other curriculum can be experience-based, movie-based, play-based, or project-based.

52

When the Curriculum Isn't Working

The one most challenging part of homeschooling is the selection of a curriculum that will work for the child, or multiple children, and can be administered by a working parent who has limited time and energy to actually teach the classes. When a working parent who is taking on homeschooling gets started, they have to consider the curriculum, the way their child learns, and time constraints. This can cause a great curriculum for their child, which may work but takes tons of time to administer, to be left out of the selection process.

Don't be discouraged. Understand that this is typical and that changing or augmenting a curriculum to meet your needs is completely fine.

Consider Issues like Learning Gaps, Learning Style and Personality Traits

Take a moment to consider how you selected the curriculum of choice. Make sure it was a good fit for the child's learning style. Talk to the child and ask them questions about the curriculum, what worked, what didn't work, what they would like, and how they want to learn the topic in question. The child's personality also responds to teaching methods differently. If the curriculum moves too fast and the child has some educational gaps, slowing down to teach those lessons in different ways or repeating them may be necessary.

Supplement it

Sometimes the problem is not the curriculum but the teaching method. In those situations, getting a tutor, adding a video supplement, or extra practice work may be able to save a curriculum from being eliminated. By supplementing, sometimes you find that the curriculum worked fine, but the child may have some learning challenges with the material.

Slow it Down

Some curriculums are rather advanced in portions and may seem easy when initially started but speed up, leaving kids behind. Take time to evaluate when the curriculum stopped working. List which portions were attempted and how successful the child was at finishing them. This can be discovered early if the parent is doing accountability checks with the child daily or, at least, weekly. Ask the child what happened, where it started getting too difficult, boring, hard, or frustrating. Those sections may be able to be taught in another way or can be broken into smaller pieces.

Is it a Study Skills Issue?

In advanced grades, students may have curriculums that expect a level of memorization or retention of the topic. In those situations, many kids may not know how to take notes or even study for retention. In some private schools, study skills are taught starting in 4th and 5th grades as it is a valuable skill. Taking the time to teach this may give a child success in a curriculum that is especially challenging.

Use an online Video, a Tutor, or an Online Teacher

There are times when a child just needs someone to explain a topic to them differently. When that happens, you can do a small phased approach to see which works. Starting with a video instruction from some of the free sources first, watch them with your child, ask them questions, have them take notes, then have them attempt the lesson again. Use a tutor or online teacher with the intent for specific results. When using tutors, be clear on what specifically you desire to focus on. Then have them report to you the child's issue and how you can repeat what they shared. Ask if they have any resources for help with retention and reinforcement of the lesson.

Selecting an online teacher should include sampling an online lesson, researching reviews, and sharing sample lessons with your child to see how the child responds to the teacher and the methods of teaching.

Redirect Learning to Different Format or New Curriculum

When all else fails, change the method. Go completely opposite of a standard curriculum, and try unschooling for a few months. Your child will let you know if they feel something is lacking. You have the freedom and flexibility to change directions. Have the child point out when learning is happening. It also gives them an eye for creative ways to teach themselves and guide you in what is working at the time for them.

53

Tips for Overactive Child or Inattentive Child

Having overactive and inattentive children is common, especially in certain age ranges. Kids need to get extra energy out of their systems and really don't start to calm down in general until around thirteen years old. Many studies on this show that children are supposed to have the level of energy they do, so keep that in mind when having the freedom to homeschool. Take the time to understand your specific child's personality, needs for activity, and quirks that we all have. Work education around those learning styles, environment needs, and tastes. Also, use homeschooling as a way to teach your child to control some of their overactive impulses. Don't force it. Realize this takes years for some kids to grasp, but it can be done.

Focus on Action-Based and Short Sprint Curriculum

Do not do a typical sit-down, lecture-based, or total video-based curriculum all the time. If this is a consistent challenge for your child, make sure you select a curriculum that is hands-on, project-based, and experience-based and unit-study based. Another great curriculum for overactive and inattentive kids is

Charlotte Mason through My Father's Word (find more about this in the Cathy Duffy's Reviews website: https://cathyduffyreviews.com/) which keeps lessons short. Be eclectic, and mix up different types of curriculum to build the best fit for your child. These curriculums are made to teach with action, and it helps overactive kids grasp concepts by doing it with movement or giving it to them in small bites. For a working and home-schooling parent, make note of the time loss and the focus time for your child to get a clear picture of what can realistically be accomplished in your schooling day.

Develop the Skill of Sitting Still

Sitting still, focusing, and self-control can be taught – within reason. This should be integrated with the teaching day for your child. Realize that even adults have this challenge and that it's something that can be cultivated. There are tools to use to improve sit down and focus time.

- **Be consistent.** Have a consistent method of teaching your child to sit still. Make the rules the same, and progress the expectations based on their consistent ability to remain still for short periods of time. Start with five minutes, to ten minutes, to fifteen minutes up to thirty minutes based on the child's age.
- **Make being still a game.** Play the Freeze Game or Be Still Game. Use a game to tell them to 'Move' and 'fast.' Then yell 'Be Still,' and see who can stay still the longest, or time the duration to stay still. There is also Freeze Tag where kids act out different lights from yellow, green, red, which is the stop light, then they freeze.
- **Use a timer.** This tool allows them to manage their focus time. It can also be a game.
- **Working with them through a tough focused time.** Sometimes we just need companionship to finish a

task. Sitting and doing the lesson with your child can get them over a period of boredom.

- **Have a routine.** For overactive and inattentive kids, keeping a routine, using a checklist, and letting their schedule be something they can walk through blindfolded can help them get things done.
- **Teach them relaxation techniques.** Kids can stretch, do breathing exercises, concentration exercises, and more while sitting.

Getting Back Their Attention

There are ways to redirect or recapture your child's attentiveness by augmenting the methods in which instruction and topics are presented. Below are some tips and lessons for working with kids that are inattentive and overactive.

- **Keep lessons short.** This will make sure the child's interest doesn't diminish too fast.
- **Bite Sized Expectations with timed and directed tasks.** Give the child one thing to do, and time them finishing it. Then add two additional tasks with timer, and so on.
- **Go to game-based learning.** Having games on hand to switch the focus of a lesson that may not be as interesting is a great option and complement to a day of inattentiveness.
- **Accommodate them for periods of time.** Get desks that have pedals and desks that allow them to move while they work.
- **Study while doing pushups or using resistant bands.** Exercise is a way to get their blood pumping, get them fit while they learn. Read a colorful card, review pictures with math facts to recite to keep them learning while moving.
- **Fidget Tools when needed.** Kids can use these when

they need them. They are tiny rubber and safe toys kids can squish and squeeze as in the palm of their hands.

- **Checklist to show progression or activity.** For kids that like movement, the movement of checking off items helps them and gives them some movement.
- **Chunk the directions.** Review directions one sentence at a time, and have them repeat the directions back with their own interpretation of them.
- **Make task and checklist short and focused.** Don't overwhelm them with a long list that seems impossible. Keep everything short and focused in fifteen to twenty-minute timeframes.
- **Alternate sitting and standing.** While doing work, have times that they have to sit to work and times they have to stand for work then times to move around to do work.
- **Make it fun.** Build an enjoyable interactive activity, game, hand playing, artful, or strategy activity into each lesson.
- **Get the most difficult subject done when child is being supervised or as first thing.** Sometimes getting the worst out of the way is best. Make those subjects/topics done with supervision and done with some kind of fun activity at the end.
- **Know your child's limits.** Watch your child to see when they typically start to crash, and give breaks at those times. Make it part of your expectations and their schedule.
- **Make sure they got some rest.** If the child is tired, you may have to get a naptime in their day, no matter what the age. Make sure they are active enough during the day that they get proper sleep at night.
- **Give them their own dry erase Boards for showing work or working out exercises.** These are great tools, and finding a dry erase board that also sends

the pages to the computer for safekeeping can really get these kids writing and working in short sprints.

- **Make the indoor space to inspire learning.** Having an environment that makes kids want to reach out and touch, learn, and get motivated will help foster motivation.
- **Give them rewards.** Prizes and rewards can motivate a child out of their slump.
- **Watch that sugar.** Make sure the child hasn't consumed sugar or carbs that could make them overactive. Sometimes though, kids may need that extra helping of carbs to get them through the work. Using it as a reward or as a push can help.
- **Let them tell you.** Getting your kid to decide what subjects they want to work on first, which ones they don't like, what topics they want to change will help decide if a method or curriculum may need to wait.

54

Math and Writing Evil Twins

Math and writing are some of the hardest and most consistently needed skills in all the school subjects. They are the foundation courses, along with reading, that if your child can do well, it will help them immensely in all other subjects. It is frustrating when there are subjects that your child can't absorb independently. Usually, the main topics that give children the most challenge are math and writing.

First understand that kids are basically taught and reinforced with the same math facts from 6th grade until 8th grade. In traditional school, the child may be considered advanced and will move to pre-algebra as early as 8th grade. The staples of math that include addition, subtraction, division, multiplication, decimals, fractions, and measurements will be used in one way or another by the child for the rest of their lives. If the child doesn't know this extremely well, advanced math will certainly be a struggle.

Core Math Facts Typically are Taught until 7th Grade

Realizing that the core math facts are taught for at least eight years makes it less daunting. If you have to get your kid on grade level and your child doesn't seem to grasp all the facts, you have plenty of time to teach, fill in gaps, recover or restart their learning. The focus should be on: addition, subtraction, multiplication, division, measurements, factoring, decimals, percent arithmetic, dividing fractions arithmetic, word problems, ratios, metric, time measures, roman numerals, and temperatures.

Surviving Math

Many parents and kids stress about math. There is a new math that our kids learn, and many people oppose memorization. However, if your kid has the ability to memorize the basics, it will help them in the long-term for quick recall. The method for quick recall of basic math—addition, subtraction, multiplication, and division are up to you.

As far as Common Core math, remember that colleges are still teaching math the old fashion way. They will gladly take those common core math students with their international students and all other students who are struggling with math and build courses to get them to the level of college mathematics that combines algebra and geometry facts. So, just remember, your child can be successful with a deep and well-balanced understanding of math facts up to the math 8th grade, geometry, and some algebra.

Tips to help child solidify math skills:

- **Memorize basics for quick recall.** Taking the time to solidify quick recall of the basics is a must. Some methods for this are memorization and logical understanding of how to get the answer.
- **Write out methods in steps.** When children learn long addition, subtraction, complex division, complex multiplication, decimals, and fractional equations, knowing the different steps from decoding, checking, and answering is important. Have them write the steps before they start the problem, then have them verbally explain how they will attempt to get the answer. After they can

do that effectively without assistance, have them solve the problems. Having a quick recall of basic math facts will all fall in place.

- **Reinforce core recall skills at every level.** Even when your child moves on to advanced math, have weekly drills or math fact recall games to make sure they don't get rusty in those quick recall skills. They will need those fast skills for tests such as college entry, military entry, and sometimes job entry tests.

- **Be willing to teach the same topics but with different curriculum or different methods each time.** If you tried one method to teach fractions one year, and your kid did okay but needs more practice, use another curriculum or method to teach them the same topic. It will give the topic a fresh perspective. For example, if you taught addition to your child in 1st grade with a workbook style, change it up by teaching them the same topic with manipulatives which are hands on teaching tools for learning like used in Math U See curriculum.

- **Don't get discouraged.** Realize that this is the long game, and don't move on until a good foundation is built and your child is comfortable with all math facts at each level building up to the next level. Consider a mastery-based curriculum with a small spiral back to the previously built on facts.

Writing, the Skill Used for Everything

In order to grasp writing, the child should be able to read well and comprehend what they are reading. Once they have mastered that skill, writing by hand and typing comes in to play. Spelling is a frustrating part of the writing process for kids at advanced levels, so teaching spelling at a young age is important. Phonetic spelling and memorization or sight words are something that is developed from kindergarten until 3rd grade, and by fourth grade most kids are writing detailed papers of a page or more. Vocabulary is built with spelling memorization classes. It all folds together to build a potentially strong writer. When parts of these interwoven skills in English aren't strong, it shows up in the final product of writing and researching in-depth papers. Comprehension plays a major role in reading and researching topics that the student will later write about. Therefore, make sure that comprehension skills are well developed.

- **The skill of writing with pen in cursive and print.** This helps the child to: (1) solidify a fact written to memory, (2) to think through what they are trying to say, (3) writing in cursive will allow them to sign their name and write in a way that people don't even learn to master in schools in current day.
- **Vocabulary, spelling, comprehending and defining words.** This skill should be mastered by the end of elementary school and refined through middle school. Learning to break down words and their meaning helps. Many parents teach some form of the Latin language to help their kids' break down words better.
- **Being able to write a 350-page essay in less than one hour.** This is used for test taking, writing great papers in a short period of time, for college entry exams, and more. Learning to gather thoughts quickly and write a paper by hand or type within an hour is useful and will springboard a child's after high school career.

Surviving Writing Skill Development

The act of actually writing isn't fun for some kids. Finding a way to incorporate spelling and the act of writing and comprehension all in one can be difficult. Make sure your child understands the parts of a paper to include a thesis, body, and conclusion from the beginning will help them to stay focused. Building the writing assignments into small pieces can help get through it and solidify the parts of the puzzle for your child.

- **Try copywriting.** This helps the child with the thought process of reading something, holding the thought, then writing it. It's a form of note-taking practice. Find curriculums that have this as part of the spelling program.
- **Interactive writing games.** Creating writing games and sentence building games can help a child with the building blocks of comprehension and the thought process behind writing.
- **Creating a list of the steps.** Having a checklist of the steps in writing a paper, the different types of essays that can be created (persuasive, descriptive, argumentative, and a research Paper) can assist the child in making sure they understand the mechanics of each type of paper.
- **Practice makes perfect.** Incorporating writing into different subjects as part of a project or a way of demonstrating their understanding instead of active testing can be an incentive for some children. Writing a paper is sometimes easier than taking a test.

55

Job Change or Parental Support Change

Life happens and has a way of encroaching on homeschooling. Family dynamics change, and parental support shifts can be upsetting and can bring the entire family and schooling momentum to a halt. Well, that doesn't mean the end of the world. It means finding a way to capitalize on the freedom of homeschooling and make it work. Please remember, the way you educate your child is a choice. That means, if you send them back to traditional school, it can be a temporary reprieve with the knowledge that when you resettle your circumstances, homeschooling is still attainable. You can also after-school them, using the concepts and lessons you've learned in home-schooling and working. Know that you have the freedom and flexibility to choose educational options for your child.

Make sure Childcare is Secure

Being a working parent, you have to think in terms of proper childcare and keeping those options flexible while having a backup plan for unforeseen circumstances. Childcare options are discussed in detail in Chapters 11, 12, and 13. In situations where there is a huge transition such as odd hours of work, family change in circumstances where an in-house nanny may be needed, use the creative options for childcare mentioned.

Use the Flexibility of Homeschooling in Your Favor

Remember you are in control of your child's education, and that means if the family needs to just get through a short period of chaos like moving, environment changes, schedule changes, or more, use flexibly to your benefit. Change the form of educating from a structured to an unschooling method by strewing items around the house for the kid to use at their will. Educate with movies, games, projects, field trips, experiences, or just playing video games.

Be open to All Other Educational Options

Homeschooling is a great option, but it isn't the only one. Think of educating your children as a journey of options, and evaluate what is working for you each year or even half a year. Realize that changing from homeschooling to another mode of educating using Co-ops, tutorial, online school, or sending the child back to traditional school isn't failure; it's utilizing your freedom of choice and doing what is best for your child during the circumstances.

56

Remember Learning Comes from Many Places

There is a mindset most people have about schooling that stems from the traditional way most have learned. Open your mind and realize that learning comes in all forms, locations, places, methods, and experiences. Take the time to see the lesson in all of your children's experiences. This is helpful when you feel as though you aren't doing enough to educate your child. These experiences and forms of learning were always there even when kids did learn before being homeschooled.

Log It Daily

Every day, jot down what was done during the day where the child used skills for a particular subject. For example, if your child helped you cook by measuring the quantities, went to the store and paid for the food with money, and added the change, then researched a recipe—all that covers subjects in math, reading, chemistry, and even logic.

Keep a notebook where you log learning then weekly, put it in spreadsheet per subject.

Use Excel Spreadsheet to Log Learning by subject

Learning Log	Math	Writing	Reading	Logic	Science	Geoghraphy	Art	Language
Watched Japanese Cartoon (reading caption)			x					x
Played Minecraft	x			x	x		x	
Made Cookies From Recipe	x	x	x				x	
Watched Discovery Channel Animal Planet					x	x		
Played Pokeman Go	x			x		x		
Played Scrabble			x					x

Teach your child to think of what skills they are using

Getting the child on board and teaching them how to assess which subjects or topics they are learning in a day will make your job easier. Use checklists for them to check off what skill they exercised for the day, and have a note section for them to write down what they did. For example, they played a video game and, in that game, they had to follow a map, find a villain, communicate with characters along the way, unravel a puzzle, and read messages. A teenager can easily identify which skills they used if given a checklist of choices.

Examples of Hidden Forms of Learning Experiences

When you consider all that most kids are exposed to, you realize they are learning even when they aren't holding a book, writing in a workbook, or watching a lecture.

Use tools like Evernote to organize learning by subjects and days. Below are some ways kids learn besides traditionally:

- Music lessons
- Creating artwork
- Listening to different styles of music
- Reading
- Nature walks and hiking
- Research
- Watching fun movies
- Going to see a play
- Visiting new places
- Playing video games
- Typing
- Navigating to new locations
- Listening to an audio book

- Doing craftwork
- Volunteering
- Trips to the store and involved in shopping and purchases
- Star gazing
- Watching YouTube videos
- Cleaning the house
- Traveling to new states or countries
- Cooking
- Fixing something or learning to fix something
- Teaching another child something
- Communicating on different media
- Creating a video or taking pictures
- Writing a blog post
- Going to camp and recording what they learn or do there

57

The Power of Positive Words

The main reason we started homeschooling our son was to replace the negative words and phrases thrown at him with positive speak. One major benefit of homeschooling and working is that you get to take the time you have with your child to build positive voices for them. Many kids that are in school have to combat negative chatter around them and directed at them. Imagining having those many negative voices in your head every day and moment can become daunting. Homeschooling your child gives them the opportunity to hear and believe they are capable of anything to which they set their minds. Always give them more positive voices than negative.

In my book *Building Your Empowered Steps*, there is a chapter on the power of words, and that stands true for children as well as adults.

The Power of Positive Affirmations

It's about changing our mindset. Learning to see the glass as half full instead of boarding on empty. That glass many times is a representation of ourselves and the world around us. A survivor and thriving person has to believe there is something good about themselves. They find the silver lining in a situation and hold onto it until they are able to change it for the good. Teaching your child this will help them to believe in themselves, heal from hurt, encourage themselves through difficult situations, show love to others and themselves, express a positive perspective, and create connections.

Have their words and yours that you use with them build bridges instead of walls. Show them forgiveness so they will learn to show it to others. Use your words to build them up and show them acceptance.

Ways to Give Positive Words to Kids

Homeschooling and working are stressful. Always try to think through what you want to say before blurting out what you may be feeling. Put a positive spin on the words.

1. Give them praise before correction.
2. Specifically point out what they did well and ask them questions to get them to expand on that behavior or way of thought.
3. Focus positive encouragement on the effort or thought process, and not the superficial.
4. Don't undermine positive words with negatives or conditions.
5. Don't compare them in praise; let it be their own.
6. Turn their 'can't' into a 'can'; just help them define doing things in their own unique way.
7. Give them affectionate hugs, slapping hands, or thumbs-up to share a positive action.
8. Try not to give positive words for negative behavior.
9. Give them a surprise positive reinforcement phrase every morning or evening, in their lunch, or on their school board.

Have Child Recite Positive Affirmations

Sometimes we have to give ourselves a reminder of how to stay positive. Have a poster or board of positive affirmations that you can go over with your child. Something for them to say out loud to themselves and you daily.

58

Staying Motivated and Avoiding Burnout

Many homeschool journeys stop because of burnout. The sad reality is many parents try too hard to make the experience perfect, to do 'school at home' in the traditional manner that never worked for their child in the first place, or they don't take the power they have by homeschooling to their advantage. Realizing that as the parent educator, you get to speed up the learning, slow down school, change the method to accommodate what is going on, and take breaks when needed, is the power in homeschooling flexibility.

Remember and Use Your Freedom in Homeschooling

Often working and homeschooling parents forget that they have control in their educational decision. When stress piles up, take a step back, claim a school holiday, and re-evaluate a new direction. The freedom of homeschooling allows us breaks when needed, time to repair gaps in learning, creativity in the resources used to teach our kids, and more. Understand all the methods of learning, teaching, and exposing your child to knowledge makes it easy to understand that even when there isn't focused instruction going on, kids are still learning and using their skills learned every day.

- Make sure the issue isn't about discipline and parenting of the child over trying to get homeschooling done.
- Reset goals and schedule to reasonable bites.
- Go on a social media, computer, cellphone electronic family break (cut off electronics) and play with kids, take adventures with kids, talk to your kids.
- Take a mini-mental health vacation and just do nothing.
- Come up with a short-term solution to give yourself time to evaluate a turn-around method.
- Ask for help if you need it or if your child needs it.
- Take time to think on, observe, and build the full picture of the areas causing the burnout.
- Share the challenges with your support system and your children. Kids can give a great perspective on things.

Watch for the Signs of Breaking Point

Evaluate when either the child or the parent is getting close to their breaking point. If the child is the one showing signs of being overworked and overwhelmed, take measures to slow them down, either by taking off items of responsibility one by one or changing the direction and methods of teaching. If the parent is feeling overwhelmed, reduce the parental responsibility with teaching by diverting to using a tutor, sending child to a live online class, or in-person class.

Some signs are:
What's Going on in the Mind?

- Showing outward signs and verbal statements of frustration contrary to the child or parent's norm.
- Giving up and not taking on topics, subjects, or giving opinions where there was once active engagement.
- Loss of confidence in themselves, ideas, answers, and responses.

What's happening with The Body?

- Body Language shows tense and jerky movements in response to minor things.
- Being more tired than usual.
- Tense muscles, headaches, vision issues, stomach aches.
- Eating or not eating more than normal.

Where Are the Emotions

- Oversensitive or desensitized to others and their comments.
- Problems concentrating.
- Runaway emotional responses.
- Feeling numb about things that usually got a response from you or your child.

Actions Speak Louder Than Words

- Learn to observe your child's actions.
- Note triggers for certain outward movements, reactions, and responses to stress and boredom.

Using a Block Schedule to Ramp up and Down

Using a block schedule gives you time to catch up or get a great strong start with the curriculum when everyone is ready to dive into challenging topics. This form of scheduling allows for makeup time and ramp up time for subjects and allows for a cool-down or deep-dive into specific subjects during a condensed period of time.

Practice the Power of Saying No

The child or parent may tend to overbook. This can creep up on a schedule and make lives so jammed packed that the time to do what needs to be done is in competition with so many other responsibilities. Reserve taking on more activities until you have referred to your schedule. Don't feel guilty if you have to back out of something planned in order to focus on what's important to the family.

Go Back to the Basics

When the schedule is too hectic, take a step back. Start with just one or two courses a day. Restart with the principles noted in Chapter 39, and start slow by easing back into a more challenging pace.

59

Set the Priority of a Loving Relationship with Your Child

Never forget why you started homeschooling while working. It's because you want to go above and beyond the norm to provide a loving and supportive atmosphere for your child. Continue to remind yourself and your child of this when it gets challenging. Remember that when your child was in traditional school, there were many challenges, but they were likely not seen or dealt with until the situation was dire. When you homeschool, you can adjust to the circumstances as needed.

Start Off by Building a Healthy Foundation

Kids don't come with directions, but one thing is for sure; everyone benefits from knowing they are loved. Talking to your child no matter what age they are is important. Make them feel as though their thoughts, dreams, and purpose matter. Give children and even teenagers' hugs, kisses, and affection. Share positive words with them, and teach them to share those with you.

- Hug them daily.
- Tell them you love them daily.

- Find time to play with them.
- Focus on them, turn off the phone, television, and put down the book.
- Look them in the eye to prepare them for times of change.
- Make one-on-one time a priority.
- Let them share their emotions.
- Support them in their endeavors.
- Realize that they are always watching, listening, and learning from their parents.

Constantly Work at Keeping Communication Open

Building a relationship with your child includes many factors. Understanding their personality, their needs, and their thoughts is important to building this. Constantly seek ways to improve the relationship, and shift it as the child grows and the parent deals with different circumstances. Being honest with your kids about your humanistic qualities allow them to see that perfection isn't necessary.

Make Time to Focus on Each Child

Planning a few hours per month, with each child individually, to do something they love to do is important. Make it so they don't have to compete with a sibling for focused time and communication. Let them select the activity. Talk about things they love, are interested in, and let them lead the conversation or activity.

Teach them to Respect you, by Giving Respect

It's challenging to speak to a child in a manner you want them to speak to you, but doing so will give them an example of how to respond to your requests. Also, teach them the level of respect due to a person's role, position, and age. Even so, let them know that even in those situations, they have a voice; they just need to use it respectfully.

Don't Internalize Challenges with Your Children

Try not to take your child's attitude, responses, and actions personally. Give yourself space and permission to detach and observe without feeling as though everything about them is in your control.

Listen First, Think on it, Then Speak

The hardest part of building depth to the relationship with your child is not telling them what to do right away. Take the time to really listen. Let them get out their feelings, dilemmas, and thoughts. Hear them out by:

- Digesting what was said.
- Asking them the right questions to lead them to the solution with their own words, not yours.

Apologize if you are wrong – Make them also Apologize

Lead by example. If you were wrong in judgments, actions, or responses, take the time to apologize to your child. Do it without a 'but' for justification. Then, let some time pass before addressing the other issues that caused the loss of parental control.

An apology is the first step in learning the actions of acknowledgement of doing something wrong. Whether the apology is given from the heart or not, having the child apologize as well as doing so yourself teaches them what the give and take of reconciliation and how it feels when someone accepts your apology and how it feels when it is given.

Affirm to them a Non-Judgmental or Conditional Love

Never let them forget that they have a safe haven at home in your arms. Give them the reminder when they need it and even when they don't seem to. Letting your child know that you are on their team, by their side, and in their corner, gives them an open door to share all with you.

Cheer Them On

Kids benefit from having a cheerleader even when they act like they don't want one. Attending their events, telling them they have the capacity to do anything in their own unique way, and congratulating them when they do, will go leaps and bounds in their growth.

60

Transform a Strong-Willed Child into a Strong Adult

This is the long game. When you have a strong-willed child, there is no immediate solution for teaching them the valuable lessons of self-control, respect for authority, keeping destructive reactions in check, and just being obedient when the time dictates it. Your commitment to transform your strong-willed child into a strong man or woman is a journey that will teach you more about yourself than you thought possible. It will test your patience, your ability to hold your temper, your reasoning, your capacity for love and energy. Managing all of this and continuing to work and homeschool will seem nearly impossible. It can be done when you use all the tools shared in this book.

Positive adults and leaders can be born of this tedious work. My husband and I have seen the fruits of this with our four children, all of whom were strong-willed. Truth is, my husband and I were both strong willed and because of that have done some pretty amazing things in our lives. We just didn't accept the reality of the status quo. Our motto was, 'turning the no into our yes.' We created our own path to reach our goals.

As for our children, we didn't want to break their wills. We only wanted to give them the tools to operate in their world without becoming a destructive force within it but, instead, to become a positive force.

RECITE to make it RIGHT

When we homeschooled our youngest child, he had some self-control challenges. Those actions were the reason we invented the CALM DOWN LIST explained in Chapter 30. It was a life-saver. It did wonders and taught him how to calm down, relax, redirect, or accept his condition. We used it in addition to the below:

- Positive words
- Reciting ways to self-calm, slow down, control impulses
- Use of calming and uplifting music and songs for mindset changes
- Lots of hugs and singing with him
- Sometimes we even yelled, stomped our feet, and had tantrums with him, which made him usually appear shocked before he stopped acting out

Consistency is the Key

Being consistent in your reactions then following up with the proper response when they don't reply respectfully worked well. It can be difficult not to yell, scream, and curse (Oh yeah, they can take you there.), but strive for consistency, being non-affected outwardly by their actions. Don't be a robot, but try to work on yourself as you work on them. Sometimes they frustrate you, but through their testing of you, they are learning to be the best they can be by the way you respond to them.

Consequences That Are Thoughtful

If there is a punishment to give for a behavior, think on it, make it compatible to the lesson you want to teach the child. Then discuss with your parenting partner the best options, and have a united front. Kids can see a separation of opinion a mile away. They know you more than you may even know yourselves and will use that break in communication between you and your partner against you both. However, for typical behavior, have a consequence board that leaves no argument or debate on the punishment.

An example of this is when my oldest daughter yelled at her sister that "at school you are not my sister!" This was after numerous warnings about her alienating and mean words to her sister. That day, her punishment was that we took her own bedroom from her. She had to share with her sister until she learned humility and kindness. Six months later, we redecorated and opened her own bedroom for her because she had changed greatly.

Building a Friendly Relationship makes a Difference

These kids have lots of energy. You have to play with them. Not just parenting them will work; you have to build a level of respect that comes with spending time in their space. Interact with them, talk to them, every single day. Work at building a deep and trusting relationship. If they tell you they did something freely (even if it is punishable) don't punish all the time, but talk them through it. This friendship will blossom into adulthood and is truly the solidifying glue to working with a strong-willed child.

ASK THE RIGHT QUESTIONS that lead them to THE RIGHT SOLUTION

Learn to ask them questions instead of always telling them what to do. Ask them the questions to lead them to *their own* answers. Guide them to find the right and wrong in the specific situation. When they answer in the right manner—rarely can they dispute the facts. Also, the exercise of questions that lead them to the right answers teaches them to reason with themselves when they are being talked into or out of a situation.

Don't Take It Personally

Kids with strong personalities are rather good at figuring a way to get under your skin. They want to know what makes you tick. They could probably tell you how you will react to a word or an action with clarity once they have learned to respect you. Staying calm may make their behavior become worse before getting better. You have to learn to observe their body language and assess the best method to interact with them under the circumstances. Understand their mind in order to determine what is working and what does not.

You have to Earn Their Respect

Respect for a strong-willed child starts with the parent. Parents have to earn the respect of these children. It can't be earned by fear, anger, or restrictiveness. It is a tedious process of give and take with a huge helping of forgiveness and love. It's as though they need to constantly test that love and your capacity to give it to them. They are usually disagreeable, which makes it challenging even for parents to have the energy to work on their behavior. The building of this is through constant positive as well as corrective communication given in ways the child will accept it, remember it, and recall when they need. Soft reminders of the consequences of their actions should be noted. Having a board in place for some of the challenges help and saves the parent from repeating the need to: (1) talk respectfully, (2) think before you act, (3) apologize when needed, (4) decide to turn my day around, (5) own your actions. Lastly, keep your emotions, impulses and responses in check or it can go from bad to worse fast.

Find Them the Right Tribe of Friends

In adolescence, kids value friendships and using the benefits of homeschooling; take the time to build friendships with people that are a healthy and positive influence. Birds of a feather typically flock together. Kids conform (good or bad) to kids around them who they want to have as friends. It is not wrong to end a friend-ship, cultivate new ones, or select opportunities to meet positive thinking friends.

Sports and ROTC programs like the Civil Air Patrol (CAP) program camps that teach discipline all have been a great outlet for my sons. Those activities had structure that also gave them a great group of friends who are focused on positive things. It also came with positive oversight from strong male role models.

Consider putting them in programs just for the experience even though it likely won't be their final career. For example, I also put my oldest son through EMT training if for nothing but to teach him discipline, to foster his desire to help others. That training and volunteering matured him in many ways. It also gave him other strong male mentors besides his great supportive dad who coached him in most all his sports teams.

Teach them to:

- Respect others feelings
- To slow themselves down to observe how the other child is responding to them
- To ask their friends questions and wait for answers

As parents:

- Act out scenarios of healthy behaviors for friendships so they understand when someone is a good friend to them and they are being a good friend.
- Make them feel comfortable expressing their feelings, working out their over active frustrations, growing with each friendship

The Making And Breaking Of Friendships

Strong willed kids can make and break friendships easily; help them to recover and accept that friendships sometimes have time limits. It's about learning from the relationship and making improvements for selecting good friend groups, treating friends fairly, and knowing when the friendship's time is up.

Don't take lost friendships personally. Consider every friendship a learning experience and chat about the benefits and costs of the friendships they've had. If they made a mistake in the friendship, or the other kid made a mistake, talk with them about scenarios that could have changed the outcome of the friendship or circumstance. These kids will gain and lose them frequently as do most kids. Part of building them up is teaching them how to control their reactions to the changes in relationships. They should learn from their mistakes and positive growth in these relationships.

Key Points in Time You will see Development

Kids under teenaged years are supposed to be active, impulsive, and have lack of control. Why? They have never been to this exciting place before and they are growing. It isn't exactly natural for them to sit still for long periods of time. Most adults don't want to sit still in meetings that are over 20 minutes and we forget that when we set expectations for our children.

There are actual stages and ages that kids seem to calm down and do a better job controlling their impulses (Anumeha Bhagat, Rashimi Vyas, Tejinder Singh, 2015). Understanding these modes and changes in maturity gives a parent a basic marker when understanding what drives their child's decision making, impulsivity, and lack of self-control.

- **Age 12 years** old is when kids start to slow down and think more, consider the consequences first, and gain an understanding of their actions.
- **Age 15 years** is when they think about the outcomes to their actions and take longer to react. However, they are still fueled by peers over parental influence.
- **Age 17 to 22 years** old, kids fight fiercely for their independence, rely greatly on their peer relationships,

become opinionated, and like to argue and fight parents' control in their lives.

- **Age 24 years** is a pinnacle point where kids start to make mature decisions, become less inclined to go with peer groups, and feel comfortable assessing consequences for their actions.

Realize you have a Potential Leader, a Strong and Determined person in a Tiny Body

It's like watching *The Incredibles* movie when they show the skit about the baby, Jack Jack, who now has all these uncontrollable super powers. Most strong-willed children remind me of that baby. So much potential to go against the grain, to become some great force in changing the world, all in that itty-bitty package. If raised to harness those abilities, they grow up to utilize those gifts of creativity, quick intelligence, ability to read people, and determination to do the impossible beyond expectations. They become world changers, strong enough, focused enough to make the big stuff happen if they so desire.

Keep them BUSY, BUSY, BUSY

My kids didn't have too much idle time. Being involved in structured activities kept them out of trouble and tired enough to get good sleep. Breakdancing, track, canoe racing, lacrosse, football, soccer, skateboarding, surfing, swimming, jujitsu, and capoeira were great tools for my kids. Also, running. It gave them something to do with all of that nervous energy and taught them self-discipline. It put them more strong male role models and teachers.

Let Them Sleep However They Want

Sleep was a big factor. Make sure there isn't a mild 'sleep apnea' or insomnia health issue that is affecting their rest. If you suspect this, get medical direction and accommodate their weird sleeping needs. As a homeschooling parent, you have the ability to just let them sleep when they want. A small battle is to let them manage their sleep habits in their own way. You can make them stay in their room, but they can sleep and wake whenever they want. For some reason, kids who are strong-willed tend to have the oddest sleep habits. Take the time to learn ways to accommodate it so they are in the best mood during their waking hours.

Be Careful with Labeling

Words have power. Sometimes, deciding not to label your child based on your or someone else's assumptions can reveal the positives of their characteristics instead of the negatives. In the current years, I've met so many adults who are not medical doctors but who like to throw around the label, diagnosis of "ADD" or "ADHD" like it's a title for every single child who is over-active, mouthy, impulsive, and more. This has been proven to be one of the most misdiagnosed conditions, especially in the US compared to other nations, now more than ever before.

When I was young, you never heard the term. People focused on mitigating the behaviors, not medicating. When you medicate a child, you alter them, their ability to grow, and their minds. So, do not take medicating lightly. Research the medication, its origins and most you will find have a close link to mind altering drugs that when taken for long periods of time can seriously damage a child and give them markers for addiction later in life. Remember, you are the parent, the one in control and should make the decisions about your child using all options before medication. Even with medicating, you will have to consistently work through the behaviors with your child.

Changing behavior, teaching the child to manage and under-stand themselves and to develop alternate methods to cope with them is better than just giving them a label and writing them off. This is what has driven many people to homeschool their children. The schools use the labels to separate children and stigmatize them instead of creating an environment for all types of learning styles, personalities, maturity levels, and abilities.

If you are going to give them labels, make them positive to their actions and not a condition that has a negative history and tone to it. Don't use the label as a crutch or a way to explain away the child's challenges instead of helping the child through therapy or consistent work to overcome their hurdles. At the end of the day, we have to love ourselves just the way we are. Doing so without labels makes the positive strides the child makes shine brighter than what they've overcome.

SECTION THREE

CREATING
AN AMAZING
LEARNER

Introduction

An amazing learner is about your child's personal and unique makeup, and ways to improve on their desire and capacity to learn at a rate that is beyond their own personal 'normal'. As a home-schooling and working parent, you don't have to compare your child's success to anyone else's. You rate their success in their own uniqueness.

There is one key ingredient needed in building an eager learner – it's parental involvement through interaction, direction, and the creation of the opportunities to learn differently. This is a relationship building and motivational skill that can be improved a little each year. The skill of using their curiosity to deepen their level and capacity to learn.

Some ways to integrate learning into your relationship building with your child is to do the following:

- Share your passion and interests with your child.
- Introduce them to new experiences, places, and things.
- Actively create mock experiences with them through play, camps, immersion courses, career role playing.
- Read with them by creating your own home book club.

- Focus their learning on their growing areas of interest.
- Involve them in the educational process, curriculum selection, experience selection.
- Take a step back, and let them fly into deep discovery of their own interests.
- Ask them the right questions to spark their interest.
- Enjoy and grow through the process of learning, not the testing of it.
- Mix up the learning styles.
- Share in their excitement for a topic.

61

How to Create an Amazing Learner

Children are little beings filled with possibilities. Just because your child isn't overly gifted in math or science doesn't mean you can't cultivate strength and confidence in those areas. Use the fact that you are homeschooling to repeat and reteach what they don't know. You have the time to do it. This book has mention various ways to overlay learning so the child is exposed to topics in many different ways. Use their interest in subjects where they are extremely passionate and talented; therefore, cultivate their interest in those areas to improve all others. The key is to make learning fun for your child and get their buy-in and involvement early in the game.

Solidify the Foundation

Take the extra time to deepen their foundations in the core subjects of Math, Writing and Reading. Don't let some deficits hold them back from other subjects where they soar; just find easy methods to explore those topics.

Overlap Learning by Using Several Different Methods to Teach

Learning one topic in various ways overlaps learning and makes it solidify without necessarily having long study sessions. Take a topic the child needs to reinforce, and have them work on that subject more than once in a day but in a different way. With math, be cautious as you don't want to go over one hour of math instruction a day. An example for math could be to do a five-minute math drill in the morning, and teach a new math fact as the third subject of the day by game, quick video, or copywriting steps with examples for twenty minutes. Then have them do twenty minutes of practice problems either by hand or interactive program.

Keep Going with no Long Breaks to Work Right Through

The time wasted re-teaching subjects and skills in math, writing, and other subjects can be erased when a student works right through. Basically, having a year-round schedule with short breaks. Do this by letting the child go directly from basic math, take two weeks off, and then dive into pre-algebra and geometry which can be taken at the same time. Take three weeks off, then finish algebra 1. After they finish algebra 1, remove the repeated curriculum in the first few lessons and dive into algebra 2.

Limited breaks can still have math, writing and grammar drill work to keep skills current. This can virtually eradicate middle school 6th, 7th and 8th grades. Remember, middle school is virtually a repeat of most subjects to solidify and reteach what was taught in elementary.

Share Ownership for Learning with your Child

Involve your child in the process to get their enthusiasm for growing and learning. You can easily overload subjects by condensing and teaching them in ways that aren't traditional, and kids won't even realize they are doing more than the typical course load. Cover more subjects by teaching them in different ways or methods that don't seem as though they are taking on another subject. History can be an experienced-based curriculum where the child goes on field trips, watches movies with family, creates crafts and food for the period.

Let Their Passionate Interests Run Wild then Fold Curriculum into It

Expose your kids to many things even when they don't seem interested. When they get absorbed in a topic or subject, let them take over deep-diving into the topic, and surround all other subjects with as much of the areas of their interest as possible. For example, my friend's daughter loved gaming and Sims. She found an online school that was conducted in a virtual reality world. The school was named WiloStar3d, and her daughter loved that it was similar to Minecraft. She covered additional courses through a Minecraft homeschool curriculum that her daughter enjoyed so much she didn't want to stop doing schoolwork in the summer. My daughter is an artist, a video-gamer, a programmer, and a writer. All of these passions were developed through her years of homeschooling. She watched more YouTube videos on gaming, game development, and art than I can name. It helped us condense her years in school, and she even worked through summers to feed her thirst for knowledge in those areas.

62

Skills That Give Your Kid a Competitive Edge

There are certain skills that boost a person's ability to navigate different subjects and challenges. Some of them I will name below, but for your child, think about all the things you wished someone had taught you. Then add them into your curriculum to teach those skills to your child.

As far as education goes, solidifying the foundation makes everything so much easier to grasp. However, there are different skills that kids don't typically learn in traditional school that a homeschooler or after-schooling parent can help their children to develop.

Speed Reading

After your child is comfortable reading both phonetically and with sight words, introducing the art of speed-reading is a wonderful addition to their ability to self-teach.

Comprehension in Reading

Improving comprehension takes practice. Building a child's vocabulary is a great tool for improving comprehension. Take that understanding and ask questions about the person, the place, or the thing that happened. Pinpoint the main idea, main characters, the thesis, main point in reading. It allows them to think and consider what is being read on a deeper level than just completing the act of reading.

Logic

Building the skill of thinking logically is a precision tool that can be used for test taking, science, and building skills of critical thinking. This can be done through games, curriculum, debate teams, logical series of questions, and answers to practice skills.

Fast Computational Math

There is value in learning tricks and tips for fast mind-driven computation. Use curriculums that teach 'mental math' that can be learned once the child has a good understanding of math facts. My kids took several courses on the Secrets of Mental Math to learn these techniques and tricks. It helped them immensely.

Research

Researching skills are valuable life lessons. They are also skills that will assist the student in high school, a military career, trade careers, and more. Teach them to research from sources besides just doing an internet search. Take them to the library for research, have them view movies, interview people, create experimentation to evolve their understanding of researching a fact or theory. Use questions to spark their research and desire to find answers to support their understanding.

Speech and Debate

Learning to write speeches and give speeches to people other than parents hones the skill of critical thinking and the ability to share those thoughts with others. The more it's practiced the easier it gets.

Test Taking

Many homeschoolers love the freedom of throwing away the testing conforms of schools. However, test taking is a skill that can be used in college, careers, and beyond. Learning the techniques behind improving testing methods and outcome is a skill that is used even after school. Even the military requires testing; most careers require online testing for entry and the skill is needed.

Writing Papers Fast

Speed-writing papers is a skill many kids worked on in preparation for the SATs. It is a talent that can be used for more than just preparing for a high school or college test. This is an ability that can be utilized in day-to-day life after school and definitely in many work places. Taking an SAT review course that is focused on the writing of the paper portion is a must, and it encourages actual hand writing of the 300-word paper that is required. This is another form of thinking and processing that many students don't develop well when they only type their papers.

Focus on:

- Analysis of information
- Writing a paper by hand in one hour
- Total word count of about 300 words written by hand

How to Take Notes

This is a difficult skill to build, but with practice, it becomes second nature. Learning the different ways and formats for note-taking from reading, lectures, videos, and the environment will help solidify and build study techniques.

Study Methods

Learning how to study is something even traditional schools no longer teach. Don't let your kid wing this; teach them this skill. Studying can help in later careers, college, and life in general. Find the method that is most aligned with your child's learning style and personality.

Networking Skills and Interpersonal Communication

Communication skills are key. Teaching your child to improve their networking, people meeting, small talk, and comfort around groups is a great tool. Interpersonal communication is the way to interact with people in one-on-one settings. Also, skills as the interviewee or interviewer can be used beyond school.

Life Skills

Life skills such as cooking, cleaning, paying bills, making a budget, renting a place, buying a car, searching for a college, or making a shopping list, are all part of life skills. Think about all the things you have to do as an adult, and take the time to teach your child to do them for themselves before they leave for college, a career, or your home.

Music

Playing an instrument and learning to read music is something your child can use in their adult life. It can also assist them with learning other topics and give them an outlet for stress and creativity.

Art

Numerous great artists were taught to draw, sculpt, and paint even though they didn't have an innate skill to do so. It is a form of expression that can be taught. It is useable in many ways and into their adult life.

Languages

It is amazing when you travel to other countries and the people there actively attempt the language of your country, yet it's frustrating when you can't do the same. Teaching children to speak another language or two will be necessary for the ever-changing economy and world where we live.

Athletic Sports

Team sports, singular sports, and nutrition are lifelong skills many kids will use for the rest of their lives. Have them attempt different sports, forms of working out, and foods to learn how their body works. Exercise and stretching with proper diet will go a long way in helping them to learn to regulate the way they feel and respond to the world around them.

Business and Marketing

Even if your child has no desire to start their own business, teach them anyway. The work that goes into building a micro business, marketing that business, and managing the budget, teaches so many other lessons and skills.

Leadership and Mentoring Skills

Have your student participate in activities that will give them leadership skills and cultivate mentoring. They can tutor their siblings or other children. They can volunteer as a camp teen assistant or participate in summer camp that teaches leadership.

63

Encourage Child to Delve Into Something New Every Year

If your child is like most kids, trying something for the first time is scary. My kids didn't want to do about half of the activities, experiences, subjects, topics, or anything I suggested—at first. We make the mistake of thinking that kids know what they will like. How is that possible if they haven't been here before and they are still learning about themselves? Many adults find their passions late in life because they weren't exposed to them sooner. While your child is still a child, and basically you have control over what they are exposed to, use that time to expose them to new things, people, experiences, and possibilities.

If Your Child Has No Idea What They Want to Do or Be – Pick Something For them

Picking a career focus or teasing a child's interest by giving them direction is not a bad thing. Many parents feel that the child can figure it out. How can they? Kids haven't been here before and can't possibly know all the different career choices or life paths they can take. Our job as parents is to expose them to as many as possible so they can try them.

Most successful actors, athletes, child prodigies became so because their parents led them on a path and helped motivate them to stay there to achieve something great. Some kids can decide what their areas of interest are, others don't have a clue, and may never will. Of my four kids, only one knew what they wanted to do when they grew up, and even so, she has changed direction somewhat. Therefore, giving your child a direction can help them immensely by giving them some sort of focus.

- Write down possibilities for career discovery and interest discovery for your kids. There is a test that can help you guide them:
- Career Aptitude Test for Kids: you may have to help them
- MAPP Career Test: https://www.assessment.com/
- Focus2: https://www.focus2career.com/
- Your Free Career Test: https://www.yourfreecareertest.com/
- Have them focus on one or two of them every six months and decide what to move forward with more discovery. Then add another possible career to explore.

Approach Learning in Full View

To approach learning in a holistic method that gives the child ownership and breaks the monotony of a traditional lecture, book, study and test method, consider filling their curriculum with an immersion method.

Aspects to include middle school and high school years

- **Research based learning**: Have students do research work that ends in projects, papers, or presentations for all topics and subjects throughout their school year.
- **Online Interactive Courses**: Plan to have an exposure to online courses that are both asynchronous

and synchronous to round their approach and experience in learning in various independent ways.

- **Certificate Programs**: Add in a course or two that gains them a certificate that can be added to the resumé. This could be CPR, computer, or any number of fields or areas of exposure that is interest-led by the student.
- **Internships, Part-Time Jobs, and Volunteer Programs**: Use these as complements to your student's education plan that falls in line with their interest or an area that complements their learning.
- **Conferences**: Have your child attend a conference or two that will build leadership skills, team building skills, or areas of interest exposure.
- **Field Trips with Purpose that include Workshops and Classes**: These are offered by many local institutions, museums, state and government agencies, and camps.
- **University Extension Programs or Apprentice Programs**: These are usually offered in the summer. For apprentice programs, those can easily be found by personal request.
- **Speech and Debate Program**: Have the child get involved in a speech writing, debate program that improves their comfort in speaking.
- **Intensives**: These are great summer camp experiences for kids that can allow them to deep-dive into areas of interest.
- **Literature in Live Plays and Movies**: Reading literature is a key skill, but being able to view it when it comes to life is another where kids will value exposure when transitioning beyond high school.
- **Manners and Etiquette**: Having students take etiquette classes or even have those experiences practiced at home will help them when they have to attend events after to high school.
- **Interest-Led Using their Hobbies and Curiosity**

for Deep Diving in Topics: Have your high school student help build a curriculum for them that integrates other subjects but is based in their areas of interest with hobbies that they are already pursuing. Build discovery of topics or subjects that they are curious about to experience. These can help the student get to know different possible career paths or build their life experience by following their curiosity of a topic or area of interest not explored. Help them build a list and build their expression of learning into it.

Enroll Them in Activities that complement them

Taking the time to find activities that complement your child's interests and abilities and more can be a challenge. For instance, for a child has a ton of energy, finding a sport to complement that level of high intensity could be a great opening to a new passion for the child. That means that as a parent, you will have to seek activities that you aren't as familiar with to open them to new possibilities that fit their personality.

New Things to learn what they like and overcome Fear

Don't get discouraged when your child is afraid to try something new. Sometimes doing the activity with them makes it more interesting, less intimidating. The newer things they try, the more willing they will become in doing so.

Something that will Mature, Teach, or Improve Outlooks

Don't overlook activities that teach manners, self-care, talking to others, or ones that show positive reinforcement. These activities build great comfort in a child's ability to network and meet people that can open their eyes to different opportunities that aren't readily apparent to them.

Stimulate Creativity

For some children, creativity may be hidden. If they don't have the traditional forms of creativity, many things can be taught. For instance, if your child seems uncoordinated and can't dance, sign them up for a class. Dance can be taught. If they aren't artful and don't know how to draw, sign them up for an art class, drawing can be taught. Consider the many creative forms of expression, and find ways to teach the core principles of it to your kids in order to expose them to it. Those experiences will broaden their ability to understand that just because something doesn't come naturally, with hard work and learning of skills, it can be enjoyable.

Complement a Skill or Ability They Already Have

If your child has an interest in flying planes, put them in activities that teach them to build the planes, understand the computer systems that run them, and get to know the industry. Build on something they enjoy to show them as many aspects of it as possible to give them a full picture and rewarding experiences.

Build Job Skills through Volunteering, Internships, Part-time Jobs, Job Shadowing, and Events for High schoolers

Groom your child to have a great work ethic by exposing them to working, owning a business, volunteering, and more before they finish high school. You want to give them an opportunity to make mistakes, learn about the working environment while building skills they can put on their resumé. Start these activities as early as fifteen years old.

Teen Resumé Building to Visualize the Importance of What They Are Learning and Volunteering

Teach your child how to build their resumé, starting with what they have learned through volunteering, focused camps, courses they've taken, and skills they have gained. Have them build their dream career resumé that they based on samples they have found on the internet. The sample dream career resumé will give them a road map of possibilities for themselves by researching and learning how others have reached that goal.

Give Them a Diversion

Sometimes kids need a diversion from home, boredom, and negative influences. If they aren't self-motivated to find things to do on their own, take the time to find things to fill empty time. It will keep them out of trouble, give them new perspectives, and allow them to better compartmentalize their day.

Reasons to Expose Them to Something New

Expose your child to something new even when they complain about it. Help them through the anxiety and stress, and reward them when they have conquered a new thing. Doing so will help them to better navigate feeling intimidated by something new.

- It forces child to grow and mature
- Shows them they are capable of more than they thought
- Can cause a positive ripple effect
- Teaches them to take control of their life experiences
- Teaches to make less excuses
- Builds character and belief in themselves

64

Benefits of a Rigorous, Challenging Curriculum

A rigorously challenging curriculum isn't for everyone. However, if you build your child up to the rigor, it gets easier and more manageable for them in time. Private schools thrive on offering rigorous academics that are college preparatory in nature. Being a product of private school then going to public school later, I felt public school was too easy and that I was slipping from my former training to learn at a level that challenged the abilities built over the years. I requested to be sent back to private school after one year spent in public school.

A rigorous educational framework is a form of homeschooling that can take your child way beyond what a private school can offer. Homeschooling makes it easy to customize rigor to a point where they are academically and mentally mature enough to handle it, all within their own time. It allows a slow build of rigor to the point where the child is learning way beyond the limitations of some schools. The rigor can also be focused on their preferred subjects and topics, making the load of subject matter seem like an exploration of an area of interest. You can have a child that isn't necessarily a whiz in memorization and can build up to the rigor that fits them nicely and without stress.

Consider Rigor – With No Stress

This doesn't have to be a dump-them-right-into-it approach. This should be gradual, with the adding of subjects once the child is comfortable and growing bored. Doing this by solidifying their foundation in being well read, comfortable writing fast, comfortable reading fast, quick recall of math core facts, and able to self-manage (especially for working parents). When the child's core learning areas are a comfortable fit, adding more won't stress them; it will challenge them. Keeping the stress low is a trick of combining various methods of teaching and expanding the topics of focus. By differentiating the methods of teaching, you are overlaying different perspectives of one topic, which makes it easier for the child to solidify a depth into each topic without having to study for an abundance of hours to do so.

The Benefits of Rigor

Primary and secondary education can be the training for a bigger race, college, and beyond. If your child has a desire to pursue an interest in challenging subjects or careers, teaching them to be comfortable in rigor and a difficult curriculum or subject matter prepares them for when they are pursuing those areas in college, the military, a volunteer opportunity, on-the-job training, and more. A rigorous curriculum will enable them to be able to navigate high-pressured scholastics, or work-based endeavors, and work naturally at a higher quality level.

Mix in Fun with Rigorous Subjects

In order for the experience of rigor to become positive, make it all about the child's interests. Don't teach every subject the same way. Have no more than two difficult courses at one time. The other courses should have some really easy classes, some medium challenge level courses, and if possible, tie them all into the same topic or subject area.

Gradual Build up then Scale down To Measure Student Tolerance

In order to build tolerance to a rigorous curriculum, condition your student for it. Self-discipline is necessary, and some students don't have it until they are in their teens. However, if you do a gradual build by stacking classes when they feel comfortable with their current load, or adding on a summer semester, the student becomes able to manage more topics. For instance, if you want your child to advance in math, but they are mediocre at it and take longer to finish it, have them only take the math class with an easier class that interests them. You can also break up the course, do part with other courses, then save it for summer when the child can focus on only that topic.

Slide in College Related Topics in Gradual Method

For a college-bound child, find ways to weave in courses that are the core courses all students generally take in college. Start with courses that are in the areas of their personal interest and level of maturity. Some of those courses are World History, US History, American Government, Biology, Chemistry, Psychology, Sociology, Business Management, Literature, Technical Writing, and many more. Take the time to research multiple colleges' required courses and water them down for the student. You can start by offering the subject matter in a light manner with a fun curriculum to introduce them to the topics. Then overlay it the next year with more in-depth and challenging assignments.

Weave in Testing, Projects and Writing Papers Quickly

Training your child to do well on tests by gaining study skills, writing skills, and project building skills should be woven into subjects in order to build the skill. Get your student to the point of being comfortable with testing, checking their results, revisiting areas that they didn't understand well, and resubmitting their understanding of the topic by either another test, a follow-up on the project, or presentation only on the information they didn't understand the first time. Try test prep camps, tutoring programs, and immersion courses that can be taken by your child in a class or small group setting outside of homeschool. It would be a good experience for them to see how other kids their age learn.

Build Up to a College Level Packed Schedule

As the child is comfortable through eighth grade, turn their schedule into one that emulates a college schedule. Preferably, model after one that seems in line with the type of field they are most interested. If they want to be a doctor, have them take several years of Latin, memory skills courses, word decoding, and medical terminology.

Include Student in Assessment of Grade

Getting the student used to grading is a way to make them comfortable with it. However, get them involved in the process. Let them argue a grade value either with a letter or presentation. Give them a chance to revisit a course, topic, or subject that the grade wasn't to their liking. Don't punish them for the grade, but have them address or understand that they need to revisit the topic in order to improve. It's about learning, not necessarily the grade. Giving them some level of control over the grading helps them to understand that, as does allowing them to revisit the topic. This is the freedom that homeschool gives when it comes to rigor, the ability to change the lack of control in it and give it back to the child.

Assess Grade, but allow Ways to Improve Learning Focus with Student Input

Use the grade as a way to reevaluate the method of teaching the subject. Get the child involved in this process by asking them what they believe would help them to better grasp the material. Ask them what is challenging with the topic, at what point they started to feel overwhelmed or unchallenged.

You and the child create a grading scale and criteria focused on how well the material did the job and not necessarily how the student did in completion of the work. This approach allows the child to gain ownership in the success of the learning topics, sources, and methods. The goal should always be on them learning, not a grade focused on their inability to perform perfectly.

No More than two Challenging Courses at a Time

Limiting the number of challenging classes makes sure the child is successful and doesn't become overwhelmed. Also, in order to allow a deep understanding of the more difficult courses, having them limited and mixed in with less challenging courses is best.

Focus on Students' Areas of Interest-Research Courses, Knowledge Areas that fit their Way Forward

This is especially powerful when the challenging curriculum surrounds an area of deep interest for the child. For example, my daughter was passionately interested in video games. We researched skills needed to complete building a game from beginning to end and built her entire high school curriculum around learning every aspect of the process, gaining key skills in the industry, articulating those skills which gave her confidence to consider starting her own business in the area of choice. Her high school curriculum involved online courses in visual design, art, coding for video game development, story development, and more. The goal isn't necessarily for her to stick with the career but to be able to dive-deep enough to see if she wants to continue or to add to her overall learning experience.

Make Study Skills Part of Every School Year

Learning to take notes, creating picture flashcards, mindmapping and memorizing facts are utilized in many fields. Learning the skill of studying is important and should be refreshed every year with a different perspective. Teach ways to take notes, study for a test, and solidify facts that can assist students in all careers, life adventures, and experiences going forward.

Have Reasonable Break Times

Giving a child a break after short, intense rigorous work is the best way to keep them motivated and revitalize their learning. You can break this into four eight-week semesters where the student takes a heavy load every other session, has two to three week's break in between to do nothing, or something fun, then start again.

Teach Difficult Subjects in More than One Way

When the child is learning a difficult topic, try to have two or more ways to teach that topic. Finding visually based ways to share the information, then having them write about topic, followed by presenting solidifies it in multiple ways. Being exposed to information at least three times further implants it into their memory. The forms of doing this are by listening, seeing, and writing.

Make Sure to Back off When Student Shows Stress

Take the time to observe your child. Encourage them to let you know when they are tired of a subject, overwhelmed, or just stressed. Also, communicate with them to identify whether it's the way the subject is presented, if there's just too much busy work, or the topic is boring (although learning boring topics is a skill they should have since many students in trade programs, college programs, and job training programs can run across material that doesn't interest them).

65

Accelerate Learning & High school to College Dual Enrollment

The average kid of age fifteen and above are academically mature enough to attack college courses if they are comfortable with reading, reading comprehension, vocabulary, writing papers by hand and typing them, analysis, logic, math (Basic, Geometry and Algebra 1 concepts), test taking, research, and comfort with technology. The reason they are usually held back is to allow the physical and mental maturity to catch up with their knowledge, and to practice, then solidify concepts.

However, you can easily prepare your child for accelerated learning, and they don't have to be a gifted, exceptionally bright, or overly intelligent child to do this. Acceleration for public or private school students can be done in high school, provided they are proficient in the topics noted above.

Our children had blended 4th and 5th grades and blended 7th and 8th grades. We condensed high school by doing Math and English for year-round schooling. All other subjects were given deep focus into college semester weeks of eight to twelve weeks to groom them to be used to a college schedule. High school was finished in two years and we started dual enrollment into college credit courses for two and a half years so they would graduate from homeschool high school with a college degree also.

A full course on Dual Enrollment is offered by LM Preston's www.EmpoweredSteps.com (course name: College The Radical Way).

Consider Your End Game for Your Child's Educational Journey

Think beyond getting the student through elementary, middle, and high school. Consider the path that you and your child are developing together during their educational journey. Be flexible as the child will change their minds, directions, and focus many times before they reach the end goal. That is what they should be able to do in order to find a path that works for them. Every year, evaluate their interest, goals, and desired life after college, military, trade school, or on-the-job training.

- Multiple disciplines are best – it allows the child to have various experiences that make them employable in many different fields of work and focus.
- Changing gears is alright – it widens their areas of knowledge.
- When the child wants to end an activity or study, have them present all they have learned on the topic. They should give a viable reason for wanting to move on to something different.

The Positives of Accelerating

Accelerating your child's education to include college in high school has some positives. The parent is in the position to manage the child's orientation to college level material. It allows the parent to have more control and involvement in the selection of courses, the growth and direction of the student, the cost of the classes, the method of the teaching, and so much more. It opens the child up to having time to explore other options if they finish their degree early. Dual enrollment gives them the opportunity to start faster or slower and take longer to finish a degree. It can also potentially free them up for a gap year to experience different things while staying on course to finish school in the allotted time.

Some highlighted benefits are:

- Save on overall cost of college (if pursued using CLEP, DSST, AP exams, cheaper community college courses, ACE accredited courses that transfer – these cost less per course by taking the test than paying for the course at a university).
- Allows child time to condense education if they want to pursue careers with a vigorous schooling requirement (doctors, lawyers, nurses).
- The child has time to do double majors in college or a major and a minor.
- A child that may not be 'college material' will be able to get at least an associate's degree that will give them a boost in any career area and make it easier to finish a degree at a later time if they so desire. Having a parent coaching them through helps immensely.
- Gives student opportunity to finish college and pursue other interests without having to jump right into working. They could do a yearlong volunteer program, study abroad, pursue their dream to travel the world, start a business, have a gap year (but their school work is already done so they lose nothing by continuing a path of discovery).

The Negatives of Accelerating

This approach changes the learning structure of most colleges regarding age, internships, scholarships, financial aid, and more. Dual enrollment can be stressful for the child to attend courses with adults and interact with them without being intimidated. It can force them into mature situations earlier than they may be ready.

- Scholarships for freshmen may not be available if the child has completed too many credits prior to starting a four-year college in the traditional way.
- If they desire to play sports in college, it could affect their eligibility to play.
- May desire to have a 'college campus' experience – this can be gained if the child wants the experience and already has their degree by enrolling for one semester at a university for additional courses. As long as the student has the money, they can live on campus.
- May not be a typical college experience.
- Networking opportunities could be lost.
- They may graduate too early to be of age to start their chosen profession.

The Wonderful Possibilities in Accelerating

Having had three of my four kids pursue and benefit from accelerating their education and graduating from college at ages seventeen and nineteen, I can say that for us, the benefits far outweighed the risks. My graduates were able to start working in their chosen profession at age seventeen with no problem. One child had to submit a work permit for her corporate job. Here are some ways my kids personally benefited from graduating college early:

- A gap year to explore a study abroad, a passion in a sport, build a business.
- Being able to have multiple disciplines because they have the time to pursue them. Accomplishing something that would've been more cumbersome at an older age.
- Having time to pursue a passion in dance, music, the arts, and other interest without stressing about time for college.

- Finishing their advance degrees early and getting noticed by their university.
- No distractions such as dating, friends' negative influences, or rebellion since they were still under eighteen years old and felt more inclined to be obedient instead of trying to prove they were an adult.
- Being free to do anything they wanted since they didn't spend four to five years sitting on a college campus.
- Early savings of the money they earned by working early to be set up to basically retire early if they so desire.
- Little or no student loan debt.

Elementary school Blending

Elementary school for most kids doesn't have to be from kindergarten until fifth grade. There are grades that can be combined and subjects that can be focused to continuous learning. An approach can be to have a year-round schedule with only the fall, winter months with focused instruction, but the spring and summer months with forms of learning that are fun and that solidify math, reading, writing by use of games, projects, experiences, and more. The continuous solidifying of the core skills in each can remove the need to have a 5th grade when you blend 4th and 5th grade curriculum. Traditional school has spread out the grades in order to assist with review time and maturity for the student. Consider these when contemplating blending grades.

Middle School Acceleration

Middle school in some cases is essentially a review, solidification, maturity-focused time in the educational growth of a student. Many students need the time to mature and constant review in Math, Writing and Reading to get comfortable with the coming advanced concepts. Look over the curriculum that you wish to use for middle school and high school to best determine what grade could be combined or removed. Combining 6th and 7th grade won't deter student's overall progress if they are proficient in the core subjects mentioned above.

Consider moving student from 5th grade to 8th grade to do only one year of recap before moving forward to 9th grade curriculum. Eighth grade is the final recap with pre-algebra and pre-geometry concepts to prep the student for Algebra and Geometry.

Math Acceleration

The best way to determine how to accelerate math is to determine what your child plans on doing after high school. Depending on what field of interest they have, math can play a major part in their success in college.

If they are pursuing a Bachelor's of Arts degree that supports fields in business, economics, sociology, psychology, then they would only require math up to college mathematics that includes some algebra, geometry and trigonometry.

For technology- or science-based degrees in in engineering, computers, technology, and science, then math up to calculus is necessary.

Students that aren't interested in college (those who decide to go in the military or work a non-technical job) should at least finish geometry and algebra 1.

Look at the local colleges or universities' course catalogs and see what they require for each type of degree program as far as math goes. Doing so will give you an idea of what to have your child complete.

Pre-calculus and calculus are not a requirement in most majors. However, algebra 1 and 2, geometry, and possibly trigonometry are the least amount of math that "most" college majors require.

Our Math Path

After graduating a homeschool student and now having one doing dual enrollment, we documented our math path to college.

Each child seemed to gravitate towards the sciences. However, when we began homeschooling, I found they all had the below challenges:

CHALLENGES WITH MATH: These were the challenges two of our kids had when transitioning to homeschool.
1) Forget accuracy, recall, and math rules from basic math taken up to 8th grade.
2) Solidification of Algebra and Geometry Facts
3) Planned to take College Accuplacer Exam which is a College Entry Exam that reviews students' basic math, geometry, algebra and trigonometry - most students forget the basic math, geometry by the time they take the test.

SOLUTION: This was our solution.
1) Build in a curriculum of review
2) Once student knows the information - test out of the college course or take the college class for that subject

OUR FAMILY MATH PATH: The curriculum that worked best for us may not work for you. This is to be used as an example only. The tricks we used:
1) Teach each math topic area in a different method/curriculum
2) Keep math review lessons under twenty minutes
3) Separate each math course for the day with two other courses
4) Only go up to math that is required for your child's desired area for college study

Accelerate Math			
Year	Course	Curriculum	Milestone
I	Algebra I	Saxon w/ Dive	
I	Geometry	Teaching Textbooks	
I	Basic Math Review	CTCMath.com [or] XtraMath.com [or] Drill sheets	
2	Algebra 2	Saxon w/Dive	CLEP: College Math
2	Basic Math Review	CTCMath.com	
2	Geometry Review	CTCMath.com	
3	Pre-Calculus	LiveOnlineMath.com	CLEP: Algebra
3	Basic Math Review	IXL	
3	Algebra Review	IXL	
4	Calculus	Saxon w/Dive	Dual Enrolled College Class OR CLEP: Calculus
4	Basic Math	IXL	

High School Acceleration and Homeschooling College

High school Math and English are usually four years and distinctly different degrees of learning. For those courses, it's hard to accelerate. Year-round school is one method to consider. Doing school year-round, only for those topics, will allow the student to finish the Math and English requirements in two years.

The general math path includes: algebra 1, geometry, algebra 2, and either finite math. Depending on the child's chosen path after high school, pre-calculus and calculus may be required. English has two years that include English 1 and 2, which focus on in-depth writing, grammar skills solidification, vocabulary growth, and more. Then, English and American literature, both of which a student can learn again in college and is logic-based writing.

In high school, the opportunity to introduce college credit is easy. As far as English after 10th grade, if you have exposed your child to the classics in literature (either in reading, movies or type of curriculum), then consider finishing the English requirements at an online community college or in person. Otherwise, have them take the two-literature based English courses, and then follow them with a final exam that gains them college credit.

If your student is proficient in certain topics finished through homeschooling, they can test out of the college course for the subject. Pursuing the test out method, allows the parent to use a CLEP, DSST or AP test, to name a few, as a final exam to subjects' math, English, social sciences, history, art, business, economics and more. For example, when instruction for US History is completed, have the child study for and take a CLEP exam that will give them college credits (at only certain colleges, so research the various colleges of interest to see if it's accepted as transfer credit).

Research Points:

- **CLEP**: https://clep.collegeboard.org/exams
- **DSST**: https://www.getcollegecredit.com/
- **A/P Exams**: This is the page reference for homeschoolers, https://apcentral.collegeboard.org/ap-coordinators/exam-ordering-fees/ordering-materials/home-schooled-students
- **Test Prep Lesson Plans FREE for Homeschoolers**: Also, see book by Tricia McQuarrie where she provided these homeschool high school study plans http://clepprep.tripod.com/cleplessonplans/id4.html
- **Test Prep for all**: These are study focused web-based flashcards and used to help the student prepare for the CLEPs and DSST. The key is for the student to practice

to the point of scoring over 75% consecutively in order to be ready to sit for the exam. A passing score is 50% for most colleges to give credit.

- Instantcert (https://www.instantcert.com/ and visit their *Degree Forum* for free help https://www.degreeforum.net)
- SpeedyPrep (has video lessons also https://www.speedyprep.com/)
- **Dual Credit at Home**: You can use a study plan program that can be purchased. It sends study plans daily to the student (https://dualcreditathome.com/2016/03/how-dual-credit-works-for-homeschooled-students/)
- **ACE**: Use this site to see what sources you can qualify for credit. These will transfer to colleges that accept ACE transcripts: https://www2.acenet.edu/credit/?fuseaction=transcripts.main
- **Individual State Profile of Dual Enrollment by The Education Commission of The States**: http://ecs.force.com/mbdata/mbprofallRT?Rep=DE15A

For The Child Who Does Not Want To Go To College

There are some children that do not want to go to college, but want to accelerate high school to move on to other things. For kids with the mindset to discover their way, some options are to work, travel, or volunteer.

Work After High School: If your child wants to just work after high school, have them plan a pathway to possible other careers or jobs that may ignite their curiosity. Have your child create a 5-year plan to include:

- *Budget for*: Paying their rent outside the home, utilities, transportation, savings, food, incidentals
- *From Job to Career*: They should research their growth plan from their current job, to a career that will sustain them

and enable them to live independently outside the home in 2 years

- *Pathway To Live Independently*: Walk them through planning their pathway to living independently and staying independent

Volunteer After High School: Have them complete the plan in the work after school section. Then they should research volunteer opportunities that fit their interest. There are many volunteer programs that are free and offer room and board for high school graduates that are seeking a life altering move to adulthood. Some to consider are: Americorps, Femacorps, YearUp, Helpx.net, Surf The Nations, GVI high school team, Love Volunteers, GoEco, The Experiment in International Living, World Wide Opportunities on Organic Farms and many others.

Military After High School: Homeschooled high school graduates can use their homeschool diploma to enlist in military service. If they want to go into the military at a higher rank, taking some college classes, participating in ROTC programs, CAP programs and other military based high school programs will give them a rank or pay boost.

Always work with your child through the process of enlistment for the best possible scenario and results. If there is a family member or friend that was in military service have them mentor you and your child through the process. These are some steps they should take to prepare for seeking a military career:

- Consider the military reserves which is part-time military, and only one weekend a month after boot camp and training, but gives military benefits and allows the young adult to pursue other interest and decide if full-time military is for them.
- Research the pros and cons of military enlistment
- Research the branches of service and the cost benefits to each
- Research the criteria for entry for each branch of service

- Research jobs in the military that lead to after service careers
- Research the criteria for each job desired in the branch of service
- Research the bonuses offered and how to get them

For the Child Who is College Bound
High School to College Dual Enrollment Basics for Success

This is where a parent teacher becomes an educational coach and less of a homeschooling parent. In order to ensure the best possible scenario when considering dual enrollment, the parent and child should spend time exploring career paths, life paths, goals, interests, and what happens after dual enrollment, college, and graduation. The child should be involved and have experiences to help them feel comfortable telling you where they want to possibly focus their career. If they don't know, help them find one through a career test (see chapter 63 for ideas).

Support your child by walking them through the process, giving them a voice in the method they want to approach dual enrollment as there are so many paths to gaining college credit while at home.

List of Items to Research and Prep for Dual Enrollment

- **Transcripts** should be created by parent (see Appendix J) to account for all courses up to the point of enrollment into:
- Homeschool courses and curriculum
- Community college dual enrollment programs
- Prior to taking CLEP, DSST, AP or other exams (ACE courses)
- Prior to attending universities that have early entrance programs and early college scholars' programs
- University summer college programs for high schoolers (research universities of interest for these programs, it's

not easily located, but many universities have them see FastWeb for these: https://www.fastweb.com/college-search/articles/summer-programs-for-high-school-students)

- Online providers dual enrollment programs (visit Straighterline.com and Study.com to name a few and to research additional programs go to Ace: https://www.acenet.edu/higher-education/topics/Pages/Credit-Evaluations.aspx)

- Scholarship programs to pay for CLEP test and give free training for exams (Modern States: https://modernstates.org/faq/)

- **Test to prep**: *College Accuplacer Exam* is used by many colleges to decide what level course in Math and English where the student should be placed

- Sample Accuplacer exams: https://www.accuplacerpracticetest.com/ (Math/English if attending community college or university for early admission and the courses planned on taking require a Math or English college level course as a pre-requisite)

- Placement of student into Math or English can be decided based on: (1) SAT scores, or (2) Accuplacer Exam – which student has two attempts at taking

- **PSAT/SAT and ACT**: Can be taken in preparation to dual enrollment but is **NOT necessary in most cases for dual enrollment or early entrance** community colleges (also note, if your child takes community college courses of up to thirty credit hours, most universities do not require a transcript or SAT score for the child to qualify for transfer student status). As far as a subject test like ACT, the student needs to take the test after they have actually finished learning the particular subject in order for the student to be able to get their best score.

- **Letters of recommendations**: This is required for some programs. It is good to have at least two in case your child needs them for program entry, scholarships, or financial aid.

- **Personal essay:** These are usually written when needed, but student should be able to write a 350-word essay on any topic fairly quickly.
- **Scholarships and FAFSA (Financial Aid):** This isn't usually offered until you, the parent, officially graduate your child with completed transcripts and diploma. However, researching the specifics of what scholarships and financial aid is available makes the transition from dual enrollment (high school while taking college classes) to freshman or transfer student college enrollment much easier.
- **The Common App:** Even though the student isn't applying for their four-year degree, getting to know how the Common App works can help in learning requirements for freshman and transfer student admissions. Research and understand the Common App, which is used for application to multiple universities and colleges. Take a further step and research the universities and see if any of them offer a summer early college program. Also, go into this application with an email address that you don't plan on using to actually enroll your child into university prior to your child attending college (it is cleared every year in July) in order to view what each university's requirements are for your student.
- **The Coalition App:** This is another application that allows the application to various universities and colleges, but it is not as extensive as the Common App. This application is there to help students that aren't as well represented as the Common App users.
- **Take the time to call Admissions:** Taking the extra step and calling the college admissions department and asking them all the questions you have saves time and reveals opportunities offered by the school.

University (4 Year Colleges) High school Parallel Enrollment

In addition to community colleges having dual enrollment programs, four-year colleges also have a similar program. They call it High school Parallel Enrollment. By taking the time to search the college website, and to contact their admissions department, you may find that many state universities have this program and have specific requirements for students to enroll in the parallel High school Enrollment programs.

Get their Associates or Bachelor Degrees while Homeschooling High school

Your child can complete their degrees as a combination to their homeschool diplomas. There are many online college programs that make it simple to do a degree by using tests, transfer credits, and taking a few courses online at their university. If trying to save money, the goal would be to get as many credits as possible from alternate sources.

Local community colleges have great dual enrollment programs that transition perfectly to state universities that allow the student a smooth transfer and sometimes scholarships for students that started in the community college system of the participating state. Some universities to research initially are: Thomas Edison College, Excelsior College, Charter Oak, Western Governors University, then take your search to other schools of interest to see if they have similar streamlined programs. In our home state, the community colleges gave a scholarship to students that received an associate's degree and transferred to an in-state college.

Dual Enrollment for Kids in Public and Private Schools

If your child is enrolled in a traditional public or private school, they can still do dual enrollment by way of community college dual enrollment programs, universities that have a parallel high school and college program, through CLEP, DSST, ACE credit as well as AP (even if they aren't in an AP class). If they plan on pursuing gaining college credits while in traditional high school, here are some ways to approach it:

- Have the child take CLEP, DSST or AP exams the summer after they have finished the courses that coincide with the test. Exams like history, biology, chemistry, Spanish, analyzing literature, English composition, and some other CLEP exams and AP exams will only require the child practicing taking the exam after they finished the high school course and final exam.
- AP exams are harder than CLEP test. If your child is taking an AP course and fails the exam, have them take the corresponding CLEP exam, which happens to be a bit easier than the AP exam. *Note:* your child doesn't have to be in an AP class to take the AP exam. It is opened to anyone, and if the child studies, they can pass.
- Get the Admissions Counselor at the high school to explain the high school policy on dual enrollment.
- Contact the community college to get its perspective and rules based on dual enrollment of students that are from the local high schools.
- Get the guidance counselor at the high school to sign off on any documentation required by the college for enrollment.
- Register the child in local community college the summer after their 10th grade year in high school. Have them take one course in an area they like that doesn't require the Math or English Accuplacer exam.
- Have them take the math and English Accuplacer exam after they finish geometry and algebra 2. There are free practice exams at the library.
- The summer of their 11th grade year, increase the number of classes to two classes for the summer.
- If they are interested in doing so, have them take one

course a semester online at the community college during their high school junior year, but make sure that the courses they are taking in high school are not too vigorous (do not have them take the High school AP course that has tons of homework and enroll them in a college course – if you do they will burn out fast.

- Senior year, increase to two college classes a semester, but only have the student takes the minimum required courses for high school to graduate (usually the student has to take an English and possibly a Math course their senior year of most state high schools that require three years of Math and four years of English)
- If they'd rather take time to learn a course, consider enrolling them in Straighterline (which offers an Associate's Degree Program, transfer of credits to partner colleges and colleges that accept ACE credit) that cost $59 per course and $100 a month. Study.com has a similar program, but the cost is a bit higher.

Speed Up Homeschooling and College to Earn Degree by High School Graduation

There are many ways a motivated child can speed up earning a degree (see my course *College The Radical Way* www. empoweredstep.com) for details. A quick list of ways to do this is:

- Test out of courses: Use CLEPs, DSST, AP test to earn credit
- Start Early: Dual Enroll in College or University with Short Courses (8weeks, 4weeks)
- Earn credits through partnerships: Use companies that have partnerships with colleges / universities to finish course fast: (with ACE approved colleges and universities: www2.acenet.edu/credit)
- Straighterline
- Study.com

- Sophia.org
- Saylor.org
- edX
- Davar Academy
- Shmoop
- Aleks
- Overloading classes: While enrolled in college, overload classes by taking the maximum number of credits for each semester. The student can finish a semester or even a year faster, especially if they go to a college that has shortened semesters.

Acting as Your Child's High school and College Educational Coach

An academic coach is a role I became familiar with while watching a sports documentary with my son. He pointed out that I do everything for him that the athletic academic coach was doing for these football players that were going to the college. The duties of an athletic academic advisor is to work with the student-athletes to ensure their optimum academic performance to keep them eligible to play their sport by assessing their grades, their academic performance, hiring tutors to assist them in difficult topics, supporting them through selection of courses, dropping of courses, selection of degree path, study skill strategies to ensure their ability to maintain grades in order to keep their academic scholarships. After researching the job, I realized that as a parent who is helping their high school student through dual enrollment, that is basically the same role.

One main benefit to dual enrollment is that it is easier to assist your student with success. As a parent, you want to be involved in checking their progress, making sure they aren't overwhelmed, and helping them with the paper as well as working with their guidance counselor with them. This is something most young people don't mind their parent assisting with until they get older. Through the process of coaching them, don't do the work for them, but walk them through doing what has to be done themselves so they are better prepared later to manage the tasks for themselves.

Some ways to be your child's educational coach for dual enrollment and early college:

- Your child should sign paperwork with the college to give you permission to call about their account and grades on their behalf.
- Have your child give you access to their online classroom so you can walk them through the syllabus and the level of effort for the class.
- Go over the community college or university course catalog with your student, and have them understand what courses will be needed to be completed.
- Review the quality of their work prior to them turning it in, and if it isn't college level: (1) have them work with a tutor, (2) help them formulate emails and contact with their professors for assistance, (3) help them decide to drop a class that may be too challenging for them.
- Check their grades frequently.
- Be their liaison if they are having problems with teachers or faculty.

How My Family Approached Early College Admission

With my four children, we have approached education in many varied ways. We made sure to involve our children in the process by helping them complete some life path scenarios. Then we asked them about their comfort in attending college classes in person, online, living on campus, and more.

Our oldest son and daughter attended both private and public schools up to high school. Our oldest son played high school sports and even played at his community college. Our oldest daughter started homeschooling in the middle of tenth grade then went to community college. She walked onto the lacrosse field, tried out, and started playing. After her first semester playing at just sixteen years old, she earned a scholarship for lacrosse. Our youngest two kids were homeschooled from elementary to high school. They finished college at the ages of sixteen and seventeen.

Traditional with creativity: My oldest son, although going to a traditional public high school, benefited from the high school training programs in applied nursing and EMT certification in 11th and 12th grades. In the summer of his 11th grade, we also enrolled him into the local community college where he took two classes in the summer then two classes a semester during his senior year of high school. He also played football, lacrosse, and ran track at his high school. He was a young student, graduating from high school at seventeen years old due to us putting him in private school since he had a late birthday. His only regret for being a younger student was when it came to sports. He'd wished that he were older so his body would be taller and thicker for competing. Even so, he did well at all of his sports.

Traditional until tenth grade: My oldest daughter was always in gifted and talented programs. She was in line to graduate from high school at eighteen years old. However, we started home-schooling her in the 10th grade. Then enrolled her into the local community college. She took a few CLEP tests for credit, overloaded classes with taking from eighteen to twenty-one credits a semester. She finished her Associates in BioInformatics at age seventeen. She graduated from her four-year college at age nineteen with honors after two years with a degree in BioInformatics with a minor in Computer Science. Then spoke at her graduation. Her first two degrees took 3.5 years to finish.

Homeschooled from middle school and dual Enrolled: Our youngest children decided to go to college online as neither wanted to be tied to a classroom. They studied for the CLEP and DSST exams for college credit and attended Straighterline and Study.com for the ability to transfer up to sixty college credits in an accelerated time period. They liked the program because it had eight-week courses and year-round semesters.

My youngest daughter graduated from college at seventeen

years old, traveled with the family for a month (she wasn't interested in study abroad), started her own online graphic art business, worked a summer internship that she loved, then started working in her field of choice. Her major was Information Systems with a minor in Computer Science and Graphic Design. She is now eighteen, getting paid to finish her Masters in Data Analytics that she will finish by her nineteenth birthday. She says she doesn't have regrets since she is doing what she loves, has her own set of friends and interests.

The youngest son is currently fifteen years old, a junior in college, pursuing a BS in Information Systems. He desires to be a pilot and go into the aviation field. To do so, the plan is to finish his BS degree by age sixteen years. Then pursue his private pilot license. Once he turns seventeen years old, he wants to start the local community college's airplane program where he has to attend in-person courses in Airplane Mechanics. We decided to have him earn his online BS first since he didn't want to attend the community college program until he was closer to the age of his peers.

Our Total Cost Savings by Doing College Non-Traditionally

Many people worry about the loss of those freshmen year scholarships if the child pursues early college credit. My children graduated from reputable colleges that accepted their transfer credits from CLEPs, DSST, and ACE approved courses. As I used this method with each child, the approach was different, but the savings in cost was obvious.

Most colleges have a monthly payment plan, so we didn't pay these in lump sums (with the exception of the first semester of attendance where you have to have the money for the courses upfront. Then we were able to pay each school on a monthly payment plan for the coming semesters).

My oldest kids wanted to live for one year on a college campus; the cost for living on campus dramatically increased their tuition.

Both children wanted to move off of campus after the first year, which is a typical request of most college students.

Here is the total cost for college in each of my children's scenarios:

- Child 1: traditional high school, community college, state university
- Community college $21,000 + university $30,000 = Associates Degree and Bachelor's Degree cost $51,000
- Additional cost of living on campus for 1 year $12,000
- Finished both Associates and Bachelor degrees in 5 years
- Child 2: homeschool high school, community college (overloaded classes by taking twenty-one credits a semester + summer and winter courses-finished Associates in 1.5 years), CLEP test, state university
- Community college $14,500 +CLEP cost $320 + university $20,000 − scholarship $5000 = Associates Degree and Bachelor's Degree cost $29,820
- Additional cost of living on campus for 1 year $12,000
- Finished both Associates (age 17) and Bachelor (age 19) degrees in 3.5 years
- Child 3: homeschooled high school, CLEP test, community college, university
- Community college courses $2000 + CLEP cost $160 + university $26,400 = Bachelor Degree cost $28,620
- No cost for living on campus
- Finished bachelors (age 17) with major and minor in 3.5 years
- Child 4: Homeschooled high school, ACE approved courses and transfer to partner school
- ACE approved courses $1,544 + University $16,800 = Bachelor Degree cost $18,344
- No cost for living on campus
- Finished Bachelors (age 16.5) degree in 2.5 years

What Is NOT NEEDED to Apply for Dual Enrollment

A misconception about college entry the masses believe is that there is only way to get into a college. Well, as a homeschooling and working parent, you naturally go in the direction of finding your own way.

Colleges have to accommodate many different types of students. These non-traditional student programs have been around for decades. I know because I taught at the university level for five years. These programs for dual enrollment for high schoolers are very similar to their non-traditional student programs.

Not Needed for Dual Enrolled Student College Entry	Dual Enrollment to Community Colleges or Universities with Parallel High school and College Programs
SAT	SAT scores aren't usually needed for acceptance into dual enrollment or parallel high school and university programs
ACT	ACT aren't usually needed for acceptance into dual enrollment or parallel high school and university programs
Transcripts	In some cases, transcripts aren't needed for homeschoolers for dual enrollment courses if the child is enrolling in the remedial math or English level course and works their way up through the college level courses by taking the classes • Required if child is considered graduated from homeschool high school Required by some community colleges with list of curriculums used

Steps to Lead to Dual Enrollment
And Possible Early College Graduation

Time Frame & Steps
Prior To Dual Enrollment

- Research and decide on three possible career choices with your child. (They can change their mind; you are only working towards general requirements of most all universities.)

- Research dual enrollment programs at local community college and universities.
- Research universities child may attend after earning either an associate's degree or thirty credit hours of college credit.
- Verify and build a personal list of all sources planned for your child's transfer credits: See: ACE credit. (ACE http://www.acenet.edu check the website for list of transfer credit sources.)

Evaluate How Best Your Child Can Earn Credit

- Is your child good at studying and taking a multiple-choice test? (If so, consider CLEP, DSST or AP test prep.)
- Is your child better at learning the information independently than taking test? (If so, consider CLEP, DSST or AP test prep using study plans.)
- Does your child do well in online courses that are expected to self-teach and take quizzes, tests, and finals on their own? (If this is a better option, consider Study.com, Straighterline, Shmoop, Saylor or any of the other choices of credit sources found on the ACE website: http://www.acenet.edu.)

Create a Degree Map Spreadsheet

Build a spreadsheet with the following:
-community college (CC) or university (U) **Required courses for ALL possible majors** (see row below for details)
-CC or U **Required Courses for your child's specific Major**
-CC or U **Accepted Transfer Credit from ACE, CLEP, DSST, AP**

List the source that your child will attempt to gain college credit from.

Courses to Attempt for Dual Enrollment or Credit Transfer that are Required for All College Freshmen and Sophomore

- English Composition 1
- English Composition 2 (Analyzing Literature)
- Psychology (Social Science usually required)
- Sociology (Social Science usually required)
- Humanities (Art Appreciation)
- Social Science (2 courses or more) US History 1 and 2, American History, Government, Western Civilization
- Speech (or Interpersonal Communication)
- Science (Biology + Lab for most majors + Any other Science that doesn't need a lab)
- General electives (any course that the college can use for an elective – check the college of choice elective list and descriptions to see what will transfer)

Note: *Foreign language* is not a required college course for all colleges or college majors. However, it is usually a requirement for their high school students to have two years of language. Taking a CLEP (for French, Spanish or German) or an AP (for Chinese, French, German, Italian, Japanese, Latin or Spanish) can show a college the child's language requirement for high school AND give them either a Social Science credit/language college credit or general elective credit.

Register for Dual Enrollment at Community College

- Review the general overview of colleges in your state: See Education Commission of the States overview for a quick start: http://ecs.force.com/mbdata/mbprofallRT? Rep=DE15A

- Call the community college and ask them to meet with guidance counselor that works with homeschooling students, dual enrollment students (or) transfer student if your student has earned thirty credits or more through other sources.
- Make an appointment, meet with counselor, request course catalogue.
- Determine the type of enrollment your child will select. Choices are in order of preference: non-traditional student, transfer student, dual enrollment/high school parallel/early entrance.
- Before filling out the application: (1) See if you can register your child as a non-traditional student – this will give them the freedom to take all the courses they prefer, and it doesn't require an SAT exam score or transcript, (2) If you can't register them as a non-traditional student, see if they qualify as a transfer student – if you have CLEPs, DSST, or ACE credit to transfer in, (3) dual enrollment/high school parallel program/early entry program applicant.
- Fill out community college admission form online or call college for direction if requirements are different for dual enrollment or parallel high school program.
- Schedule child's Accuplacer exam (Math and English).
- Send transcripts for CLEPS, DSST, ACE courses to community college. Have all transcripts for external courses sent to college.
- Note: If your child isn't ready to take math or English exam, you can register them for any class where college math/college English is not a prerequisite.

SECTION FOUR

MAINTAINING YOUR SANITY

Introduction

Many working parents get seriously overwhelmed to the point of anxiety and depression. When these frustrations grow, it results in anger, frustration, and impatience with their family. In most cases, the working environment gets the best part and performance of their day. That's not the way it was intended. The best part of yourself should be given to your family. In order to do that, prioritization is best. Realizing you can't give everyone one-hundred-percent all the time is a good start. That is the point where sanity stays intact. Learn to take a moment to gather your thoughts, control your actions, and notice signs of being overwhelmed.

This section will address ways to keep your cool, feed your spirit and health while maintaining a challenging lifestyle of home-schooling while working. Some tips in doing this successfully are:

- Don't give up proper sleep. Know your body's needs and put rest at a priority.
- Don't depend on coffee, energy drinks, or artificial energy to refuel your body.
- Be realistic in your goal setting.

- Pad your schedule with ten-minutes between tasks to see the true amount of time needed in your day.
- Don't strive for perfection, just be happy for what you effectively get done.
- Give up the television and web surfing, they eat up many hours in a day if use goes unchecked.
- Don't take on more than you should and be comfortable saying 'no' to activities.
- Focus on your family and limit what you give outside of that by putting your family needs first.
- Delegate as much as you can.

66

How to Do It All ~ Setting Priorities

When you work and homeschool, stress is a major opponent in your success. Many of our tips and organization of priorities came with being a working parent who had four kids in various grades in school or daycare. In order to survive, you need to adopt a delegate or forget-it technique.

As you consider doing it all, write down what is most important. If you don't mind a messy basement, but the living room has to be clean every day, then make that the priority, and get to that basement once a month. If sports are more important, and it's a hassle to pre-cook food or meal prep, eat out when you have a sports day.

At the end of the day, you want your kid to learn, be safe, be happy, and for you to get proper sleep so that you can also be happy. That may mean that the house is wrecked until Saturday morning cleanup. It can mean that you don't put the kids in as many activities because having a clean home is really soothing to you, so you want to clean.

The Number One Rule is to never beat yourself up if you can't do it all. Instances where the kids didn't finish their work on time, you came home from work each day that week and needed a nap, or whatever didn't get done, don't remain upset about it. Own the power of homeschooling flexibility and choices. Scale back where you need to, delegate tasks, let things go in areas that don't impact the goals of the family, and find a way to redefine what is working for your family.

Get Organized

Organization takes a change of mindset. It takes practice and works best if everyone has the same priorities. When you see that you are the only one passionate enough to keep the house running, that's the beginning of a slow climb to burnout. This means everyone needs to voice what is important to them in the home. Then, people need to be assigned to be part of the organization of the household. When that falls on one person, especially when that person is working, schooling kids, then doing all the work, it hinders the benefits and freedoms of homeschooling and working.

Some basic steps to get your mind in organization:

- Select a day to plan what needs to get done.
- Do it on the computer so you can do planning at work on lunch break if necessary.
- Have the calendar and plan open for all adults to update to view or update.
- Create a list with each family member's name on it, and the one thing about the house and homeschooling that is most important to them. Place them in charge of planning and executing that item.

Chore Day and Planning Day

Have a day of doing chores and a separate day for planning. Sometimes putting too much on one day makes life hectic.

- Clean in 15-minute sprints. (See Chapter 46)
- Use dry erase boards for calendar and plans, and make

sure everyone looks at it instead of asking you what is planned.

Laundry Quick Tip

Have a place in each bedroom or bathroom where dirty laundry is collected. Decide if everyone can be responsible for their own laundry and what day they will wash their clothes.

- Wash clothes daily or weekly.
- Delegate it. There are laundry services that will wash and fold your clothes for you. If this is a problem for management in the household, sometimes delegating it out helps immensely.

Meal Prep

Approach meals with the forethought to know what is realistic for your family. Plan when it's likely to eat carry-out food that fits in budget and diet. Meal prep should be a priority in saving money and time. In order to do it effectively, you have to know what works for your family. Make time to meal prep, getting everyone involved. The best scenario is to do monthly meal prep. Meal prep companies can help by fixing the meals for you in advance, providing you a place to prep your meals, and more. See Chapter 47 for more.

Letting Things Go

Have a let-it-go list that you post that reminds you that it's okay to let the laundry go for two weeks, let the meal prep go for a week, to not clean the living room for a few days. Sometimes we need reminders that all doesn't have to be perfect. The let-it-go list should be for every one of the planners in the household.

Building the let-it-go list means taking the time to assess the tolerance of not having certain things done. For instance, if no one cares that you eat on actual dishes, then invest in paper plates and plastic. If the let-it-go list is Mommy's room is messy all week, then add it to the list.

Separate Work from Home Expectations

Working is demanding. Sometimes the persona we have at work is intense, focused, and all about perfection. Having that attitude and managing a home, homeschool, and a marriage can be defeating. Learn to turn off the work attitude. Take that extra thirty minutes when you get in the house to unwind. Make that time just as important as anything else. If you don't give yourself time to redirect your mindset, mood, and attitude, it will set a bad tone for productivity for everyone the rest of the day.

Put It on the Family Calendar

Have a place where you share daily itinerary, like a dry-erase board or calendar. The calendar is the life in movement for the family. Using tools like online calendars or mobile reminders will allow the automation and organization of every single task the family has to get done.

Give Up Social Media and TV

It can be painful, but it is obvious that social media and television are major distractions. I realized that when I got home from work, as a working and homeschooling parent, my kids needed my focused attention, so the television went off, our cellphones went off, and we interacted with our kids. They knew it was their time, and soon our friends knew not to expect us to hang out during the weekdays on Tuesday through Thursday, or the evenings on the weekend.

All Hands-on Deck

Some households rely only on one spouse to do all the homeschooling work, housework, contribute by working outside the home or managing the business and so on. This isn't the best way to run a homeschool and working household. It breeds resentment, exhaustion, and burnout of the spouse maintaining it all. If one spouse isn't interested in workbooks or going over work, then have them do something whether it is cleaning, cooking dinner, administering the movie-based, project-based, experienced-based or the game-based curriculum with the children. Find something they can own and be a part of in the teaching and bonding with the kids. It is important for children to know they have the support of both adults in the home. Homeschooling and working aren't just about homeschooling; it's about bonding and building a closer relationship and partnership in learning with the parent and the child.

Don't Expect Perfection or Beat Up Yourself

A major way to sabotage success is to have unrealistic expectations of perfection. Taking on homeschooling is not a recipe for perfection, it's accepting that everyday won't be perfect. Your child won't become a genius just because you are teaching them. And homeschooling isn't automatically better than other choices. Only accept that this is a journey your family is willing to explore; there will be learning curves, messy middles, and perfection has left the room. However, you and your kids will see the adventure as completely fulfilling and opened the possibilities beyond what you've considered before.

Automate as Much as Possible

For working and homeschooling parents, automation is a key. It will save many hours of frustration, stress, and time. Finding curriculum that teaches the child through videos, online, and audio helps immensely. Having tablets for providing instruction, for kids to check through their schedule, to see their calendar.

Realize that there isn't always Balance with Work, Life, Homeschooling

Once you stop trying to juggle everything and focus on the positives of what was accomplished, you can put it all in perspective. Sometimes you have positive outcomes with schooling, but the house was wrecked for two weeks. Or the house has been clean for the last few weeks, but school has been stagnant. The balance is about flexibility.

Rest and Self-Care and Relationship Care

Rest is the healing balm for stress. Schedule in the time to do it each week. We have to feed our soul, our strength, and our ability to continue to give what is given each day to manage a home, work, a marriage, and nurture of children. Do not cheat yourself out of this. Self-care means taking the time to do something that feeds you as an individual. A paint night, a dinner with kids, or whatever allows you to relax. Taking a date night or a dinner out with your spouse, is important. Remember to always feed the roots that build the family. The parents are the roots, and if you aren't taking care of yourself, it all falls apart.

67

The Mindset for Success

The mindset for your success means you learned from the experience of it all. Being a working parent is not easy. Truthfully, being a parent isn't. It teaches you more about yourself than any other experience in your life. Parenting tests you in methods you have no way to prepare yourself for, no matter how many parenting books you read. The success is not just about what subjects were taught or what classes the child finished, it's about the relationship you build with your kids through this experience. It has the potential to be the most powerful connection and experience that shapes the rest of their lives and your relationship with them.

You Can Do this

Keep reminding yourself that you are the one in control of the schooling, work situation, bill situation, home situation, and life situation. Flexibility is key, so own it. The areas you can change to make the time or situation more bearable is really about how you approach it. Make changes in areas that will lessen your stress. If the job schedule is not working, find another job. If the curriculum isn't working, change it. When the house isn't getting clean, then take a day off from everything and clean it. Don't be afraid to make positive changes that will get you through the various phases of your life.

Talking yourself out of the stress or deflating attitude will work when you own your choices and the many options available for you. Changing gears temporarily does not mean failure. It means adjustments, and life is all about adjustments.

Enjoy the Freedom of Homeschooling even when you have to Work

Some people hate the fact that they have to work, maintain a household, school their children, and all other aspects of being an adult who just has to get stuff done. It's not always easy, but keep trying to manage it; you will get better as time goes on. Remind yourself of the benefits of working and homeschooling. Know that this is only a season of many in your life.

Budget in Delegation of Subjects

The reason for working while homeschooling is usually because you need to work for financial reasons, self-goal reasons, or even sanity reasons. If you are going to work, budget in the delegation of subjects you don't have the time or inclination to teach your child. It will free up some of your time and give your child exposure to other teachers.

Focus on Milestones in Learning not getting Daily Lessons Done

When you get out of the stress of "we didn't do lessons today" or "we didn't do school today" and focus on solidifying the core concepts of the cornerstone courses in math, reading, writing, and comprehension, your child will be able to build on those concepts. Break up each phase of their schooling into what milestones you want them to reach. Build your list of learning from everywhere (see Chapter 56) by listing all aspects of what the child learns just by doing things they like to do during the day. It will give you a better view of what the child is taking in without formal instruction.

Schedule and Give One-on-One Time the Same Respect as Work Time

Many parents put working hours and other family activities ahead of the time they actually need to spend with their kids teaching them, helping them understand a concept, correcting their work, and spending that one-on-one time with their kid. Do not put anything before that time. If you have to basically cut off the phone, the television, social media, let your friends know not to call or bother you during a specific time each day, then do that. Treat that schooling time as a no-holds-barred, no interruption time.

Hang a Reminder of why you chose this Method of Schooling

Sometimes in the midst of the challenges in running a household, managing a school, feeding everyone, and working a job, people forget why they decided on the chosen method of educating their children. Keep a sign, note, and/or poster of why you decided to homeschool your children. List all the reasons, the benefits, the positive outcomes made, and read it when you get discouraged. **At the top of that list put, "We Are in Control of Our Flexibility in Homeschooling!"**

Ditch the Resentment

Resentment has a way of creeping in when we hate change. The change of coming from a stay-at-home parent to a working and homeschooling parent runs deep with many people in the homeschooling community who also find they have to work to sustain their household. That is a horrible emotion if you allow it to take root. Doing so will lead to depression, anger, and burnout.

Negative emotions and anger have a way of wearing a person out, exhausting them, and creeping into the failure of all they touch. If you feel you are starting to resent working, tell yourself all the benefits of doing so. Talk yourself out of that negative space, and realize that as parents and adults, we just need to do what we have to do to survive, feed our family, and have a roof over our heads. All of the negative resistance to doing what you have to do only makes your possibilities shrivel up, because you are too upset to pursue them.

Making a living is part of being a team in the management of your household; it's a season of life and can benefit a family in many ways. Use the ability to be flexible by thinking outside the box about career choices, budgeting choices, schooling choices that benefit the family as a whole.

I grew up with a single mom whom I truly can't remember ever expressing anger at having to work three jobs to support my brother and me. She only expected us to be a partner in maintaining the house since she was at work, and we wanted the time she was home spent with us. Her positive attitude was an example to sustain me through many desperate situations as a young woman. Be that example to your kids, the example that no matter what we are doing, whether we like it or not, we adjust our attitude to get the job done and focus on the positives of our situation, and look toward the possibilities it brings.

See the Benefits in Working and Homeschooling

There are truly benefits in working and homeschooling. For us, they have gained my husband and me employment opportunities for each other through our networking. We have met amazing people; built friendships with families we never would have met if either of us were not working. Our kids have gotten scholarships and opportunities from the jobs we've worked. The extra money from both of us contributing fiscally has provided more opportunities for our kids and allowed us to pay for their college education outright, to travel, to give them foresight in getting employment, education, and even visiting our work place. Also, it's been the one place I can get thirty minutes to myself during lunch break and even meet a friend for lunch. Lastly, work gives both my husband and me something to talk about besides the kids, homeschooling, and the house.

68

My Lessons Learned

The lessons I've learned in working and homeschooling while working were valuable. The most hard-won lesson was that it wasn't just about getting to know my kids, educating them, and more. It was what I learned about myself. In order to pull this off, my husband and I had to learn that what worked for our family meant being able to adjust, change, evolve, devolve, grow, wait, and even shrink to build children who are truly an amazing gift to us. As a working parent, I didn't realize how much of my kid's time was spent hearing the negative voices of someone who didn't love them. My husband and I made it our mission to replace all that negative with our positive voices telling them, "You can do it. Just figure out how to do it your own way."

Focus on the Relationship

It is so important to make the journey of homeschooling and working about focusing on the family relationship. The relationship of parent to kids and spouses to each other. Put those first, and everything else will fall into place.

Playing with the Kids, no Matter How Old They are, Has helped Us mitigate our own stress

If all else fails, play hide and seek, capture the flag, sock attack, anything to get everyone laughing and bonding again. This is so important in building the relationship and taking the stress out of the situation. Besides, adults need to play more, and kids are the best teachers to take parents minds off of the challenging aspects of life.

Ask Them Questions, let them Find Their Own Answers

The skill of conversation and questioning to build thoughts, ideas, and ownership of a concept can take a while to cultivate. Doing so has made my kid's analytical thinkers and myself more than I ever was. It allows us to have deeper conversations. It is refreshing when they can ask thoughtful and pointed questions to get answers from their educators.

Teach Them by Guidance, Not Telling

Kids are much smarter than we give them credit. They can learn when taught the method on how to get their answers. That has been the best technique for us, but we had to evolve into it. Kids needed to learn that the process of finding the answer in itself is a method of learning. Most of all, they are resilient and designed to be survivors.

There is Freedom in Being the Teacher & Boss of Your Home Life

It can take a while to get used to owning your schedule and the schooling of your children to make it flexible around your work schedule. Many get caught up thinking about the traditional way children learn and all the subjects and lessons that they must finish. When you are comfortable moving around your goals, time for teaching, and even having school on the weekend, then it's not hard at all to maintain.

There Is No Right Way to Do It except Your Own Way

You can read many books, blogs, and attend tons of conferences on how to successfully homeschool your child. In the end, the best and only effective way to do it is…your own way. Make it work for you, have your goals, the kid's goals, and your family goals, and meet them based on the path and road you set. Own it, there are no boundaries.

69

Consultation and Course Offerings

My company Empowered Steps (www.empoweredsteps.com) strives to offer coaching in homeschooling, working, education, college-based methods to save, career re-imagination and coaching. If this book has helped you in any way, and you need or want more personal one-on-one, please take a moment to consider some of the services offered.

Online School Empowered Steps

We have created an online school for courses specifically as a companion for this book. It can serve as a mentoring tool for your family's journey in the following: www.empoweredsteps.com

Free   Mini-Course: https://empowered-steps. teachable.com/courses

- Kickstarting Homeschooling and Working
- College The Radical Way
- Secrets to Homeschooling and Working

Please review homeschooling and work: *Homeschooling While Working to shape Amazing Learners* (www.empoweredsteps.com)

- **Homeschooling While Working to Raise Amazing Learners Facebook Group:** Join here: https://www.facebook.com/ groups/homeschoolwhileworking/
- **Homeschooling and Working Online Course**: Find here: https://empowered-steps. teachable.com/courses
- **Homeschooling and Work Blog**: http://www. homeschoolandwork.blogspot.com/

APPENDIXES

Appendix A:
Sample Schedule Template Work and Homeschool for the Parent Point of View

When planning a schedule to work and homeschool, it's best to make a schedule from two points of view:

- Parent's schedule
- Child's work schedule

Sample Parent's Schedule – Working outside the Home

Consider working inside the home the same as outside the home since the parent will need time to actually work with external sources.

Schedule Considerations:

We changed our schedule at times to three to five days alternating weekly. When schedule was only three days a week, we did school year around.

1. Mon, Wed, Sat (school) – one-on-one parental instruction, and kids did independent work on Mon, Tue, Wed.
2. Tue, Thu, Sun (school) one-on-one parental instruction, and kids did independent work on Tue, Wed, Thu.
3. Wed, Sat, Sun (school) one-on-one time, and kids independent work would be on the same day.

Short school week setup

-Year around school

-One-on-one instruction and child's independent work on same day

-School two to three days a week

-Structured instruction only in math, reading, writing, spelling/vocabulary

-All other instruction using unstructured recording of learning, other curriculums (game schooling, project based, unit studies, question based, classical using audio books and movies, movie based)

TIME	SUN	MON	TUES	WED	THURS	FRI	SAT
6:00 AM		Mom Leave for work		Mom Leave for work		Mom Leave for Work	
6:30 AM			Mom Leave for work		Mom Leave for work		
7:00 AM		Dad Wakes up kids	Dad Wakes up kids	Dad Wakes up kids	Dad Wakes up kids	Dad Wakes up kids	
7:30 AM		Kids get prepped breakfast from refrigerator	Kids get prepped breakfast from refrigerator	Kids get prepped breakfast from refrigerator	Kids get prepped breakfast from refrigerator	Kids get prepped breakfast from refrigerator	
8:00 AM		Dad Prep For Work		Dad Prep For Work	Kids do Instruction [MATH] with online teacher/course or video	Dad Prep For Work	
8:30 AM		Kids do Instruction [MATH] with online teacher/course or video	Kids do Instruction [MATH] with online teacher/course or video	Kids do Instruction [MATH] with online teacher/course or video	Dad Prep For Work	Kids do Instruction [MATH] with online teacher/course or video	
9:00 AM		Kids [5-Min-MATH DRILL] with DAD	Kids [5-Min-MATH DRILL] with DAD	Kids [5-Min-MATH DRILL] with DAD	Kids [5-Min-MATH DRILL] with DAD	Kids [5-Min-MATH DRILL] with DAD	
9:30 AM		Nanny or Childcare Provider	Dad Prep For Work	Nanny or Childcare Provider	Nanny or Childcare Provider	Nanny or Childcare Provider	

See next graphic on the next page...

10:00 AM	Dad Leave For work	Nanny or Childcare Provider	Dad Leave For work	Dad Leave For work	Dad Leave For work
10:30 AM	Kids do Instruction and workbox work with nanny [PE/Language/Reading/Art and Craft]	Dad Leave For Work	Kids do Instruction and workbox work with nanny [PE/Language/Reading/Art and Craft]	Kids do Instruction and workbox work with nanny [PE/Language/Reading/Art and Craft]	Kids do Instruction and workbox work with nanny [PE/Language/Reading/Art and Craft]
5:00 PM		Kids do Instruction and workbox work with nanny [PE/Language/Reading/Art and Craft]			
5:30 PM					
6:00 PM		Kids Play Sports with Rec Team		Kids Play Sports with Rec Team	
6:30 PM					School Work Review with Mom or Dad
7:00 PM	School Work Review with Mom or Dad		School Work Review with Mom or Dad		
7:30 PM					
8:00 PM					

Appendix B:
Sample Homeschool Schedules Elementary school for the Child

The children should have their own schedule that is posted where they can see and check off.

Considerations:

Work not finished or extra review time is on the weekends.
School can also be done on the weekends.
Most hands-on work will be done with parent, but nanny or other childcare provider can facilitate art, project fun, or what is agreed on.

TIME	MON May 2, 2016	TUES May 3, 2016	WED May 4, 2016	THURS May 5, 2016	FRI May 6, 2016
8:30 AM					
9:00 AM	MATH [with Dad] -5 Min Drill -Learn New Lesson -Practice	MATH [with Dad] -5 Min Drill -Learn New Lesson -Practice	MATH [with Dad] -5 Min Drill -Learn New Lesson -Practice	MATH [with Dad] -5 Min Drill -Learn New Lesson -Practice	MATH [with Dad] -5 Min Drill -Learn New Lesson -Practice
9:30 AM					
10:00 AM	ART or Project - Self Directed [With Nanny or Daycare]	ART or Project - Self Directed [With Nanny or Daycare]	ART or Project - Self Directed [With Nanny or Daycare]	ART or Project - Self Directed [With Nanny or Daycare]	ART or Project - Self Directed [With Nanny or Daycare]
10:30 AM	Writing Practice / Copy Work [with Mom]	Writing Practice / Copy Work	Writing Practice / Copy Work	Writing Practice / Copy Work	

See next graphic on the next page...

5:00 PM	Phonics/Language Arts [with Mom]			Phonics/Language Arts [with Mom]		Phonics/Language Arts [with Mom]
5:30 PM						
6:00 PM	Spelling / Poetry [with Mom]			Spelling / Poetry [with Mom]		Spelling / Poetry [with Mom]
6:30 PM	Reading [with Dad]	PE - Recreation Sports Team		Reading [with Dad]	PE - Recreation Sports Team	Reading [with Dad]
7:00 PM						

Appendix C:
Sample Working and Homeschool Schedules Grades 3rd to 8th

From this age on, students can use several forms of their schedule. The schedule below is an example of a set schedule. However, using a checklist schedule at this age will allow the child more freedom to manage themselves and their time.

Tips:

- Groom them to be independent learners at this stage.
- Save topics that they need help with to be done with parent present or available to help.
- Weekends, early mornings, or late nights are to be used as part of schedule. If the child is rather dependent, save school time for those times when parent is available.

Course Additions to Consider

- Speed-reading
- Logic
- Latin (for word and vocabulary deciphering)

See graphic on the next page…

TIME	MON May 2, 2016	TUES May 3, 2016	WED May 4, 2016	THURS May 5, 2016	FRI May 6, 2016
10:00 AM	Grammar	Grammar	Grammar	Grammar	Grammar
10:30 AM	Reading & Comprehension Drills	Science	Reading & Comprehension Drills	Science	Reading & Comprehension Drills
11:00 AM	Art or Project		Art or Project		Art or Project
11:30 AM	Spelling	Spelling	Spelling	Spelling	Spelling
12:00 PM					
12:30 PM					
1:00 PM	History	Fine Art Study	History	Fine Art Study	History
1:30 PM		Logic Practice		Logic Practice	
2:00 PM	Vocabulary Practice	Vocabulary Practice	Vocabulary Practice	Vocabulary Practice	Vocabulary Practice
2:30 PM	Copywork / Writing	Copywork / Writing	Copywork / Writing	Copywork / Writing	Copywork / Writing
3:00 PM					
3:30 PM					
4:00 PM					
4:30 PM					
5:00 PM	MATH [with Mom]	MATH [with Mom]	MATH [with Mom]	MATH [with Mom]	MATH [with Mom]
5:30 PM	-5 Min Drill -Learn New Lesson	-5 Min Drill -Learn New Lesson	-5 Min Drill -Learn New Lesson	-5 Min Drill -Learn New Lesson	-5 Min Drill -Learn New Lesson
6:00 PM	-Practice	-Practice	-Practice	-Practice	-Practice
6:30 PM	English [with Dad]	English	English	English	English

Appendix D:
Sample Working and Homeschool Schedules High school

High school planning should coincide with the requirements for the student's state. Also, consider if the student will plan to dual enroll, take CLEP or DSST tests, AP courses, and condense high school for college combination.

Typical Required Courses for Each State:

Math: 4 classes / 4 credits (some states only require 3, and you can select different math courses; the below are recommended for children attending college)

- Algebra 1
- Geometry
- Algebra 2
- Trigonometry

English: 4 classes / 4 credits

- English 9
- English 10
- American Literature
- British Literature

Science: 3 classes / 3 credits

- Earth Science / Life Science
- Biology
- Chemistry

Fine Arts: 1 class / 1 credit

- Theatre, Art, Dance

PE: ½ semester / ½ credit
Health: ½ semester / ½ credit
Social Studies: 3 classes / 3 credits

- US History
- World History
- American Government

Technology: 1 class / 1 credit
World Language: 2 classes / 2 credits
ADDITIONAL COURSES TO CONSIDER:

- Logic
- Speed reading
- Speed writing
- Passion-based project work (focused on the child's interest-based studies)
- Interpersonal communication

See graphic on the next page...

Appendix D: Sample Working and Homeschool Schedules High school

TIME	MON May 2, 2016	TUES May 3, 2016	WED May 4, 2016	THURS May 5, 2016	FRI May 6, 2016
10:00 AM	Speed Reading Online course	Speed Reading	Speed Reading	Speed Reading	Speed Reading
10:30 AM	Technology Online Course	Science	Technology	Science	Technology
11:00 AM	Vocabulary Building Online Course	Science	Vocabulary Building	Science	Vocabulary Building
11:30 AM	Spanish Online Course	Spanish	Spanish	Spanish	Spanish
12:00 PM					
12:30 PM					
1:00 PM	History Through movies, games	Passion Focused Study	History	Passion Focused Study	History
1:30 PM	History Through movies, games	Logic Practice Online Course	History	Logic Practice	History
2:00 PM	Speed Writing Course	Health project based	Speed Writing Course	Health	Speed Writing Course
5:00 PM	MATH [with Tutor] -5 Min Drill -Learn New	MATH [with Mom] -5 Min Drill -Learn New	MATH [with Dad] -5 Min Drill -Learn New	MATH [with Mom] -5 Min Drill -Learn New	MATH [with Tutor] -5 Min Drill -Learn New
5:30 PM	Lesson -Practice	Lesson -Practice	Lesson -Practice	Lesson -Practice	Lesson -Practice
6:00 PM					
6:30 PM	English [with Tutor]	English	English	English	English [with Tutor]
7:00 PM					
7:30 PM		PE - Recreational Sport		PE - Recreational Sport	

Appendix E:
Sample Weekly Curriculum Plans Elementary

This curriculum plan is an example only. We encourage you to build your own by sampling different curriculum offerings that fit your homeschool needs. The goal of this book is that you use the tools to customize what works for your homeschool, your child's learning style, your child's personality type, and your time constraints. The ideal curriculum for most homeschooling and working parents will be a curriculum that does the topic teaching for the parent, can self-grade, has tracking for the student, is easy for the parent to give reinforcement and provides hands-on practice for subjects in math and writing.

Curriculum plans are interchangeable and can be used for the type of phase where you are in life or your homeschool. Curriculum chosen is homeschooling and working friendly.

Please note: only core classes mentioned in plan.

Core Courses that are more formal in instruction:

- Math
- Writing
- Grammar
- Spelling

Curriculum-Go eclectic if possible

(1) Use standard curriculum that meets child's learning style for math, writing, reading.
(2) Use overlapping of curriculums to solidify past and current facts. This includes game-based, experienced based, question based, project based curriculums.

Add these courses to your Plan:

- Science
- History
- Social Studies
- Speed Reading

Course Curriculum Planner

	Light Curriculum	Standard	Accelerated	Additional Practice
Math	Teaching Textbooks	Math-U-See	Abeka	xtramath.org
	Math Mammoth	Acellus/PowerSchool	Bob Jones	Khan Academy
	CTCMath	Mobymax	Saxon	IXL
	Singapore			
Reading	LearnWithHomer	Clicknkids	Abeka	Read Out Loud
	ABC Mouse	Phonics My Way	Bob Jones	IXL
	Kizphonics	Acellus/PowerSchool		Reading Assistant
	AllInOneHomeschool	Mobymax		
Spelling	Spelling-U-See	MovingBeyondPage	Abeka	IXL
	Sequential Spelling	Acellus/PowerSchool	Bob Jones	
	All About Spelling	Mobymax		
Grammar	Rod & Staff	Analytical Grammar	Abeka	CrashCourse Videos
	Hake Grammar		Bob Jones	IXL
	GrammarFlip			

Appendix F:
Sample Weekly Curriculum Plans Middle school

This curriculum plan is an example only. We encourage you to build your own by sampling different curriculum offerings that fit your homeschool needs. The goal of this book is that you use the tools to customize what works for homeschool, your child's learning style, your child's personality type, and your time constraints. The ideal curriculum for most homeschooling and working parents will be a curriculum that does the topic teaching for the parent, can self-grade, has tracking for the student, is easy for the parent to give reinforcement and provides hands on practice for subjects in math and writing.

Curriculum plans are interchangeable and can be used for the type of phase where you are in life or your homeschool. Curriculum chosen is homeschooling and working friendly.

Please note: only core classes mentioned in plan.

Core Courses that are more formal in instruction:

- Math
- Writing
- Grammar
- Vocabulary
- Spelling

Curriculum-go eclectic if possible

1. Use standard curriculum that meets child's learning style for math, writing, reading
2. Use overlapping of curriculums to solidify past and current facts.

3. Use question-based curriculum (see Chapter 20) to expand on subjects or as a fill in for subjects that student isn't using a standard curriculum

Add these courses to your plan:

- Science
- History
- Social Studies
- Speed reading and comprehension (Literably and ReadWithMeFluency)
- Speed writing
- Study skills
- Logic and reasoning (*The Art of the Argument* is highly recommended)
- Typing
- Technology (consider Minecraft Homeschool, SKrafty and GameEdacademy)

See graphic on the next page...

Course Curriculum Planner

	Light Curriculum	Standard	Accelerated	Additional Practice
Math	Teaching Textbooks	Math-U-See	Abeka	xtramath.org
	Math Mammoth	Acellus/PowerSchool	Bob Jones	Khan Academy
	CTCMath	Mobymax	Saxon	IXL
	Singapore	FunCationAcademy		
English	LearnWithHomer	Clicknkids	Abeka	Read Out Loud
	ABC Mouse	Phonics My Way	Bob Jones	IXL
	Kizphonics	Acellus/PowerSchool		Reading Assistant
	AllInOneHomeschool	Mobymax		
Spelling	Spelling-U-See	MovingBeyondPage	Abeka	IXL
	Sequential Spelling	Acellus/PowerSchool	Bob Jones	
	All About Spelling	Mobymax		
Grammar	Rod & Staff	Analytical Grammar	Abeka	CrashCourse Videos
	Hake Grammar	Quill.org	Bob Jones	IXL
	GrammarFlip			
	Grammaropolis			

Appendix G:
Sample Weekly Curriculum Plans High school

This curriculum plan is an example only. The goal of this book is that you use the tools to customize what works for your homeschool, your child's learning style, your child's personality type, and your time constraints. The ideal curriculum for most homeschooling and working parents will be a curriculum that does the topic teaching for the parent, can self-grade, has tracking for the student, is easy for the parent to give reinforcement and provides hands on practice for subjects in math and writing.

Curriculum plans are interchangeable and can be used for the type of phase where you are in life or your homeschool. Curriculum chosen is homeschooling and working friendly.

Please note: only core classes mentioned in plan.

Core Courses that are more formal in instruction:

- Math
- Writing
- Coding (software programming)
- Speed reading

Curriculum-go eclectic if possible

1. Use standard curriculum that meets child's learning style for math, writing, reading
2. Use overlapping of curriculums to solidify past and current facts.
3. Use question-based curriculum (see Chapter 20) to expand on subjects or as a fill in for subjects that student isn't using a standard curriculum

Add these courses:

- Science (Standard Deviants videos, Crash Course, Uzinggo are light and fun considerations for science)
- History (world civilization, US History, government)
- Social Studies (humanities, geography)
- Science (earth, biology and chemistry)
- Study skills
- Speed reading (AceReader and 7 Speed Reading are highly recommended)
- Speed writing (Write 350-word paper in thirty minutes)
- Logic and reasoning (*The Art of the Argument* is highly recommended)
- Technology (CompuScholar and CodeAcademy is highly recommended)

Consider adding courses: (some can be added as dual enrollment courses, CLEP/DSST/AP tests for both high school and college credit)

- Speech and communications
- Financial management
- How to Start a Micro Business and Business Management
- How to build resumé, interview for job
- Psychology (prep for college curriculum)
- Sociology (prep for college curriculum)
- Latin/speed vocabulary review (Membean.com is highly recommended)
- Micro and macro economics

*See graphic on the next page…

Course Curriculum Planner

	Light Curriculum	Standard	Accelerated	Additional Practice
Math	Teaching Textbooks	Art Of Problem Solve	Abeka	Khan Academy
	UnlockMath	Mr. D Math	Saxon	IXL
	CTCMath	ChalkDust	MathUSee	
	TabletClass	LiveOnlineMath	AoPS Online	
English	Study.com	Sonlight	Abeka	IXL
	Teachwithmovies.org	TheGreatCourses	Bob Jones	Quill.org
	Sonlight	Oak Meadow		Membean
	Home2Teach	Appologia		Time4Writing
Writing	Time4Writing	Sandiego Scribblers	Abeka	IXL
	Brave Writer	Writeshop	Bob Jones	
	Fortuigence	WriteAtHome		
		IEW		

Appendix H:
List of Curriculum Options

There are several online schools that also have some accreditation affiliated with them. For homeschooling and working parents, DVD based, online courses, and tablet courses are a great help. These are some choices.

Online Schools Full Curriculums

Acellus: https://www.acellusacademy.com/
Penn Foster: https://www.pennfoster.edu/high-school/academics/tuition
Abeka Homeschool: https://www.abeka.com/Homeschool/
BJU Press Homeschool: https://www.bjupresshomeschool.com/
James Madison: https://www.jmhs.com/
Alpha Omega: https://www.aoacademy.com/
Whitmore School: https://www.whitmoreschool.org/
Smart Horizons Career Online High school:
https://smarthorizonsonline.org/
Excel High school: https://www.excelhighschool.com/
WiloStar3d:
https://wilostar3d.com/
The American Academy: https://www.theamericanacademy.com/
American School: https://www.americanschoolofcorr.com/access-student-center/
The Key School: https://www.keystoneschoolonline.com/
Laurel Springs: https://laurelsprings.com/
North Star: https://northstar-academy.org/
Forest Trail Academy: https://www.foresttrailacademy.com/
Nebraska Academy: https://highschool.nebraska.edu/

Advantages School International: https://www.
advantagesschool.com
The Oaks: https://theoaksprivateschool.org/#
Bridgeway Academy: https://www.homeschoolacademy.com/
The OgBurn School: https://ogburn.org/
K-12: https://www.k12paymentcenter.com/
Home/ParticipatingSites
Connections Academy: https://www.
connectionsacademy.com/enroll
The University of Missouri High school: Mizzou K-12:
http://mizzouk12online.missouri.edu/
PA Homeschool: http://www.aphomeschoolers.com/
Kolbe Academy: http://kolbe.org/academics/diploma-types/
magna-diploma/
For other online schools go to The Best Schools Website: https://
thebestschools.org/rankings/best-online-high-school-diploma-
programs/?
fbclid=IwAR1TBN10aQ7kDCeG4z3R9Qb4iElZikCrRNXv9ux0H
YNSojdVa_3YqT8OGDw

Curriculum Sources Online

Veritas Press: https://veritaspress.com/
Memoria Press: https://www.memoriapress.com/
Lukion Project: https://www.lukeion.org/
Homeschool Book Study: https://www.onlineg3.com/
TPS: https://at-tps.org/subjects/
Virtual Homeschool Organization: http://www.
virtualhomeschoolgroup.com
Tapestry Of Grace: http://www.tapestryofgrace.com/index.php
MobyMax: *https://www.mobymax.com*
Discovery K12: http://discoveryk12.com/dk12/
MangoMath-Game-based math: https://mangomath.com
Project Based Unit Studies: https://unitstudy.com/

Game Schooling Curriculum Sources

Math Games

- Right Start Math (Full Curriculum and Game Based)
- Prime Climb
- Equate: The Equation Thinking Game
- Educational Insights Fraction Formula Game
- Monopoly
- Sequence Numbers Game
- Phase 10
- Dominos
- Rummikub
- PayDay
- SkipBo
- MathDice
- Uno
- Clumsy Thief
- Five Crowns
- Math Explosion Game

History Games

- Timeline Card Game: Comes in many versions of historical game play
- Professor Noggin's: Game comes in different versions
- Ticket to Ride
- American History Memory Game

Language Arts

- Mad Libs
- Rory's Story Cubes
- Zingo
- Pathwords
- Scrapple
- Table Topics
- Wordical

- You've Been Sentenced

Science Games

- Science Ninjas
- Totally Gross
- Science Explosion
- Laser Maze
- Circuit Maze
- Gravity Maze
- Professor Noggins World of Science

OTHER RESOURCES

Administration: Planner Software: http://www.
homeschooltracker.com/download_basic.aspx?
Administration: Planners, Info, Lessons (K-12): http://www.
donnayoung.org/
Fine Arts: Art (K-6) http://www.nga.gov/kids/
Fine Arts: Art Appreciation Games from the National Gallery of
Art (K-8): http://www.nga.gov/kids/
Fine Arts: Art History (3-12): http://www.metmuseum.org/toah/
Fine Arts: Art Lessons (K-6): http://www.artprojectsforkids.org/
Fine Arts: Art Lessons (K-6): http://www.deepspacesparkle.com
Fine Arts: Art Prints (K-12): http://groups.yahoo.com/
group/AOArtPrints/
Fine Arts: Artist Study (K-6): http://www.cuchicago.edu/
experience/arts/visual-arts/art-lessons/
Fine Arts: Artist Study and lessons (K-6): http://kidsart.com/blog/
Fine Arts: Classical Music (K-8): http://www.classicsforkids.com/
Fine Arts: Music Theory (3-12): http://www.teoria.com/index.php
Foreign Language: French (K-6): http://ambafrance-uk.org/-Just-
4-Kids,223-
Foreign Language: German, French, Spanish (K-12) http://www.
knowitall.org/instantreplay/content/LanguageIndex.cfm?CFID=

2906044&CFTOKEN=99415101&
jsessionid=56301f3c32ada172839e592f175363657f38
Foreign Language: Japanese (9-12+) http://www.gpb.org/
irasshai/japanese-i
Foreign Language: Spanish (K-2) http://www.gpb.org/salsa
Health: Health and Safety topics (K-12): http://classroom.
kidshealth.org
History: American History (3-7) http://www.mission-us.org/
History: Ancient History (K-6): http://bringinguplearners.com/
mosaic...s-and-marvels/
Kindergarten: Lessons (K-1) http://www.
kinderthemes.com/index.html
Language Arts: Aesop Stories and Lessons (K-6): http://www.
mainlesson.com/display.ph...8ac5c6116dd093
Language Arts: Audio books (K-12): Librivox
Language Arts: Daily Grammar (K-12): http://www.
dailygrammar.com/archive.html
Language Arts: Dolch Word Lists (K-4) http://www.
mrsperkins.com/dolch.htm
Language Arts: Early Reading (K-2): http://www.
jmeacham.com/emergent.readers.htm
Language Arts: Early Reading (K-3) http://www.
1plus1plus1equals1.com/YouCanRead.html
Language Arts: Early Reading- I see Sam (K-2): http://www.
marriottmd.com/sam/index.html
Language Arts: Grammar (K-6): http://www.scholastic.com/
dodea/index2.htm
Language Arts: Grammar and Spelling (?) http://www.mhschool.
com/reading/treasure_workbooks/national.html
Language Arts: Grammar Handbook (3-8):
http://www.zaner-bloser.com/gum/gram...anics-handbook
Language Arts: Grammar- Mad Libs (K-12): http://www.wordlibs.
com/genre/?name=Childrens
Language Arts: Grammar Textbook (?):http://www.englishbanana.
com/big-grammar-book-english-worksheets.html

Language Arts: Grammar, Spelling Workbooks (K-6): http://www.mhschool.com/reading/trea.../national.html

Language Arts: Handwriting (K-6): http://donnayoung.org/penmanship/

Language Arts: Handwriting , D'Nealian (K-2) http://www.handwritingworksheets.com/flash/dnealian/sentence/index.html

Language Arts: Handwriting help (K-2) http://www.handwritinghelpforkids.com/expert.html

Language Arts: Literature (K-12): Manybooks

Language Arts: Phonics (K-2): http://www.beginningreading.com/Free%20Workshe.htm

Language Arts: Phonics (K-3) http://www.progressivephonics.com/~suzettew/

Language Arts: Phonics (K-3) http://www.readingbear.org

Language Arts: Phonics (K-3): http://www.starfall.com

Language Arts: Picture Books (K-4): http://www.wegivebooks.org/

Language Arts: Reading and Grammar (?) http://www.sfreading.com/index.html

Language Arts: Reading, word families (K-3): http://www.hubbardscupboard.org/prin...FamilyBooklets

Language Arts: Spelling (K-12) http://www.spellingcity.com

Language Arts: Word Families (K-3): http://www.wordway.us.com/

Life Skills: Character Education (K-6): http://humaneeducation.org/sections/view/childrens_character_education

Life Skills: Financial Literacy from the Actuarial Foundation (grades 9-12) http://actuarialfoundation.org/progr...urFuture.shtml

Mathematics: Algebra from Purple Math http://www.purplemath.com/index.htm

Mathematics: Comprehensive School Mathematics Program (full curriculum; grades K-6)

Mathematics: Explorations and Fun with Math from the Actuarial Foundation (grades 3-8) http://actuarialfoundation.org/progr..._academy.shtml

Mathematics: Games (K-12): http://www.learn-with-math-games.com/

Mathematics: Games and Lessons (K-12) https://www.xtramath.org/home/people

Mathematics: Games from Big Brains (multiple grades) http://www.bigbrainz.com/

Mathematics: Living Books (K-6) and Ancient History http://www.livingmath.net/LinkClick.aspx?fileticket=8k51N6evMx0%3d&tabid=1046&language=en-US

Mathematics: MEP Full Curriculum (K-12): http://www.cimt.plymouth.ac.uk/proje...ry/default.htm

Mathematics: Various topics from the Actuarial Foundation (multiple grades) http://actuarialfoundation.org/programs/youth_education.shtml

Mathematics: Virtual math manipulatives from Utah State University (multiple grades) http://nlvm.usu.edu/en/nav/vlibrary.html

Multiple Subjects: BBC (k-12) http://www.bbc.co.uk/schools/

Multiple Subjects: CM curriculum (K-12) http://www.charlottemasonhelp.com/p/...urriculum.html

Multiple Subjects: Free Textbooks, mostly science and math (9-12) http://www.ck12.org/flexbook/

Multiple Subjects: Full Curriculum (K-9) http://www.guesthollow.com/homeschool/curriculum.html

Multiple Subjects: Full Curriculum (Pre-K-5) http://www.theheadoftheclass.com

Multiple Subjects: Full Curriculum program from Ambleside (multiple ages) http://amblesideonline.org/curriculum.shtml

Multiple Subjects: Games (K-12) http://www.familygames.com/freelane.html

Multiple Subjects: Games (K-6): http://www.sheppardsoftware.com

Multiple Subjects: Lapbooks (K-12) http://www.homeschoolshare.com/Lapbooks_at_HSS.php

Multiple Subjects: Lesson Plans (K-12): http://www.lessonpathways.com

Multiple Subjects: Resources and Lessons (K-12): http://www.teacherspayteachers.com/

Multiple Subjects: Teaching Resources (K-12): http://www.learningpage.com/

Multiple Subjects: Topic Links (K-12) http://www.usborne-quicklinks.com/usa/usa_homepage.asp
Multiple Subjects: Unit Studies (K-9) http://www.thehomeschoolmom.com/schoolroom/unitstudies.php
Multiple Subjects: Units (K-12) http://www.schoolexpress.com/
Multiple Subjects: Videos and Lessons (3-12): http://www.khanacademy.org/
Preschool: Full Curriculum, Letter of the Week http://www.letteroftheweek.com/index.html
Preschool: Montessori: http://www.montessoriforeveryone.com/Free-Downloads_ep_35-1.html
Science: Animal Science (K-6): http://www.nwf.org/Kids.aspx
Science: Archeology, Dinosaurs and Fossils (3-12) http://www.fossils-facts-and-finds.com/earth_science_lesson_plans_on_geologic_time_introduction.html
Science: Astronomy (K-12): http://solarsystem.nasa.gov/eyes/
Science: Biology (9-12) http://quarksandquirks.wordpress.com/biology-hs-level/
Science: Chemistry (grades 3-6) http://www.inquiryinaction.org/
Science: Chemistry, Periodic Table (K-12): http://www.periodicvideos.com/index.htm
Science: Coloring Pages (K-12): http://www.hometrainingtools.com/sci...-pages/c/1112/
Science: Computer Programming (K-12): http://fuse.microsoft.com/page/kodu.aspx
Science: Computer Programming (K-12): http://scratch.mit.edu/
Science: Computer Science (K-12): http://csunplugged.org/
Science: Elementary Science (K-5): http://www.discoveryeducation.com/teachers/free-k-5-teacher-resources/index.cfm?campaign=footer_teacher_k5
Science: Elementary Science (K-6): http://www.hhmi.org/coolscience/forkids/
Science: Engineering (K-12) http://www.teachengineering.org/index.php

Science: Evolution (k-12): http://evolution.berkeley.edu/evolibrary/search/search_lessons.php

Science: Evolution, Tree of Life (?): http://tolweb.org/tree/home.pages/treehouses.html

Science: Experiments (K-12) http://www.sciencebuddies.org/index_A.htm

Science: Free Course (?) http://www.superchargedscience.com/a... le-classes.htm

Science: Full science courses (grades 6-9) http://www.jason.org/public/whatis/start.aspx

Science: Games (K-6): http://pbskids.org/zoom/activities/sci/

Science: Geography (K-6) http://www.gutenberg.org/files/12228/12228-h/12228-h.htm

Science: Geology (K-5): http://www.k5geosource.org/

Science: Human Evolution (K-12): http://humanorigins.si.edu/

Science: Life Science (1-6): http://www.eequalsmcq.com/classicsciinfo.htm

Science: MIT courses (9-12): http://ocw.mit.edu/courses/

Science: Multiple Subject Curriculum (K-12): http://www.msnucleus.org/membership/index.html

Science: Multiple Subjects (K-12): http://sciencenetlinks.com/

Science: National Geographic (K-6): http://kids.nationalgeographic.com/kids/

Science: National Geographic (K-9) http://www.ngsp.com/RESOURCES/TeacherResourceDownloads/ThemeSets/tabid/70/Default.aspx

Science: Nature Study (K-6): http://www.naturedetectives.org.uk/download/

Science: Physical Science, various 'ologies' (K-12): http://www.amnh.org/ology/

Science: Physics (K-9): http://www.aps.org/programs/education/k8/index.cfm

Science: Projects (K-6): http://pbskids.org/scigirls/projects

Science: Satellite Earth Science (K-12): http://scijinks.jpl.nasa.gov/

Science: Science Fair (K-9): http://www.good-science-fair-projects.com/index.html

Science: Videos (K-12): http://thehappyscientist.com/category/
free-stuff
Science: Virtual Museum (K-12): http://www.
exploratorium.edu/explore/
Science: Zoology Links (K-12): http://nationalzoo.si.edu/
Education/HomeworkHelper/
Social Science: American Folklore (K-12): http://www.
americanfolklore.net/
Social Science: American History (3-9): http://www.pbs.org/
wnet/historyofus/
Social Science: American History (K-3): https://sites.google.com/
site/mindfi...erican-history
Social Science: Current Events (3-12) http://www.timeforkids.com
Social Science: Geography (K-6): http://www.
sheppardsoftware.com/Geography.htm
Social Science: Government (K-6): http://bensguide.
gpo.gov/index.html
Social Science: Greek Myths Flashcards (3-9): http://
boggglesworldesl.com/greekmyths_flashcards.htm
Social Science: History Unit Studies (2-12) http://www.
learningthroughhistory.com/newsletter/archives/archives.php
Social Science: History, National Archives (3-12)
http://docsteach.org/
Social Science: Human Trafficking from Free the Slaves (grades 6-
12) http://www.freetheslaves.net/Page.aspx?pid=302
Social Science: Multiple Subjects (3-12) http://www.
socialstudiesforkids.com/
Social Science: Mythology (3-9): http://www.mythweb.com/
Social Science: Narrative History (K-12): http://www.
fsmitha.com/index.html
Social Science: Talking Pyramids (K-9): http://www.
talkingpyramids.com/ancie...-games-online/
Social Science: US History Timeline (3-9): http://www.factmonster.
com/ipka/A0902416.html
Social Science: Vikings (K-9): http://www.bbc.co.uk/schools/
primaryhistory/vikings/

Social Science: World History (K-12): http://worldhistoryforusall.
sdsu.edu/eras/era1.php

Social Science: World History (K-6): http://www.littlecitykids.com/
perspective/index.php

Supplemental Resources: Information (K-12): http://www.
mrdonn.org/index.html

Supplemental Resources: Maps (K-12): http://www.nationalatlas.
gov/printable/reference.html

Supplemental Resources: Worksheets (k-12): http://www.
worksheetworks.com

Supplemental Resources: Logic (7-12th): http://www.filozofia.uw.
edu.pl/kpaprzycka/Publ/xLogicSelfTaught.html

Appendix I:
List of FREE Curriculum Options

Your commitment to your empowered steps starts now. Use this to build your roadmap, your family's personal journey, and the commitment to get there. Now that you have created your Empowerment Picture, you know where you are going. Here is where you decide how you plan to get there. If you have no idea how, don't worry about that now. We will work through how to be open enough to see your way through.

Discount and Used Curriculum

Homeschool Buyer's Co-op: Discount curriculum:
https://www.homeschoolbuyersco-op.org/
Homeschool Classifieds: http://homeschoolclassifieds.com/

FREE RESOURCES for HOMESCHOOL

Whole Curriculum:

Discovery K12: http://discoveryk12.com
AllInOneHomeschool (Easy Peasy): https://allinonehome-school.com/
Ck-12.org: https://www.ck12.org/browse/
Virtual Homescchool Group - http://www.virtualhomeschoolgroup.org/
Philfour: https://philfour.com/classes/
Ambleside Online: https://www.amblesideonline.org/New.shtml
Old Fashioned Education: http://oldfashionededucation.com/
(Preschool and some elementary) http://www.letteroftheweek.com/

Puritan Homeschool Curriculum: http://www.puritans.net/puritans-home-school-curriculum/
Core Knowledge. Teacher jargon outline is at the beginning of each lesson. Scroll past this to get to the actual activity pages of the lesson. https://www.coreknowledge.org/community/teacher-workroom/teacher-created-lesson-plans/
School Yourself (High school): https://schoolyourself.org/
Lesson Pathways: https://www.curriculumpathways.com/portal/
Mater Amabilis: http://materamabilis.org/ma/
Crash Course Youtube Video Courses: https://www.youtube.com/user/crashcourse/playlists

Math:

Ray's Arithmetic: https://raysarithmetic.wordpress.com/
Khan Academy: https://www.khanacademy.org/
Free Math Program: http://www.freemathprogram.com/members1/G12345-18/Grade1/both1.htm
Practice: http://www.ipracticemath.com/
Ck-12.org - https://www.ck12.org/browse/
GCFGlobal: https://edu.gcfglobal.org/en/

Math Drill:

XtraMath - https://xtramath.org/#/home/index
Math is Free - https://www.mathsisfun.com/links/index-curriculum.html
Hippocampus - https://www.hippocampus.org/
Math Mammoth - https://www.youtube.com/user/MathMammoth/playlists
Math Drills - https://www.math-drills.com/
Homeschool Math - https://www.homeschoolmath.net/worksheets/
Math U See: https://www.mathusee.com/e-learning/drills/
Math Worksheets to create and print: http://themathworksheetsite.com/

Flipped Math: http://algebra1cc.flippedmath.com/
MasterMath: http://mastermath.info/

Phonics:

Word Mastery: http://donpotter.net...ery - Typed.pdf
Starfall: https://www.starfall.com/h/
Blend Phonics: http://blendphonics.org/

Spelling/Vocab.:

Membean: http://membean.com/
A2z: https://a2zhomeschooling.com/explore/
language_arts_kids/spelling_homeschoolers/
Spelling City Online Spelling Program*-*SpellingCity.com

Handwriting:

ZB Online: https://www.zaner-bloser.com/products/zb-fontsonline-plus.php
Writing Wizard: http://www.writingwizard.
longcountdown.com/handwriting_practice_worksheet_maker.html
Custom Tracer Pages: https://www.kidzone.ws/tracers/

Grammar and creative Writing:

Quill.org: https://www.quill.org
Grammar Bytes: http://www.chompchomp.com/menu.htm
Daily Grammar: http://www.dailygrammar.com/

History:

EdX: https://www.edx.org/learn/history
Crash Course Youtube Videos: https://www.youtube.com/user/
crashcourse/playlists

Geography:

Sheppard Software Geography (Online): http://www.
sheppardsoftware.com/African_Geography.htm
Crash Course Youtube Videos: https://www.youtube.com/user/
crashcourse/playlists

Current Events:

TIME for kids: https://www.timeforkids.com/
NY Times Learning Network: https://www.nytimes.com/
section/learning

Science:

Try engineering: https://tryengineering.org/teachers/lesson-plans/
Crash Course Youtube Videos: https://www.youtube.com/user/
crashcourse/playlists

Computer Science:

Blender 3D animation creation: https://cloud.blender.org/courses
Computer Programming Courses: TheNewBoston Playlist: https://
www.youtube.com/user/thenewboston/playlists
GCFGlobal: https://edu.gcfglobal.org/en/

Art:

The Virtual Instructor: https://thevirtualinstructor.com/
Dick Blick Lessons: https://www.dickblick.com/lesson-plans/

Typing

Typing Clut:
https://www.typingclub.com/sportal/program-3.game
Dance Mat Typing: https://www.bbc.com/bitesize/articles/z3c6tfr

Foreign Language:

BBC Languages: http://www.bbc.co.uk/languages/
Local Libraries: go to local library to get free language apps for downloads

High school:

HippoCampus: http://www.hippocampus.org/
edX: https://www.edx.org/
Yale University Open Courses: https://oyc.yale.edu/courses
Coursera: https://www.coursera.org/
A2Z Homeschooling: http://a2zhomeschooling.com/materials/curriculum_shop/free_curriculum/lesson_plans_free/

Minecraft Based

GameEd: https://www.gamedacademy.com/
Homeschool With Minecraft: http://www.homeschoolwithminecraft.com/
Minecraft Homeschool: https://whenyouriseup.com

Movie Based Curriculum

TeachWithMovies: http://www.teachwithmovies.org/#

Appendix J:
Creating Homeschool Transcripts and Homeschool Diplomas

For homeschoolers who have varied schedules, the best type of transcript is a subject-based transcript. With the transcript, I advise also creating a curriculum list of what was used in order to estimate the grade.

Considerations:

- Subject-based curriculum
- Map to list of curriculums used to estimate the grade per subject
- Have signature block and get it notarized for official copies
- A high school accreditation service you can use for transcripts and Diplomas from a second party.

Here's their website: Homeschool Life Accreditation service: http://www.homelifeacademy.com/Registration/start_homeschooling.aspx

Homeschool Diplomas: can be ordered online by several different sources as well as caps, gowns, class rings (ie: homeschooldiploma.com)

Subject Based
(Preferred)

High School Transcript
[School Name]

[Student Name]	Parents: [Parent Name]
[Street Address]	[Homeschool Name]
[City, State, Zip]	Years Attended: 2008-2012
[Phone Number]	Date of Graduation: May 2012
Date of Birth: 1/01/94	[Email Address of Student or Parent]
Sex: [Male/Female]	

Courses	Final Grade	Credit Awarded
English		
American Lit/Comp	A	1
World Lit/Comp	B	1
British Lit/Comp	B	1
English 101 *	B	1
Technical Writing *	B	1
Math		
Algebra 1	A	1
Algebra 2	B	1
Geometry	C	1
Trigonometry	A	1
Science		
Physical Science	B	1
Biology	B	1
Chemistry	A	1
History		
Geography	B	1
US History	A	1
World History	B	1
US Government	B	1
Economics	B	1
Foreign Language		
Japanese 1	B	1
Spanish 1	B	1
Spanish 2	C	1
Other		
Phys Ed	A	1
Health	A	½
Nutrition	A	1
Technology	A	½
Humanities	B	½
Finance	A	½
Total Credits	24	
Grade Point Average	3.15	

* Community College Course taken (name/location)
* CLEP Test / AP Test / DSST Test Taken

Date Graduated: June 6, 2011
Parental Certification:
We, [Parents Name], do hereby certify and affirm that this is the official transcript and record of [Students Name] academic studies of 2008-2012.

_____   _____
[Name of Father or Mother] administrator   [Parent Name]/teacher

_____   _____
Date   Date

Grade Based

(use the same top and bottom as the subject based)

9th grade (2002–2003)

Algebra 1	1 cr.	A
Physical Science	1 cr.	B
Geography	½ cr.	A
Am. Gov't	½ cr.	A
Lit/Comp	1 cr.	A
Spanish 1	1 cr.	B
Phys Ed	½ cr.	B
Art Appreciation	½ cr.	B
Total credits	6 cr.	
GPA	3.50	

10th grade (2003–2004)

Algebra 2	1 cr.	B
Biology	1 cr.	B
World History	1 cr.	B
World Lit/Comp	1 cr.	A
Spanish 2	1 cr.	C
Computer Graphics	½ cr.	A
Phys Ed	½ cr.	A
Total credits	6 cr.	
GPA	3.17	

11th grade (2004–2005)

Geometry	1 cr.	B
Chemistry	1 cr.	B
American History	1 cr.	A
American Lit/Comp	1 cr.	A
Spanish 3	1 cr.	C
Music Appreciation	½ cr.	A
Drama	½ cr.	A
Total credits	6 cr.	
GPA	3.33	

12th grade (2005–2006)

Consumer Math	1 cr.	A
British Lit/Comp	1 cr.	B
Economics	½ cr.	A
Debate	½ cr.	A
Physics	1 cr.	B
Accounting	1 cr.	A
Graphics Design	½ cr.	B
Database Design	½ cr.	B
Total credits	6 cr.	
GPA	3.50	

Total Cumulative GPA: 3.38
Date Graduated: June 4, 2006

Appendix K:
Dual Enrollment, College While Homeschooling, Sample Plan

There are several ways for high schoolers to earn college credit while still in high school.

This applies for homeschooling students and traditional school students. Build your student a spreadsheet college plan where you track where their transfer credits will come from.

Example Degree Plan
Note: Courses can also be BOTH college transfer compatible and high school requirement course

[Transfer to COLLEGE/UNIVERSITY NAME] Overall Credits		CLEP/DSST/AP Test	ACE Credit Accepted Source	Community College
I. General Education Requirements				
A. Communications				
■English 101	3	CLEP		
■English 102	3	CLEP		
■Speech	3	CLEP		
■Technical Writing	3	DSST		
■College Mathmatics	3			Accuplacer/Take Course at CC
B. Arts and Humanities				
■Humanities- Arts Core	3		Straighterline	
■US History	3		Study.com	

Some sources for transfer credit, see the below for just a few:

- **CLEP**: https://clep.collegeboard.org/exams
- **DSST**: https://www.getcollegecredit.com/
- **AP Exams**: Page reference for homeschoolers, https://apcentral.collegeboard.org/ap-coordinators/exam-ordering-fees/ordering-materials/home-schooled-students
- **ACE**: Use this site to see what sources you can use to gain college credit that will transfer to college that accept

ACE transcripts: https://www2.acenet.edu/credit/?
fuseaction=transcripts.main

- **Straighter line**: See partner college list – **They also offer online Associates Degree Program**
  https://www.straighterline.com/
- **Study.com**: www.study.com
- **Individual State Profile of Dual Enrollment by The Education Commission of The States**:
  http://ecs.force.com/mbdata/mbprofallRT?
  Rep=DE15A

NON-FICTION BOOKS BY
L.M. PRESTON

Please find LM Preston's books at www.EmpoweredSteps.com

REFERENCES

- Anumeha Bhagat, Rashimi Vyas, Tejinder Singh. (2015, August 5). *US National Library of Medicine*. Retrieved from NCBI: https://www.ncbi.nlm.nih.gov/pmc/articles/PMC4552069/
- Cassie. (2017, September 14). *10 Ways to Improve Student Concentration*. Retrieved from Teach Starter: https://www.teachstarter.com/au/blog/10-ways-to-improve-student-concentration/
- Duffy, C. (2019). *Cathy Duffy's Reviews*. Retrieved from Cathy Duffy: https://cathyduffyreviews.com/
- Heick, T. (2019, March 5). *6 Alternatives To Bloom's Taxonomy For Teachers*. Retrieved from TeachThought: https://www.teachthought.com/critical-thinking/5-alternatives-to-blooms-taxonomy/
- HSLDA. (2018). *Home School Legal Defense Association*. Retrieved from https://hslda.org/content/#
- Limited, N. A. (2019). *16Personalities*. Retrieved from https://www.16personalities.com
- McQuarrie, T. (2004, 05). *Clep Lesson Plans*. Retrieved from Clep Prep: http://clepprep.tripod.com/cleplessonplans/id4.html
- McShane, M. (2018, May 21). *Forbes*. Retrieved from Forbes: https://www.forbes.com/sites/mikemcshane/2018/05/21/is-hybrid-homeschooling-the-wave-of-the-future#5e6bef706bf7
- Patrick, S. (2008, 09 01). WorkBox System. WorkBoxSystem, LLC.

- Saint James School of Medicine, Kralendijk, Bonaire, The Netherlands. (2013, April 3). *Maturation of the adolescent brain*. Retrieved from US National Library of Medicine National Institues of Health: https://www.ncbi.nlm.nih.gov/pmc/articles/PMC3621648/
- Zinth, J. D. (2016, March). *Dual Enrollment - All State Profiles*. Retrieved from Education Commission of the States: http://ecs.force.com/mbdata/mbprofallRT?Rep=DE15A

HOMESCHOOLING AND WORKING

While Shaping Amazing Learners

A NOTE FROM THE AUTHOR

Thank you for reading *Homeschooling And Working, While Shaping Amazing Learners.*

If you have enjoyed it, please consider leaving a review. You can visit my Amazon page:

LM Preston
https://amzn.to/2U5kXKH

Don't forget to sign up to *LM Preston's Newsletter!*
https://landing.mailerlite.com/webforms/landing/v6q7e4

ABOUT THE AUTHOR

LM. Preston is an avid reader. She loved to create poetry and short stories as a young girl. With a thirst for knowledge she attended college and worked in the IT field as a Techie and Educator for over sixteen years. She started writing science fiction under the encouragement of her husband who was a Sci-Fi buff and her four kids. Her first published novel, Explorer X - Alpha was the beginning of her obsessive desire to write and create stories of young people who overcome unbelievable odds. She loves to write while on the porch, watching her kids play, or when she is traveling, which is another passion that encouraged her writing.

To stay updated on upcoming books, sales and new releases follow me:

For more information, please visit
www.lmpreston.com

Made in United States
Orlando, FL
30 August 2022

21730263R00220